The End of the Circus

Also available from Bloomsbury

Circus as Multimodal Discourse, by Paul Bouissac
The Languages of Humor, edited by Arie Sover
The Meaning of the Circus, by Paul Bouissac
The Semiotics of Clowns and Clowning, by Paul Bouissac
Understanding Nonverbal Communication, by Marcel Danesi

The End of the Circus

Evolutionary Semiotics and Cultural Resilience

Paul Bouissac

BLOOMSBURY ACADEMIC
LONDON • NEW YORK • OXFORD • NEW DELHI • SYDNEY

BLOOMSBURY ACADEMIC
Bloomsbury Publishing Plc
50 Bedford Square, London, WC1B 3DP, UK
1385 Broadway, New York, NY 10018, USA
29 Earlsfort Terrace, Dublin 2, Ireland

BLOOMSBURY, BLOOMSBURY ACADEMIC and the Diana logo are
trademarks of Bloomsbury Publishing Plc

First published in Great Britain 2022
Paperback edition published in 2023

Copyright © Paul Bouissac, 2022

Paul Bouissac has asserted his right under the Copyright,
Designs and Patents Act, 1988, to be identified as Author of this work.

For legal purposes the Acknowledgements on pp. xiv–xvi constitute
an extension of this copyright page.

Cover design by Rebecca Heselton
Cover photograph © Group of 5 Circus clowns including
Felix Adler / Lusha Nelson / Getty Images

All rights reserved. No part of this publication may be reproduced or
transmitted in any form or by any means, electronic or mechanical, including
photocopying, recording, or any information storage or retrieval system,
without prior permission in writing from the publishers.

Bloomsbury Publishing Plc does not have any control over, or responsibility for,
any third-party websites referred to or in this book. All internet addresses
given in this book were correct at the time of going to press. The author and
publisher regret any inconvenience caused if addresses have changed or sites
have ceased to exist, but can accept no responsibility for any such changes.

A catalogue record for this book is available from the British Library.

A catalog record for this book is available from the Library of Congress.
Library of Congress Cataloging-in-Publication Data
Names: Bouissac, Paul, author.
Title: The end of the circus : evolutionary semiotics and cultural resilience / Paul Bouissac.
Description: London, UK ; New York, NY : Bloomsbury Academic, 2021. |
Includes bibliographical references and index. |
Identifiers: LCCN 2021006793 (print) | LCCN 2021006794 (ebook) | ISBN 9781350166493
(hardback) | ISBN 9781350166509 (ebook) | ISBN 9781350166516 (epub)
Subjects: LCSH: Circus–Social aspects. | Human body–Social aspects. | Acrobatics. |
Clowns. | Circus animals. | Semiotics. Classification: LCC GV1815 .B683 2021 (print) |
LCC GV1815 (ebook) | DDC 791.3–dc23
LC record available at https://lccn.loc.gov/2021006793
LC ebook record available at https://lccn.loc.gov/2021006794

ISBN:	HB:	978-1-3501-6649-3
	PB:	978-1-3502-4476-4
	ePDF:	978-1-3501-6650-9
	eBook:	978-1-3501-6651-6

Typeset by Integra Software Services Pvt. Ltd.

To find out more about our authors and books visit www.bloomsbury.com
and sign up for our newsletters.

This book is dedicated to the memory of Alain Robba (1938–2018)

Contents

List of Figures   viii
Acknowledgments   xiv

1   Overture: *Themes and Variations*   1
2   First Movement, *Andante Sostenuto*: The Time of the Gypsies   11
3   Second Movement, *Vivace Furioso*: Animals   53
4   Third Movement, *Adagio Lamentendo*: Clowns   131
5   Fourth Movement, *Maestoso Appassionato*: Bodies   171
6   Coda, *Sforzando*   215

Bibliography   229
Index   238

List of Figures

1   Alain Robba, 1962. Author's archives   xv
2   Firmin Bouglione (1905–80): A pose among his wild animals on the cover of his memoirs, *Le Cirque est mon Royaume* [The Circus is my Kingdom]   xvii
3   This poster of the French circus Royal Kerwich was vandalized with the inscription "*A mort le cirque!*" [Death to the circus]   4
4   This French print of 1895 encapsulates the traditional interface between nomadic Gypsies and the authorities that try to control them. Its title is "Gypsy Census Caravan and Dancing Bear"   13
5   From the depth of time, through borderless lands, nomadic families with their animals have carried forward the circus trade and arts. This ageless, faded postcard from the early photography era evokes the caravans of the traveling performers who, for millennia, brought elusive wonders to the midst of sedate villages and boisterous seasonal fairs   14
6   Modern British Gypsies on their way to Appleby horse fair   14
7   Exterior view of Astley's Riding School as it appeared in 1777. The front is modeled after a typical fairground structure with a few steps up and hanging banners showing samples of the feats to be witnessed inside after payment of an admission fee: various equestrian tricks, rope dancing, and acrobatic "pyramids"   30
8   Inside view of Astley's Riding School (or Amphitheater) at Halfpenny Hatch in 1777. This configuration evokes an improvised exploitation of a vacant lot rather than the deliberate design of a spectacular premise   31
9   The author (center) with Patricia Bouillon and her husband at the Monte Carlo International Circus Festival (January 18, 2020)   38
10 My maternal grandparents in the 1930s. Théophile Eugène Frène, born in 1870, was a tinsmith and cauldron maker who had left his village in his teen years to learn his trade through travelling for several years across France and working for various metal craftsmen as an apprentice. He had rebelled against his father, who was employed as

"*régisseur*" [farm supervisor] on the behalf of local landowner nobility. I was told that he reproached his father to "spend his life on his horse watching other people work". Although there was no hint of Gypsy culture in this side of the family, reading about the Kalderash always conveyed to me a sense of affinity as I remembered the many hours I spent as a kid at the bellow of my grandfather's workshop where, after his retirement, he often enjoyed forging some implements for our household or some of his relatives and friends. My grandmother, Marthe Pitard, had worked as a teenager making cigars and cigarettes at the *Manufacture des tabacs* [Tobacco factory], then a state monopoly, in Chateauroux in central France. Although an unpalatable reference, very much at odd with reality as I perceived it, I secretly associated this detail with the notorious Carmen of Charles Bizet's opera 54

11 At seventeen, Théophile Frène obtained the legal document that allowed him to travel over the country to learn his trade with the metal craftsmen he would encounter on his way. In this identity kit, he is curiously described as "colored". The workshop owners were supposed to provide written testimonies of his training in the pages of this booklet. However, as literacy was not yet universal in those days, it seems that all the testimonies were written by the same person whose handwriting is similar to my grandfather's as I remember it. The signatures and official stamps, though, look genuine 55

12 This French booklet recounts the well-documented history of Cirque Bureau that was founded in 1854 by Jean Bureau. The poster on the cover is from the late 1940s. We knew that we would actually witness this extraordinary act in the show down to the exact number, color, and trapping of the horses as this circus was famous for its reputation of honest advertisement 56

13 Spotted hyena (*Crocuta crocuta*). Abdullahi Mohammad with the hyena Mainassara by photographer Pieter Hugo who has vividly documented the street performances of Nigerian nomads exhibiting trained hyenas. These predators remain a serious threat for humans in some African countries. *The Guardian* of November 20, 2020, provides details about the death of an old man in Zimbabwe, who was dragged from his hut during the night by a pack of hyenas. Only the upper half of his body was recovered the next day in the bush 67

14 "Traveller Attacked by Wolves" by Richard Ansdell (1815–85), Royal Academy 1854. In nineteenth-century urbanized Europe, the fear of the wolves is kept alive by rumors, tales, and popular imagery 70

15 Before photography became the main source of visual information, newspapers and magazines used drawings to illustrate their contents. Louis Bombled (1862–1927), a celebrated French artist, provided the press with realistic renderings of contemporary events 71

16 A poster advertising Rudesindo Roche's fifteen-wolf act on the stage of the Folies Bergères theater in Paris by lithographer Tom Merry (1852–1902) 72

17 The posters and banners of the traditional circuses and menageries enticed their audience with hyperbolic representations of wild predators, showing a single diminutive but bold human outnumbered by raging oversized carnivorous animals such as aggressive polar bears …Circo Orlando Orfei (Italy). The comment reads [in Italian]: "White bears from the North Pole: Fantastic !!!" 91

18 … or reluctant lions that are forcefully driven through their pace while the whole pride menacingly encircles the trainer armed with a mere whip. Italia stock poster from the late 1960s, Artwork by Marcello Colizzi 92

19 Feared predators, crocodiles are featured here being subdued by the magic power of a master who has donned the outfit of an Indian fakir Circus Krone (Germany): poster from 1987 featuring Karah Khavac with crocodiles. Artwork by Marcello Colizzi 93

20 Another genre of posters represents man as the wild master of the beasts. Here, the trainer impersonates the Cossack hero of Gogol's novella, Taras Bulba, popularized by the 1962 Hollywood movie starring Yul Brynner. It conveys the idea that one has to share the predators' wildness in order to subdue them.Circo di Budapest TARAS BULBA—Italian circus poster from the mid-1980s featuring Emilien Beautour a.k.a. Taras Bulba, a French tiger trainer. Artwork by Aller 94

21 In a totally different mode, an elegant and poised trainer demonstrates his dominance by controlling a grossly oversized tiger. In spite of the unrealistic rendering of this scene, the audience will be influenced not only in their perception but also in their memory of this act. Circus Knie (Switzerland) poster from 1960 featuring the animal trainer Gilbert Houcke. Artwork by Marcus Campbell 95

22 Female dominance over male lions or black jaguar is a powerful icon in the traditional promotion of animal acts that suggests complicit wildness. These symbolic compositions combine raw eroticism with the dramatic staging of a circus background. Note the leopard skin patterns of the minimal outfit of the trainers. Circo Braun—Italian poster from 1978   96

23 Female dominance over male lions or black jaguar is a powerful icon in the traditional promotion of animal acts that suggests complicit wildness. These symbolic compositions combine raw eroticism with the dramatic staging of a circus background. Note the leopard skin patterns of the minimal outfit of the trainers. Circo Medrano (Italy) poster from 1974. Artwork by Renato Casaro   96

24 Overcoming the fear of snakes with charm and authority is a powerful image of human supremacy that is commonly displayed in the traditional circus. The comment on the poster reads (in Italian): "Miss Chantal in a mortal hug with giant python, boa constrictor, and anaconda." Crazy Cobra Show—Italian poster from 1997 featuring Miss Chantal, snake charmer   97

25 The precondition for the emergence of civilization is the effective control of predators that are more powerful than humans. These images illustrate the mastering of the wild through skill and courage, and celebrate the triumph of the wild animal trainer as a cultural hero. Circo Rinaldo Orfei. Italian poster from 1978   98

26 The ultimate triumph of the manly hero riding the wildest of animals. Such representations feed the symbolic capital of the imaginary circus by embodying the victory over the erstwhile challenge of predators. This image extracts from a relatively common act with tame animals the ritualistic significance of the performance it advertises. Circo Medrano (Italy) poster from the mid-1980s promoting Davio Casartelli's tiger and elephant act. Artwork by Franco Picchioni   99

27 Krampus mask celebrating the winter solstice, also known as "devils of Christmas"   135

28 The Chickys, an iconic traditional duo in the circus of the twentieth century. The elegant, arrogant, and sumptuously dressed white-face clown interacts with the ill-kept, downtrodden auguste   138

29 A typical costume of white-face clown: Yann Rossi (from the duo the Rossyans) wears a creation of Gérard Vicaire made of luxurious fabric and elaborately decorated   157

30	Detail of the embroidery on a white-face's costume	158
31	"McJesus" 2015. By Jani Leinonen	164
32	British clown David Konyot writes: "My family, like many others, have plied the circus trade for centuries. From my mother side, I descend from the Blumenfelds whose ancestry can be traced back to the mid-17th century when an Emmanuel Blumenfeld, 'Gaulker and Seiltanzer' [traveling entertainer and rope walker] brought three elephants in the town of Wuppertal. On my father side, are two British circus dynasties, the Fossetts and the Yeldings. I have over 60 years of circus experience as ringmaster, producer, and clown" (2020)	168
33	The artist's body unfolds with total grace and insistence in the revealing glare of the circus ring. Here, Romina Micheletty, heir to a long family tradition of circus acrobatics, displays her contortionist and hula hoop skill in a brief pose offered to our contemplation	172
34	Magician Christopher Eötvös Dobritch, the scion of a famous Hungarian circus family, introduces his partner (Elizabeth Axt) whose shapely body will soon be folded and locked into a small container	173
35	With charm, elegance, and cruelty, Christopher will thrust through the container four sharp swords ...	174
36	... and will forcefully dislocate the pierced body that rests inside, before, like in the notorious Indian rope trick ...	174
37	... he gracefully restores the body of his victim to her full, resplendent integrity	175
38	Commenting this photo that he selected for this book, Gérard Edon mentioned that it revives for him a moment he really feels from inside	180
39	Frontal balance on the swinging trapeze. Gérard Edon's contract with the Blackpool Tower Circus specified that no safety lunge or net were to be used in this act	181
40	The Antarès. This poster of Circus Bureau from the 1940s represents the dramatic finale of an impressive aerial act. There have been two generations of this act as the children took over when the parents retired. Unfortunately, it had a tragic end when the man hanging from his teeth fell to his death in 2006 when the leather contraption he was holding in his mouth ruptured	182
41	René et Madeleine Rousseau, "The Geraldos," ca. 1950	188
42	The Geraldos: High above the ground, without a safety net, catching insteps to insteps to stop the fall	189

43	*Les Geraldos*, early promotional flyer	190
44	Alexander Lichner slowly ascends the rope to reach his trapeze with strength, poise, and elegance	196
45	Dramatic moment: the audience cannot fail to empathize with this precarious challenge to gravity	197
46	"Like an angel taking his flight," Alexander Lichner remains secured to the bar of the swinging trapeze by the sheer muscular contraction of his insteps	198
47	A moment of triumph: Alexander Lichner takes a deserved heroic pose for the posterity	199
48	Back on earth, between the shows, Alexander teaches his daughter Denise how to master handstand balancing, a staple of the acrobatic art, under the loving gaze of his wife, Nuria Torralvo Quiros, the photographer	200

Acknowledgments

As I see this book leaving its anchorage, my gratitude goes first to the many circus artists and their families I was fortunate enough to meet in my life. They have been a constant source of inspiration, courage, and resilience. I am sharing in this book both their anguish and determination in times when the course of their destiny is threatened by cultural changes and ideological forces. I wish to thank Alexander Lichner, Sascha Santus, David Konyot, Robert Gasser, and Andrea Vianello for having allowed me to quote them in this book. I wish also to thank Andrew Wardell, the Senior Commissioning Editor of Bloomsbury Academic, and his assistant, Becky Holland, for having graciously helped me nurture this challenging project during the past two years. I am indebted to the anonymous peer reviewers who have provided useful cues for improving the text. The final manuscript has greatly benefitted from the critical input of Ron Beadle, David Conway, and Basil Thomas. I want also to acknowledge the unfailing support, both moral and financial, of Victoria University, which has been crucial for completing, over the years, some of the research projects that made this book possible. Additional thanks must go to Jovan Andric and Zbigniew Roguszka for their help in providing and preparing most of the visual documents illustrating the chapters, and, last but not least, to my lifelong partner, Stephen Harold Riggins, who has always been my first reader and editor.

Figure 1 Alain Robba, 1962. Author's archives

November 2019. The old battered shoebox at the back of the top shelf has gathered dust. It bears a date: 1962. This is the year I left France and the Bouglione circus to take up an academic position in Toronto. This is also the year the book I had written on behalf of the wild animal trainer Firmin Bouglione, **Le Cirque est mon Royaume** [Circus is my Kingdom] *appeared in print. Shuffling through the contents of the box, mostly old letters and papers that once were meaningful to me, I come across a glossy photograph that has not faded. A name springs out with my breath: "Alain Robba!". Almost sixty years have gone since Alain had given me this portrait of himself stepping out of his caravan a few days before I was due to leave. Now, suddenly a huge gap opens in my life, a story that started but was cut short. The clear memory of the beginning had been at once revived in my memory, but like a book whose pages would have been torn off after the first chapter, that story would, for ever, stay both unwritten and unread. I jump to the Internet and google his name only to find his obituary that had appeared in a local press a year earlier.*

We had met at the circus when I was a part of the team manning the entrance of the traveling zoo. He was a cousin of the Bouglione and we had instruction to give free access to family members, a category that apparently applied to all Gypsies. Friendship had instantly clicked. After the end of the season, our paths crossed again by chance on the Boulevard de Montparnasse close to the room I was renting on Avenue de l'observatoire. I showed him the book that was fresh from the press and we decided to promote the sales through his own family circus that was running at the time as Zoo Circus. My publisher agreed to print their program free of charge with a full-page picture of the book. The circus of the Robba family was then a small outfit that was touring Paris's southern suburbs. The itinerary was not firmly set in advance but Alain had given me a telephone number through which I could always find out where he was.

On my way to Canada, my briefcase was stolen and I lost what was then the most precious asset of a young man on the move: my address book. Life went on. Events kept crowding my days and nights. The year 1962 was drowned in the sea of oblivion. Deep, on the bottom, though, a name was longing to resurface.

Figure 2 Firmin Bouglione (1905–80): A pose among his wild animals on the cover of his memoirs, *Le Cirque est mon Royaume* [The Circus is my Kingdom] published in 1962.

Overture

Themes and Variations

Introduction

In spite of its ominous title, this book is a hopeful attempt to document and illustrate the immemorial art of the traveling entertainers, Gypsies, and others, who brought through the centuries, if not the millennia, a measure of dreams and rapture in the midst of the often dreary, uneventful lives of sedentary populations. We have, indeed, reached a point when we may ask: can the circus in its primal nomadic form that welds humans and animals in a common destiny survive the onslaught of worldwide social and cultural transformations, and the toxic political atmosphere created by its detractors?

This book is divided into four parts, each one focusing on a fundamental aspect of traditional circus culture. Although there are many cross-references in the volume, the parts can be read as self-contained installments, somewhat like listening to separate symphonic movements without losing sight of the whole structure. The first part is devoted to the nomadic minority that has fostered the circus arts for countless generations: the Gypsies and other travelers. The second part addresses in depth the controversial issues that are raised nowadays concerning the use of animals in entertainments. The third part examines the contemporary status of the clown and its evolution in a social context that questions biases and exclusionary behaviors in the population at large. It asks: Can clowns survive as an accepted cultural institution in the age of inclusiveness and political correctness? Finally, the fourth part discusses the semiotic treatment of the body in circus performances: How do ostentation, objectification, and seduction fare in the context of contemporary legal standards and the flood of virtual images. The underlying theme in all these parts will be the tension between the ineluctable evolution of meaning-making systems and the struggling resilience of an institution rooted in the deep past of the human kind. This reflection will focus on the serious existential threats that these social, cultural, and technological transformations represent for the traditional circus in its modern form as it has flourished during the previous two centuries.

Whence and Whither the "Traditional" Circus?

The origins of the circus in Europe can be traced back to nomadic minorities that spread westward over long periods of time from the Asian subcontinent. The "traditional" or "classic" circus, as it is sometimes called nowadays, refers to a form of ritualistic entertainment that combines animals, acrobats, and clowns. The display of trained domestic and wild animals was indeed one of the assets of the trade of these itinerant performers in addition to acrobatics, playing music for special occasions, and providing other services in which they had acknowledged expertise such as basketry, metal and wood work, horse husbandry and training; as well as begging, fortune telling, casting or removing spells, and selling lucky charms and herbal medicines. These latter activities were frowned upon as forms of deviance by civil and religious authorities which periodically repressed their perpetrators with extreme violence.

On the other hand, the commodities and the crafts provided by these nomads were appreciated and rewarded by the people in the countries they roamed, although their peculiar ethos and their reliance on unlawful expediencies in times of duress often made them less than welcome. Their nomadic way of life and unusual activities embodied a fascinating otherness that was both feared and envied. Some small family groups could secure a part of their livelihood through putting on performances in villages and seasonal fairs. Extraordinary feats of acrobatics and animal control bordering on magic in the eyes of their naïve audiences captured the imagination of villagers and farmers, and the circus, under any other name, became an important part of European popular culture. At the heart of the twentieth century, films such as Ingmar Bergman's *Sawdust and Tinsel* (1953) and Federico Fellini's *La Strada* (1954) bear witness to the haunting presence of these entertainers in the cultural memory of modern Europe. Both orchestrate the powerful symbols that are nurtured by the ever marginal presence among us of the circus and its phantasms.

Historical ethnography has documented the continuing albeit elusive existence of these travelers in Europe over many centuries and the eventual rise of the modern form of the traditional circus in England and elsewhere in Europe toward the end of the eighteenth century, an era of intense industrialization and urbanization that made possible the creation of permanent premises devoted to popular entertainments. The Gypsies, as they were known in England, were the main source of talents and entrepreneurship that raised the circus in its modern form to the rank of a cultural institution. Other minorities such as the Jewish communities which were also excluded from mainstream activities in Christian European countries contributed to the development and exploitation of this traditional trade and also begot some notable circus lineages such as the families Pauwels, Lorch, and Blumenfeld to name only a few (Bensimon 2005; Meishar 2020; Otte 2006).

The nineteenth century witnessed the birth of large-scale traveling shows that became a prominent part of the cultural landscape. The financial success of some of these enterprises captured the attention of some private investors who transformed the family-based circus into a prosperous industry. Bringing novelties, thrills, and exoticism to cities for the time of a few performances under their "big tops," they fascinated urban crowds at a time when tourism was far from democratized, and television had not yet opened in every home a window to distant worlds. The numerous permanent constructions that popped up in most major European cities during that century sustained the interest of their audience through renewing regularly their programs by temporarily hiring traveling artists and their trained animals.

In the meantime, small troupes of Gypsy entertainers kept visiting lesser towns and villages, performing in open air or under tents, thus perpetuating their ancestral trade. Their nomadic way of life and the ephemeral wonders they produced were feeding the fantasies of their sedentary audiences, and elevated the circus to a powerful symbol of freedom, heroism, and license in the popular imagination.

From the mid-twentieth century on, the rise of modern technology brought so many social and cultural changes that the circus as a trade, an art, and a form of life progressively lost some of its glamour. It showed remarkable resilience, though, but on a reduced scale. Competition became more challenging and many traveling companies struggled to stay economically afloat, or simply discontinued their operation. The traditional family-based circus, even in its most successful forms, was confronted with an intense industrialization of its ancestral trade, supported by global capital and merciless marketing strategies. Today, the traditional circus that remains a source of fascination and wonderment where and when it is allowed to perform is under attack from many sides to the extent that its very existence is threatened and the possibility of its demise is on the horizon.

"Death to the Circus!"

The end of the traditional circus is indeed a persistent theme in the twenty-first century's media. Journalists started harping on this theme as early as the last decades of the previous century. An article published in *The Economist* in September 1988 bears witness to that ominous trend. The author lists the "conventional" circuses that had already gone out of business a decade earlier

Figure 3 This poster of the French circus Royal Kerwich was vandalized with the inscription "*A mort le cirque!*" [Death to the circus]. (Courtesy of William Kerwich).

and welcomes, not quite enthusiastically, the "new" circus that appeals to "sophisticated" audiences. "The death of the circus"—that is, the traditional circus—was explicitly evoked two decades later by Jon Katz (2017). Nowadays, the traditional circus in many countries keeps edging toward its twilight zone. Some people lament the decline and disappearance of prestigious companies such as the iconic *Ringling Bros, Barnum & Bailey* Circus in America; some others applaud the demise of a popular entertainment they mistakenly equate with the systematic abuse of animals and humans. Animals, though, are currently the main focus of attention and the target of a cultural revolution that proclaims the absolute value of nature and freedom, thus advocating the "liberation" of captive circus animals and the discontinuation of their use in training and performances, including, at times, their mere display in zoos. This is part of a much larger movement that also radically opposes the use of animals in medical experiments and even questions the moral legitimacy of the husbandry of species that have been domesticated for food, clothing, and work since the advent of the Neolithic Age. The radical denunciation of this way of life as cruel and unethical leads a significant number of people to renounce meat consumption and adopt strictly vegetarian diets with fanatical fervor (Berson 2019). This emergent ideology in Western Europe, America, and beyond prompts some to commit acts of sabotage and legitimize physical violence toward those they consider the perpetrators of crimes against animals. The heroic posture of the traditional wild animal trainer confronting raging lions and tigers that was displayed on circus posters has now become for many the symbol of a shameful past. On August 5, 2018, the owner of the French circus Royal, William Kerwich, posted on Facebook a photo of one of their posters that had been vandalized by the "animalists," the self-appointed defenders of "animals' rights." The colorful image had been defaced with the black inscription: "Death to the circus."

Clowns on the Wane

Another iconic figure of the traditional circus, the clown, has lost its assumed mirthful innocence and its immunity to retributions for his playful transgressions of moral and civil norms. In recent decades, clowns have become the objects of suspicion and fear. Their presence or images are no longer a marketing asset. The benign traditional duo of the white-face clown and the auguste that has been for two centuries a favorite of their European audiences is claimed to have lost its cultural relevance and to persist only as a nostalgic reference to obsolete forms of comedy. A new mode of clowning, solo performers who entice or drag some members of their audience into the circus arena and make them the butt of more or less offensive practical jokes, is becoming the norm. However, this new paradigm is received with ambiguous feelings by the public as it thrives on a blend of self-deprecation and aggressive mockery. Many in circus audiences experience the fear of being picked on by these performers. Moreover, new standards of civility, commonly referred to as "political correctness," drastically reduce the range of permissible gags and jokes. Coincidentally, the media have popularized the terrifying image of the clown as a faceless villain, if not a straightforward criminal. Such a change of attitude goes beyond the anecdotal and signals some deeper cultural evolution. As early as five decades ago, Federico Fellini, in his ominous film *The Clowns* (1970), anticipated the death of this circus icon by staging its mock funeral in a circus arena.

The Body: From Ritual to Spectacle

Acrobatics remain an accepted part of the traditional circus but the democratization of these skills, which are now taught worldwide in countless circus schools, undermines their claim to uniqueness and tends to tone down their capacity to amaze spectators beyond belief. These performers also usually refrain from deliberately arousing the libido of their spectators. In addition, younger generations all over the world are exposed very early to the wonders of virtual reality that provide visual experience of bodies bouncing out of the gravitational universe with a virtuosity that cannot be matched by the most daring circus acrobats. Moreover, the often compulsory use of safety lunges and nets, and the systematic introduction of electric and electronic means of pulling aerialists up, down, and across during their acts temper the anxiety of their audience by factoring a coefficient of artificiality in the performances. Although lethal accidents occasionally occur, the shadow of death has been mostly erased for the sake of humanitarian and social considerations. Acrobats in the industrialized modern circus tend to accomplish their feats with the precision of competent athletes or skilled laborers rather than romantic artists daringly confronting an uncertain, potentially tragic outcome. The traditional acrobats were prone to stage their performances as outwardly life-threatening challenges, even, at times, faking apparently accidental failures in order to enhance the audience's anxiety and eventual appreciation. A poster such as the one announcing the visit of the circus Sabine Rancy in the early 1960s would now be unthinkable: it advertised "the leap of death" of *The Clerans*, a risky aerialist act with an ominous skull prominently displayed in the upper part of the image. By contrast, the "new" acrobats tend to foreground their neuromuscular prowess and avoid evoking death through their demeanor and the music they choose to accompany their acts. The ancient ritualistic meaning of these performances that verged on sacrificial staging has vanished to be replaced by spectacular displays of stunning costumes and aerial choreography in which both graceful movements and physical feats are the focus of attention, and little is left to chance.

The Human Dimension: "You! Wretched Gypsies!"

The purpose of this book is to confront these cultural changes both in terms of evolutionary semiotics, that is, the way in which general systems of meanings and values are transformed over time, and in terms of the particular impact these changes have on the individuals and families who experience them from inside, so to speak, as moral frustrations and economic losses. This is why this book starts with a celebration of the nomads who, since deep time, have created and nurtured the circus skills as a way to survive the challenges of a hostile world. Although the initiator of the modern form of the traditional circus, Philip Astley, was most probably a British Gypsy himself, as we will suggest in the first part of the book, the nomadic lineages that had perpetuated the circus as an art and a way of life over countless generations, have been dispossessed of their heritage by private business companies and global industrial enterprises that now exploit their symbolic capital and their talents while adulterating the very essence of these traditions. At the same time, circus folks are under attack, both on legal and ethical grounds, for their assumed abuse of the animals they breed and train to entertain their audiences.

However, the threat does not target solely the traditional institution of the animal circus itself but extends beyond, to the ethnicity of the families which are accused of sustaining its perpetuation. The undercurrent of racist attitudes that feeds these attacks often surfaces. For example, on February 27, 2019, James Douchet, the owner of the French family circus *Sebastien Zavatta*, reported on Facebook that the afternoon performance in Bois D'Arcy, near Paris, had been marred by the protest of a small group of "animalists" from the association "Paris Zoopolis." Since the circus had obtained the official permission to play in this town, the protesters were maintained at a distance by the local police while the crowd was lining up to buy tickets and get access to the show, but one person claiming to be a journalist was allowed to approach the entrance. This was a pretext to be able to shout toward the circus folks: "You! Wretched Gypsies! [*Sales Gitans!*]" Obviously, the proclaimed defense of animal well-being is conflated with a raw hatred for the ethnic minority whose members run most family circuses under a variety of trade names. The following morning, James Douchet posted a photo of the panels advertising his circus performance that had been vandalized during the night by splashing black paint in the form of crosshair targets upon their colorful images, an explicit threat of death.

The comments triggered by this sort of posting on the social media open a reliable window on the state of mind of the population at large. Online support from other circus folks, often betraying less than optimal literacy, are confronted by hostile diatribes that gloss over animal rights to target the Gypsies themselves with calls to lynch them or demands that "their males be castrated in order to get rid of their race," thus echoing the racial policy of a not so distant sinister time. The most violent imprecations appear to occur in France and are documented on the website of the *Association des cirques de famille de France* [the Association of the French family circuses], but a long sequence of such verbal attacks can also be seen in the UK in which an abundant BBC social stream followed, in 2019, the posting by a young British Gypsy denouncing the discriminatory signs erected in Scotland and England, barring Gypsies and travelers from the premises, shops, or pubs in several cities and villages, irrespective of their involvement in the circus trade, a long-standing exclusionary behavior that is amply documented by a few literate Gypsies who chronicled their daily life (e.g. Reeve 2003 [1958]). The same signs are found in other parts of Europe, mainly on vacant lots that were previously used as "stopping places" by traveling families. This public discourse of exclusion and its official status in the form of township bylaws today perpetuate the ideologies that led to the persecutions engineered by the Nazi and Vichy governments during the Second World War. In many cases, it would seem that the declared commitment to rescuing circus animals is, in part, a way to legitimize the hostility toward the traditional circus in the service of another, less politically palatable, racist agenda.

Those whose families have been involved in the circus for countless generations as a way of life are tragically affected by such hatred. Giving a voice to their anger and anguish, while trying to understand the current cultural evolution that jeopardizes their place in society, is one of the purposes of this book. To do so will require that these events and affects be framed in the much wider perspective of historical developments, cultural evolution, and the ensuing conflicts that arise from these social and political transformations.

The challenge is to understand the forces at play in human societies since the advent of the Neolithic Age and the progressive demise of the hunter-gatherer ways of life that had defined the emerging humankind for several million years. In many respects, the Gypsies are heirs to the primal foragers who, through industry, cunning, and inventiveness, ensured the survival and development of the human species.

2

First Movement

Andante Sostenuto

The Time of the Gypsies

Koan: *"Those who do not own space own time"*

Who Are the Gypsies?

In 1960, while I was a student in Paris, I befriended a casual encounter, Ivan Yankovich, who was from a Serbian Gypsy family temporarily settled with their bears in a camp in the eastern suburban zone of the city. In good weather, they were roaming the streets in the center of Paris and presented their dancing plantigrades and trained goats wherever they could find an appropriate spot and an interested audience. As a part of their brief performances, his little sister was doing contortions on a small carpet spread on the sidewalk. Whenever I happened to come across them, Ivan would flash a smile and I would be the first one to drop a coin in the drum, a crucial move that usually prompted other spectators to follow suit.

Admittedly, in Europe, the circus in its many forms was, and still is, only a small part of the means of existence of the partly nomadic minority who are broadly known in English as *Gypsies*. However, it is not possible to fully understand the cultural dynamics and significance of the circus in modern times without first bringing into focus the people who fostered its European emergence and institutional development. It is one of the main contentions of this book that the fundamental forms and contents of the traditional circus are intimately linked with Gypsy culture. The name "Gypsies" will be used in this book instead of more precise ethnic sub-categories such as, for instance, *Rom*,

Kalderash, *Vlach*, or *Sinti* because this term has gained currency through the centuries. Although some segments of this minority resent being identified as "Gypsies" on the ground that the word often carries stigmatizing connotations in the mainstream population, its currency is usually accepted as a general self-identity indicator by the majority of those who acknowledge their belonging to one or another of these ethnic lineages. "Gypsy" is indeed adopted by large portions of these diverse communities which have endorsed it as expressing their own cultural specificity by opposition to the all-encompassing label through which they define those who are not from Gypsy ancestry for which they have coined their own exclusionary category.

Let us note, in passing, that the word "Gypsy" can be uttered with a great variety of intonations such as a stress on the first syllable indicating scorn and hostility. Instead, it will always be produced in this book with an accent that expresses affection and respect. In addition, the contents of the texts will offset, I hope, any potential discriminating attitudes and prevent misunderstandings. A private group of Facebook that is obviously run by members of the community, titled "Gypsy/Traveller times past," proudly publishes old family photos of their British members. Most pictures show men, women, and children at various periods of time, standing before their tents, horse-drawn wagons, or motorized caravans, or in settings that show that quite a few of these families settled in sedentary life. Since I joined this group in early 2020, I noted that only very few of these photos suggest a connection with the circus. Most of them indicate some other traditional trades such as basket making, metal and wood working, or seasonal farming help, in particular picking hops. Horses as a means of transportation or chattel are often visible in group photographs. This relative absence of visual reference to acrobatics in this particular set does not obfuscate, of course, the fact that the traditional circus has been associated with Gypsy culture for centuries, even millennia.

In one of the most authoritative books devoted to the history of the Gypsies, the word "circus" appears only once to briefly refer to one of these communities' traditional activities as performers (Fraser 1992: 306). Devoting too much space to an ephemeral activity that left little record, if any, would have been a distraction from the essential. Historians deal with written archives and surviving iconography. Fraser's work provides ample evidence of the most salient constant of the history of Gypsies in Europe: their relentless persecution by the powers of the time with occasional periods of respite, notably when their skills as horsemen and ironsmiths were needed in warfare. In the most recent account of the current social conditions of these nomadic families, *Romaphobia: The Last Acceptable Form of Racism* (McGarry 2017), there is no mention of the circus.

"Entertainers," though, is listed as one of their means of existence. It should be noted that the term "acceptable" in the subtitle of this book is sarcastic. It is meant to denounce a bias that mostly remains below the radar of legal and moral objection in the mainstream European population. In *The Time of the Gypsies*, an in-depth study of East European Vlachs of Hungary, ethnographer Michael Stewart (1997) has explored the social consequences of the persisting stereotypes that affect the lives of these communities. In many countries, "antisemitism" is a well-defined criminal form of behavior both verbal and physical, but there does not seem to be a legal equivalent to control and repress "anti-gypsism." The populations Stewart researched were mostly underpaid factory and farm workers rather than animal trainers or acrobats. Nevertheless, we have to keep in mind that the current crisis of the circus cannot be abstracted from its ancestral association with the nomadic Gypsies who perpetuated this form of popular entertainment as was pointed out in the introduction to this volume.

Figure 4 This French print of 1895 encapsulates the traditional interface between nomadic Gypsies and the authorities that try to control them. Its title is "Gypsy Census Caravan and Dancing Bear" (Alamy Stock Photo).

Figure 5 From the depth of time, through borderless lands, nomadic families with their animals have carried forward the circus trade and arts. This ageless, faded postcard from the early photography era evokes the caravans of the traveling performers who, for millennia, brought elusive wonders to the midst of sedate villages and boisterous seasonal fairs. (Courtesy of Nikolai Tovarich).

Figure 6 Modern British Gypsies on their way to Appleby horse fair.

Where Do Gypsies Come from?

Qalandar have numerous stories explaining their nomadic origins [...]Like the Rom. tinkers, and other nonpastoral nomads of Asia and Europe, the Qalandar maintain themselves as an economic parasitic group within a sedentary society [...] The Qalandar are considered a pariah group. This has produced a strong sense of group identity and contributes to the viability of their subsistence strategy as entertainers within the socioecological milieu of sedentists.
    Joseph Berland, *No Five Fingers Are Alike*, The Peripatetic Qalandar, 1982: 76–7

The terms "Gypsies," "Travellers," "Romanichals," "Bohemians," and their equivalents and variants in the European languages, or more generally "nomads," are labels with stigmatizing connotations that are still used by the dominant sedentary populations to refer to groups of families which are not settled in permanent places but move around in search of opportunities through peddling their various skills such as metal scraps and rags collecting, horse trading, seasonal works in farms and cities, and various forms of entertainment. Joseph Berland's ethnography of the Qalandar, a nomadic population of the Asian subcontinent that specializes in bear and monkey training among other typical circus skills, offers precious insights into the ways and means of the European Gypsies, and shows that there is a remarkable cultural continuity from India across the Eurasian peninsula. Another enlightening ethnographic source is Lee Siegel's (1991) insider's account of nomadic street magicians in India.

"Where are you from? Where do you hail from?" is a question that reveals a bias of the sedentary mind. Individuals must first be related to a determined place as the basis of their identity. When Nicephorus Gregoras (1295–1360), the Byzantine prolix astronomer and historian, asked this question to nomadic performers who were entertaining Constantinople's crowds with feats of acrobatics and horsemanship, they answered by telling him where they had been and where they were going (Bouissac 2018: 161–5). Their relation to space was in terms of transience; they carried their homestead with themselves as paradoxical as this may sound for settled people. Naturally, historians have difficulties fathoming a migrant population that did not originate from a particular geographic area and there is no shortage of theories that contend to assign a native place to these travelers and a reason for their moving out. As sedentary inquirers could not accept a response that would not fit their frame of mind, the most expedient strategy was, for the Gypsies, to comply with these expectations and invent some plausible stories.

This approach explains the origin of the word "Gypsies" that derives from "Egyptians" because the ancestors of these modern nomads, originally hailing from the Indian subcontinent where, in any case, they had probably always been nomads, claimed in the fifteenth century to be pilgrims coming from Lower Egypt, that is, Mesopotamia and the Mediterranean coast, when they migrated westwards, via Turkey and Eastern Europe in late Medieval times. Gypsy scholar, Ian Hancock (2017), proposed some controversial variants on this diaspora dynamics from Northwestern India and insisted on using the term "Romanies" or "Rromanies" rather than "Gypsies" although his perspective is admittedly biased because of his own Vlach Romani ancestry, a population that had been located for a very long time in Southeastern Europe where they had been enslaved. Angus Fraser (1992) has documented with great care the strategies used by these nomads to defuse the hostility of the populations they encountered and exploited when some clans reached the kingdoms of Western Europe in the fifteenth century. Fraser claims that there is evidence that the official letters signed by popes, princes, or other authorities supporting their claim to be "pilgrims" were forgeries. The Gypsy tradition itself refers to that scheme as the "great fat Gypsy lie." At a time when communications could not travel faster than the speed of a horse, these letters often sufficed to secure safe conduct and the procurement of subsistence. The status of Christian pilgrims was indeed, then, a legitimate and respected explanation for being on the move. These well-organized bands were supposed to accomplish a seven-year penance of vagrancy to expiate some collective sins of which there existed several versions. They were great story tellers and they managed to master the languages of the countries which they roamed. Their narratives also provided a cover for their distinct physical appearance, clothing, and customs.

Historians have retraced the movements of these troupes across the Eurasian peninsula thanks to chronicles and legal records from the fifteenth century on. These archival documents show that they were indeed sometimes treated as *bona fide* pilgrims but the historical evidence mostly points to repressive edicts that were meant to control, exclude, and ultimately eradicate these transient troupes who were often accused of thieving and deceiving the credulous and impressionable populations they encountered. At times, they were considered fair game and they were hunted and murdered by local vigilantes.

Traveling by foot and usually with some horses which carried their tents and basic tools and utensils, they temporarily settled in fields, forests, or in the margins of villages and cities. Their presence, though, was at times welcome since they also provided essential services such as metal work, small carpentry, baskets, and medicines in places that were deprived of such commodities. Some were skilled musicians, storytellers, animal trainers, and acrobats. The women were experts in palmistry. They were also very knowledgeable in horse husbandry and animal handling in general, and they were occasionally hired for temporary casual works such as harvesting crops but also enrolled in, or even forcefully recruited by the military establishments at a time when fit horses and metal working on the fly were essential assets for warfare. Their multiple skills were such an economic resource that they were eventually thrown into slavery by the rulers of countries that were parts of the Ottoman and Russian empires (Hancock 2002: 20–7).

A second wave of massive migrations occurred in the nineteenth and twentieth centuries, mostly from Eastern Europe and the Balkans when conflicts caused the shuffling of borders and the collapse of kingdoms and empires, including some in which the Gypsies had been enslaved for many generations. Now known as the Roms or Roma people who speak Romany, an Indo-European language spoken in India that had been somewhat adulterated by words borrowed from the languages of the various countries in which they had survived. These newcomers encountered the same hostility mixed with fascination as their earlier predecessors in the western European nation-states which were now equipped with efficient bureaucracies and modern methods of control. The pilgrimage narrative had lost its relevance but there were credible alternatives such as escaping Islamic persecutions or fleeing the predicaments of slavery. These nomads who by definition tended to ignore conventional borders, became a part of the European social landscape under various names with which they identified, or which were assigned to them such as Sinti, Bohemians, Romanychals, Tsiganes, and Manouches among others. Their unconventional way of life remained problematic for the long-established sedentary cultures with which they interfaced.

Then, in the aftermath of the Second World War—during which many of them were tortured and killed in the Nazi concentration camps (Hancock 2002)—and the eventual demise of the Soviet Union, the open borders of Europe allowed for a renewed unimpeded population flow westward, including Gypsies, in search of new opportunities away from the struggling economies and discriminatory contexts in which many had been trapped for generations, including the forced cultural assimilation that had been the policy implemented by the communist governments (Stewart 1997).

Now, well into the twenty-first century, the hostility toward nomads persists in Europe from Scotland to Italy with an array of official exclusions, interdictions, legislations, expulsions, prosecutions, and various kinds of spontaneous popular harassments to the point that it appears that the self-restraints entailed by the contemporary principles of civil liberties and political correctness do not fully apply to the minorities which are not permanently bound to a piece of land or a permanent home. "Forbidden to nomads" signs in any languages are erected in many European countries at places where Gypsies and other travelers were used to set up camps or build temporary structures designed to perform spectacles with their animals for local audiences. The open hostility toward the traditional circus that has emerged during the last few decades in continental Europe and the British Isles is fed, more or less tacitly, by racist arguments.

In more tolerant townships and counties, authorizations to stay and play are strictly limited in time and, often, they are assigned places in the margins of the city, if not beyond its limits. There remain, deeply rooted in the past, antagonistic attitudes that relentlessly exclude these families and the communities they form from the civil order on the basis of their reputed indifference to the notion of ownership, and foremost to the exclusive claim to portions of space that characterizes sedentary populations. As owners of traveling circuses that still attract fascinated audiences in cities and villages, they remain the target of aggressive intolerance from fanatic groups that incriminate their dependence on trained animals for entertainment, but they also confront systemic stereotyping and intolerance in the population at large.

Treating Gypsies as an undifferentiated population, though, would be mistaken. The attitude consisting of indiscriminately lumping together the members of a large part of contemporary society into a single category rife with stereotypes is precisely the hallmark of racism. The most numerous ethnic minority in Europe is indeed diverse in many respects. On the one hand, old tribal structures and cultures have survived and remain at the root of specific identities and distinct specializations, including for instance the circus; on the other hand, a Gypsy middle class has emerged over the centuries through adopting sedentary ways of life and benefitting from mainstream education and business opportunities, thus becoming invisible. Among them, some families acquired social prominence and considerable wealth by pursuing artistic careers and running extremely successful circuses. Some gifted comedians such as Charlie Chaplin, who was born to a British Gypsy mother, reached global stardom. Like middle-class Jewish families that also included prominent circus owners and artists (Meishar 2020; Otte 2006; Roth 1996 and 2021), these affluent Gypsies were victims of the policy of extermination of the Nazi regime. With the complicity of other European countries, half of the Gypsy population in Germany at the time was systematically murdered irrespective of their social distinction or artistic talents. In France, during the Second World War, traveling Gypsies were rounded up and either deported to Germany or incarcerated in camps where they were kept long after the end of the war. Afterwards, they remained subject to administrative and police surveillance through compulsory identity booklets which they were obligated to present and have regularly stamped by the local police of the places where they stayed for a while. Through all these ordeals, Gypsies with their traditional trades and customs have proved to be extraordinary resilient. With varied fortunes, they remain a robust part of the social landscape in which they can, at times, blend indistinguishably or, on the contrary, foreground and benefit from their distinctive characteristics. Through industry, cunning, and camouflage, they are the great survivors among us and whoever had the privilege of being admitted in their midst can bear witness to their human warmth and the richness of their culture.

Contrapuntal Development 1: Friendship and Loyalty

Writing on Gypsies in the scholarly, detached mode makes me feel uneasy, out of sync. Whether by chance, choice, or destiny, my life has been profoundly impacted by my friendship with two circus Gypsy men at a time, in my twenties, when I was struggling to emerge from the mold imposed on me since my birth. One of them was for a few years my mentor, of the generation of my father, and I remained in contact with him until his death; the other could have been my slightly younger brother. I was not doing academic research then, hardly knowing what ethnography was. I was not relating to them as objects of curiosity or study. They embodied human values with which I felt comfortable. I loved them as friends not as Gypsies. I will never betray their trust for the sake of a narrative. They knew by instinct on which side of the divide I was. They took for granted my loyalty. In what follows, in order to sketch out the Gypsy worldview that, I believe, is crucial for understanding the circus, I will use the accounts of others who felt free to break their promises and write more than they should have for the sake of science or fame. This is what justifies, as much as the relentless persecutions they suffered over the centuries, the deep distrust of the Gypsies for the Gorgios (Gorgers) or the Gadje, that is, all those who are not Gypsies. The relative authenticity of the autobiographical books by Pechon de Ruby (2019 [1596]), George Borrow (1851), and Jan Yoors (1987 [1967]), for instance, who shared part of their life with Gypsy bands, is unquestionable but the glimpses of empathy and gratitude that surface in their writing is too readily drowned in the rhetoric of existential distance: they made it clear that they were not the same as these "others" who had accepted them in the midst of their family. All I can say is that their attempts to expose the Gypsy ways of life and values are mostly congruent with my own experience in essence if not in the details. Though, as I perused these books during the last winter, I could not help sensing the feeling of betrayal that these men and women would have experienced if they had been able to read and decipher those works they had made possible through their trusting hospitality—and some of them certainly were able to do so and had ways to express their enduring resentment.

Being a Gypsy: The Bane or Bliss of Difference

The Romanies' tenacious grip on their culture—keeping up old ways connected to motion, even long after you've stopped—has frequently be blamed on their far-flung Indian roots: on an inescapable foreignness that survived the passage of time. But what if clinging to the trappings of nomadism simply mirrors one of the oldest facets of all human cultures: prioritizing survival, and moving about accordingly, rather than grimly staying put until whatever end?

Damian Le Bas, **The Stopping Places: A journey through Gypsy Britain**, 2018: 141–2

The current century perpetuates the systemic discrimination and hostility that targeted Gypsies in the past. Only relatively few of them can escape the hardship of living in camps or ghettolike neighborhoods, and gain access to the mainstream society at the cost of toning down their identity. As we have seen above, the circus folks who successfully manage entertainment businesses are often exposed to racial hatred. The Roma people are Europe's largest minority. It is estimated that about 80 percent of ten million Roma live in deprived neighborhoods across Europe. As the 2020 pandemic wreaks havoc in the world, the general population's anxiety is leading, as already happened several times in the past, to the scapegoating of Gypsy communities that suffer abusive segregation, excessive coercion, and medical deprivation (Walker 2020). They are victimized through an endless cycle of self-perpetuating exclusion because of their perceived differences that originate from their way of life rather than from any assumed biological specificity.

In an article published in *The Guardian* of June 15, 2020, British writer and photographer Grace Claire O'Neill asks: "I'm a Romany Gypsy—why is racism against us acceptable?" She grew up in a small town in Lancashire. She explained that her working-class family was not different from the others in their neighborhood except that her father was urging them to keep a low profile as he had suffered from discrimination all his life. Nonetheless, she remembers that she and her siblings were bullied after one of the kids had found out that they were Gypsies. They were called names such as "Gyppo" and other slurs. Later on, she lived through aggressive anti-Gypsy campaigns prompted by popular tabloids. Today, the situation has not improved. O'Neill confesses that even now she is "presented with three choices in any new environment" she enters

> whether that be a workplace, a friendship or even a relationship: 'come out' to the person and make clear my ethnicity from the start but risk unfavorable treatment; drip-feed them bits of information and hope they connect the dots themselves; or stay silent, and hope they don't say anything offensive or upsetting about my culture. I am constantly having to shrink or dilute my ethnicity to be more palatable to others.
>
> (O'Neill 2020)

What is the basis of these perceived differences that are invoked to justify the intolerance toward the Gypsies? Although it has been shown that this minority is not ethnically homogenous (Okely 1983), "Gypsies" has become in English an all-encompassing term corresponding to "Gitans" and "Tsiganes" in French, and "Zigeuner" in German. Other European countries have such designations that are used by the mainstream population as a label of exclusion rather than a denotation of mere difference as is the case when they refer to the citizens of other countries. Whether this word is uttered with fear and hatred or conveys a connotation of romantic fascination, it indicates radical otherness.

However, we must keep in mind that this term covers a great diversity of ethnic groups with different origins, cultures, and languages. Those who have acquired some insider's knowledge of these originally nomadic ways of life have reported the complexity of their distinct traditions, occupations, and dialects (e.g., Matras 2015). The tribes and clans through which they assert their relative identities among themselves are not obvious to outsiders although some ethnographers have documented at least in part this social and cultural complexity (e.g., Liegeois 1983).

All nomads who inhabit nowadays the confines of Europe, with the exception of some pastoralist communities, are commonly lumped under this category which implies for the general population some racial rather than mere cultural differences. Conversely, from the point of view of these nomads, whether or not they have become sedentary, all non-Gypsies are called "Gadjo" (plural: Gadje) or "Gorgios," also "Gorgers" in the UK, irrespective of their actual nationality or cultural identity. This is for them a broad category of people they consider of lesser value because of some aspects of their culture they find unpalatable. This counter-stigmatization gives free rein to various forms of guiltless exploitation. This divide runs deeply in European society and, to a lesser extent perhaps, in the Americas. That might be, though, a mistaken impression as Jorge Fernandez Bernal, who prefaced the 2017 book by Ian Hancock, *We are the Romani People*, stated that, as a young Gypsy in Argentina, he had to hide his true identity at school by claiming that his look and accent were due to his Greek origins in order to avoid being bullied and called names. Many young Gypsies all over the world have reported such abuses when they were sent to primary schools. Listening to Scott Redmond, a British Romany Traveller, will provide an up-to-date account of this social condition as it is experienced today: https://www.facebook.com/658551547588605/posts/2896751457101925/?vh=e&d=n

The Gypsies' distinct status, though, is based on culture rather than nature. Indeed, it should be remembered that the notion of race is a social, political, and ideological construct rather than a biological fact (Lévi-Strauss 1971; Muller-Wille 2010). It is often used to justify the exclusion and persecution of underprivileged groups. The physical appearance is only the tip of the iceberg and depends on grooming and clothing as much as physiology. Genetic variations are widespread among the humankind and most lineages bear witness to entangled DNA flows. The identification of "racial" differences based on anatomical features is a sinister chapter of recent human history that ultimately sprang from a misunderstanding of the theory of evolution and the development of social Darwinism.

Efforts have been made in recent times to use the methods of genomics to establish the genetic basis of the so-called racial difference of Gypsies (e.g., Martinez-Cruz et al. 2016). It shows at most that some lineages hail back indeed to the Indian subcontinent. However, this is also true of other members of the population at large. The western Eurasian peninsula has been a genetic melting pot for a very long time as successive waves of immigrants or invaders encountered a geographical limit to their westward and northward progress. More relevant as a basis for human differences are the various cultures that evolved in interaction with peculiar physical and social environments. A case in point is the tests that were performed on Irish travelers to find out whether they were "genetically" Gypsies. The results were negative (Gmelsh and Gmelsh 2014). However, all the cultural characteristics of supposedly authentic Gypsies are found in the way of life of the Irish travelers: nomadism, kinds of crafts, love and knowledge of horses, begging and palmistry, adoptions of local personal names and religions, and even beliefs and words that are typically Romani. The proponents of genetic "Gypsiness" invoke the influence of interethnic contacts and influences to account for these resemblances, but this is precisely the way cultures are generated and develop in conflictual contexts with a mixture of assimilation and opposition.

The fluidity of any form of open nomadism is unpalatable to sedentary populations who cannot fathom a human existence that is not anchored to a piece of land or a dwelling, either as owner or tenant. Itinerant families escape the constant watch of neighbors. This freedom marks them as suspect of having something to hide. Many countries made "vagrancy," that is, free movements from place to place, a crime, while moving from one's home temporarily or changing home for employment reasons or because of marriage remain within the social norms. Being systematically rejected, while being occasionally used as providers of goods and services, was a strong incentive to develop resilient forms of solidarity and common cultural identities in opposition to the social environment in which they had no choice but to survive. In the meantime, they preserved a pragmatic interface with the populations with which they had to deal by adopting common local patronyms and religions. Both were factors of integration that eased the securing of relative protection. Survival is the key. If indeed, the Gypsy specificity is cultural rather than biological, the discrimination they suffered, and still suffer in many circumstances, is nothing but intolerance of others' way of life in the aggressive guise of racism.

A Deeper Time Perspective

I have mentioned how humans have the capacity to develop the strangest psychology. This has developed over thousands of years—since the Neolithic Age (around 6,000 years ago) specifically—allowing severe changes to occur for tribal people in Britain and in many other parts of the world. As ancient civilizations began springing up [...] people were using sophisticated [...] technology in their almost overnight shift away from tribal structure and values. [...] Neolithic Britain not only saw the spread of farming, but as weapons were also being developed [...] social hierarchy made its debut, altering the structure within tribes, forever. [...] I feel that this social shift was the last thing that anyone needed. As a Chovihano [Gypsy shaman], I see it more as a shadow passing over the land, a bad spell, the beginning of the curse we Gypsies talk about [...]

Patrick Jasper Lee, ***We Borrow the Earth***, 2015: 224–5

To understand the mismatch between the Gypsy way of life and the conventions of the settled populations among which they transit, we have indeed to consider the larger context of the deep time of cultural evolution within which, eventually, the circus emerged. The archaeological records show that hunter-gatherers roamed the earth for at least two million years before some tribes settled down in convenient places where they had discovered how to grow nutritious plants and breed captive animals instead of chasing these life-sustaining resources across open space. The settlers called these portions of land theirs and defended them against predators and intruders. At the same time, technological innovations improved their ability to exploit their surroundings. However, the advent of the Neolithic age was not an instant wholesome transformation. Both modes of survival coexisted for a very long time not only as distinct cultures but also as mixed means of existence. Hunter-gatherers still prosper in some parts of the planet but they are increasingly confronted with pressure to abandon their mode of life and become sedentary. Some are simply slaughtered under the cover of the forest so that industrial logging and farming can progress unimpeded.

In the farmlands and urban settlements of Europe and Asia, the two cultures have long coexisted in a pervasively conflicting mode. Constant mobility is unfathomable for people who define themselves through their belonging to a place and their ownership of a piece of the earth. How can an identity be maintained in the absence of a geographical anchorage? The nomads are a constant challenge to the tenets of civilization as it is conceived and enforced by the various forms of political authority and cultural institutions. In a world whose space is structured by exclusive collective or individual possessions, the nomads can be defined only negatively as never being at home anywhere, or behaving abusively as if the whole world belonged to them. By contrast, as Patrick Jasper Lee declares through the title of his book, Gypsies "borrow the earth." Their perception and conception of space is alien to the worldview of the mainstream population and commands a different practical and ethical behavior. As hunter-gatherers, foragers, or scavengers, they are bound to be opportunistic because what they can catch one day might not be available the next day, let it be a hedgehog, a hare, a chicken, or some more valuable items that can be transported easily, if not move on its own like a scooter or a horse. They take enough to satisfy their present needs in calories but they cannot hoard goods in excess of what they can carry with them when they move.

For sedentary populations, they have a well-established reputation of being parasites in the European countries they have crisscrossed over the centuries because they tend to consider the notion of land ownership as illegitimate.

They don't believe that the earth can truly be divided and that any part of it can exclusively belong to anybody. At most, one can borrow a place for a while, close to a stream of fresh water that ultimately comes from the sky and runs toward the sea. Who can claim to own the forces of nature that make plants grow and animals reproduce. The settled human populations experience them as pilferers, thieves, raiders, or pirates. They are also reproached to obtain resources through begging, deceiving, and scheming. By many of its aspects, the magic of the circus is a mixture of all these skills. As the father of my mentor used to tell his sons when they hit the road with their menagerie and circus: "You must make people dream!"

When historians want to explain the so-called migration of a population that shares some genetic indicators with the current inhabitants of northwestern India, they try to relate this demographic movement to some particular events. For some, it is under the pressure of the expansion of Islam; for others, the ancestors of the modern Gypsies would have been a caste-based part of military campaigns that followed advances or retreats and found themselves stranded at some point in what is now Turkey; in other explanations, it is suggested that there was a decision to migrate, although the reasons proposed vary greatly: escaping misery, slavery, or looking for greener pastures? An alternative, cultural view is that a non-Neolithic relationship to space is alien to the notion of moving out of a determined region to exploit another one. There is no obvious constraint to movements except high mountains, large deserts, and deep rivers. Areas of less resistance always offer opportunities to search for subsistence if it is not encroaching on other tribes' foraging territory, whose members may resort to violence to protect their turf. The rise of civilization transformed the earth by covering it with a network of paths and roads, and by concentrating vital resources in permanent settlements that hoard significant surpluses but are far apart. The spaces between are a welcome affordance since they mostly escape the continuing watch of the land owners and allow for fluid, unimpeded movements.

Therefore, rather than conceiving the appearance of the Gypsies in Europe as resulting from some kind of historical event that triggered a "migration," it seems more plausible that it was a continuous, progressive move whose directions and modalities were both constrained and helped by the emerging forms of Neolithic modernity. Where the natural environment was not touched by the drastic reshaping of space through construction and cultivation, those who are now classified as "forest tribes," for instance, in the Indian polity nomenclature kept roaming territories with which they had been familiar for ages, using trails and tracks made by animals and themselves, and coping with the uncertainties of their natural environment. There were still until recently such nomadic populations as the *Jenu Korubas* of the Deccan plateau in India, that built temporary foliage huts, devising ways of surviving predators and unpredictable wild elephants, until the local and national governments forced sedentarism upon them in the form of clusters of concrete shelters forming villages on the edge of the forests. Until that moment, they had escaped the strangling effect of urban and agricultural obstacles to their free movement. We can easily figure out that the nomads that still are commonly encountered in India in the vacant spaces that are found in sprawling cities are the descendants of early hunter-gatherers who adapted to drastic changes in their original environment, using domestic horses to cover a new magnitude of distances thanks to the creation of trade roads and paths.

Sedentary populations, made efficient by their new technology and exploitation of forced human labor, produced a surplus of goods, cattle, poultry, and other means of survival that they could store in premises and fenced fields. These were obvious opportunities for hunter-gatherers who would find violent or cunning ways to wrestle from them their daily ration of proteins. Being constantly on the move, though, would prevent them from hoarding quantities beyond the short-term necessities. Securing these goods, however, could be done through other means than sheer stealing such as offering actual or imaginary services in exchange, or inventing cunning methods of manipulating the sedentary owners of fertile lands and other resources so that they would part voluntarily from the products of their own properties. Hunter-gatherers usually do not exhaust the source of meat and vegetables beyond their needs. Obviously, it is impossible to carry around excessive weight of food, and the need to keep the source producing these goods alive required that they keep a balance between exploiting and gratifying the sedentary people. The traditional Gypsy way of life represents an optimal, albeit rife with risks, exploitation of their human and natural environment.

At a time when horses were at the center of civilization, they offered exceptional equine knowledge due undoubtedly to their own dependence on this means of transportation and their constant close contact with these animals. There was always a need for good or beautiful horses that had given rise to intense trading. On horse fairs, those from afar were famous for their expertise in equine husbandry and the quality of their stock. Where the horse that one bought was from was irrelevant if it appeared to be a good deal. Gypsies could be honest and trade gem animals but they were not above improving on the short term the quality of their offering. Piebald or pinto horses became their specialty probably because, originally, a "painted" coat can be both natural or artificial, and any animal can be transformed into a painted one rather quickly by expert traders. These horses are still a hallmark of traditional family circus. Known as "Gypsy horses" in the UK, they are still seen in abundance in Appleby and other horse fairs, as well as favorites of traveling family circuses all over Europe.

One of the Hungarian Gypsy informants of ethnographer Michael Stewart, Šošoj, emphatically declared:

> We deal with horses; it is in our hair. I grew up with horses, and I simply couldn't live without them. I'm completely used to having them by me, although, as you know, they don't work for us. We keep the horses rather than the horses keeping us. We could put the money to other uses, for instance, to buy the children what they need. But, you see, with horses it's like, if one hasn't got them, others say, 'Let God strike him down; he's like a poor Romungro [a Gypsy who has renounced his tradition to integrate into regular Magyar life] who hasn't got anything.' That's why I have horses. Not just me but the Rom in general. We go to the market, we sell and we buy, we swap: We know how to do it.
>
> (Stewart 1997: 141).

Horses, that are central to Gypsy cultures, are also a major component of the traditional circus. *Le cirque commence à cheval* [Circus starts on horseback] declares the title of a historical account of the circus by French librarian Paul Adrian (1979 [1968]). We can also invoke the popular injunction that was shouted by impatient audiences when the announcer happened to be too longwinded for their taste: "Cut the talk! Send in the horses!"

The Circus Enters History: Was Phillip Astley a Gypsy?

For all that Philip Astley was well known during his lifetime, little is actually known about his early life. Most of the information we have about him comes from secondary sources, the vast majority of which were written after his death.

Steve Ward, **The Life & Times of Philip Astley**, 2018: 10

Astley's Riding School was merely the draft of a circus. It was "enclosed partly by sheds and partly by rough palings, and in its centre was a pigeon-house that became a bandstand.

Dominique Jando, **Philip Astley & The Horsemen who Invented the Circus**, 2018: 30

Sedentary, literate cultures are averse to people and objects that cannot be firmly anchored in space and time. They treasure property deeds, treatises that establish boundaries, walls that can contain and protect goods, symbols, and memorials carved in stone. In the Western European civil order individuals are taken into account only as long as their existence is supported by an administrative document established by the officials of their city or their church that specifies their date of birth and the name of their parents as well as an address or at least a locality. When people move or when their status changes, they are supposed to have their records updated lest they lose their legitimate claim to civil existence. They are considered to be dead only once they are certified to be so. The conservation of successive layers of archives, sometimes covering centuries, provides evidence for narratives that are precisely mapped upon space and time.

The form of entertainment that would eventually be called the circus escaped for a very long time the scrutiny of historians. The ephemeral, fluid reality of nomadic troupes leaves only elusive archives, if any marks at all of their passage. Their tracks quickly dissolve to be overridden by new ones. Indirect evidence, though, indicates that entertainers continuously roamed the Eurasian peninsula and its islands, providing excitement with daring acrobatics, animals performing tricks, and salacious buffooneries. However, it took the social and artistic revolutions of the twentieth century for popular entertainments to be considered worthy of political and scholarly attention. In 1919, Lenin declared the circus to be an essential part of cultural institutions on par with ballet and opera. In eighteenth-century England as elsewhere in Europe, equestrian shows, trick riders' spectacles, and other forms of popular distractions abounded at a time when the dawn of the industrial age caused people to gather in settlements larger than traditional villages. Progressively, the rhythm of the periodic fairs was superseded by the shorter timing of the work week and the punctuation of national celebrations. Regular potential audiences had now various degrees of disposable income. Ever resourceful Gypsies who have always been expert in horsemanship and other spectacular performances naturally exploited this changing social context. Their shows were at times advertised on ephemeral printed bills. This, however, is not sufficient to secure one's place in history. Historians need permanent traces in the form of land deeds and buildings, written and printed reports, lasting archives. This is how the establishment of a specialized spot, whatever its degree of improvisation, on London's map by Philip Astley in 1768 was construed by historians as the point of origin of the modern circus whose 250th anniversary, in 2018, was celebrated in some quarters such as the International Circus Festival of Monte Carlo, as the "birth of the circus." Many institutions organized events and publishers exploited the occasion. Even new acrobatic companies claimed a part of the festive celebration by setting up thematic theatrical performances that had little to do with the traditional circus. In France, a family circus whose head is known to profess admiration for authoritarian regimes took this opportunity to re-enact the supposed anniversary of the circus under the aegis of a heroic military man, with a show full of uniforms, swords, guns, and charging horses, thus appropriating the prestigious trappings of the military cavalry and implicitly claiming for his own family a very improbable lineage in spite of their well-documented Gypsy or traveler background. In an Op Ed published in Circus Alive, British clown David Konyot offers an alternative view on the origin of the so-called modern circus whose "birth" cannot be pinpointed to the initiative of a Sergeant Major in 1768 in London. https://semioticon.com/circus-alive/

Philip Astley is consistently referred to as Sergeant Major Astley because this is the military rank he had reached after seven years serving in a cavalry regiment. This detail was emphasized again and again during the celebrations as if the circus had branched out from the army and the young man had learned all his horsemanship there. This makes historians still more comfortable as it takes the origin of the modern circus away from disreputable nomadic entertainers.

Probably, the truth is much different. What if Philip Astley was in fact a British Gypsy who had a brilliant knack for business like many other Gypsies have proved to possess in the course of history? They usually have clever ways of obfuscating their ostracized origins through popularizing self-serving narratives that fit the legend of a lineage coming from some heroic founding father or historical event.

The two most interesting books that were published on the occasion of the "birthday" of the circus are Dominique Jando's *Philip Astley: The Horsemen Who Invented the Circus* (2018) and Steve Ward's *Father of the Modern Circus. "Billy Buttons": The Life & Times of Philip Astley* (2018). In both books, the parts dedicated to the early life of Philip Astley are cursory and the dearth of hard evidence they can muster is compensated by plausible imaginary circumstances. Ward's title for the second chapter in his book dedicated to Astley's biography acknowledges the paucity of available information: "The mysterious early years." The most essential biographical data comes from what was written after Astley became a self-promoting celebrity in the show business world, often from incidental remarks in other people's memoirs. Depending on the sources, their hero was born on January 8, 1742, in Newcastle-under-Lyme, or on January 20, 1741. When he died in Paris on January 27, 1814, his age was variously given in his obituaries as 71 and 75. All biographers have produced apparently authentic documents from the time he enrolled in the cavalry because the military bureaucracy produced some written sources bearing his name. Then, after he was discharged from the army, there is hardly anything concerning his life until he rented open-air premises for horsemanship displays in South London. There is a gap of two years in between. Historians have not reached agreement on his activities nor on the date and circumstances of his marriage, including some uncertainties regarding the identity of his wife, whether, for instance, her maiden name was Charlotte Taylor or Patty Jones. Church registries constitute only relative evidence because "Philip Astley" was indeed a common name in England and the information provided to Church officials was not commonly verified. Some inconsistencies have been noted.

The main substance of Philip Astley's biographies emphasizes his life as a noted showman. As he eventually became a kind of historical hero of the circus saga, as the one who gave the circus a place of birth on the London map, and thus ushered the circus from vagrancy into history. This is a typical golden legend, in part generated by himself, developed from century to century until today. Taking, as a visual reference, prints of Astley's Olympic Theater in 1808 and 1810, with the imposing stage overlooking the ring, is misleading. At his historical beginning, Astley's amphitheater at Halfpenny Hatch was a rather shabby construction, improvised with wooden panels and canvasses that were characterized as unsafe and a fire hazard by contemporary chroniclers. It actually collapsed and burnt down several times. It appears that the birth of the circus emerged seamlessly from a Gypsy showman tradition. It exploited the

Figure 7 Exterior view of Astley's Riding School as it appeared in 1777. The front is modeled after a typical fairground structure with a few steps up and hanging banners showing samples of the feats to be witnessed inside after payment of an admission fee: various equestrian tricks, rope dancing, and acrobatic "pyramids" (Alamy Stock Photo).

Figure 8 Inside view of Astley's Riding School (or Amphitheater) at Halfpenny Hatch in 1777. This configuration evokes an improvised exploitation of a vacant lot rather than the deliberate design of a spectacular premise (Alamy Stock Photo).

opportunities offered by the transitioning from seasonal fairs to populous urban settings rather than being the absolute beginning of a spectacular institution created from scratch by a military hero of the Seven Year's War.

At least three main arguments can be offered to support the hypothesis that Philip Astley was a British Gypsy whose equestrian skills and knack for business were rooted in a long tradition of surviving on the road in the midst of a hostile social environment thanks, in part, to their capacity to amaze and entertain an audience.

First, the name Astley is found, albeit not too frequently, in British Gypsy genealogies that can be found on the Internet. It is a rather common name in England but we must keep in mind that Gypsies, as a rule, adopted familiar patronyms in the countries in which they lived in search of relative invisibility. If they could not provide the authorities with a permanent address, at least they could offer a name that sounded local. There are various other ways of confusing the hostile social environment in which they survived. First names can be reused from generation to generation. Family members know who is who but outsiders get lost in trying to map individuals upon a precise chronology. Since their appearance in Europe, Gypsies have been expert in outflanking civil documentary control (Fraser 1992: 180–3; Yoors 1967: 110–15).

Secondly, Philip's father, and Philip himself were cabinet makers. This was one of the special trades of Gypsies although not the main one. There are many references to this particular skill with wood in addition to metal working, such as tinsmith and cauldron making, in the literature discussing Gypsy activities in other parts of Europe. Cabinet making was one of their traditional skills that would become more prominent later when itinerant troupes in England started to build wagons instead of setting up tents. Looking at these wooden wagons and the scale of the furniture that fit into them supports the idea that Gypsies were already skilled in making small cabinets.

Thirdly, we are told that a strong interest in horses was running in the Astley family. This special love, of course, was certainly common among the class that could afford to indulge in leisure horsemanship independently of the necessary use of horses for work and transportation. However, Gypsies and generally travelers have always been tightly associated with horses, and this knowledge made them occasional assets for the military command at a time when efficient cavalry was the nerve of the war. In his carefully documented work on the history of Gypsies, Angus Fraser mentions several instances in which Gypsy men were recruited to handle horses, and forge bullets and cannon balls during wars (Fraser 1992: passim). There is in fact a long tradition of the involvement of Gypsies in the military institutions of the countries in which they lived. Even as late as the First World War, a mobilized Gypsy circus owner was appointed veterinarian in the French cavalry in spite of being illiterate, because of his acknowledged skill in training and taking care of horses (Bouglione 1962: 15). Regarding Philip Astley, historians assume in general that this young daring man learned his horsemanship in the army whereas, looking at the evidence, it seems that he actually was one of those who contributed to the management and training of military horses. There is archival evidence that Philip Astley joined the Army precisely when the British military was developing a light cavalry, as opposed to the heavy war horses that were still the rule, as an innovative new tactical tool that brought speed and maneuverability on the battlefields. He may have taken part in some daring skirmishes, including the rescuing of a high officer but his main task was to break horses and ready them for fight. Several anecdotes establish his reputation as a "horse whisperer," a talent that is learned early in the midst of a Gypsy family. It seems that it is only the distinction of his services in this capacity that could have prompted his commander to present him with a prize horse when he left his regiment.

We can also note that it has been difficult to locate with precision the geographic origin of the Astley lineage as they seem to have been at least partly itinerant, a euphemism for nomadic life. It is, though, a misconception to think that all Gypsies were (and are still) continuously on the move. Many were settled as innkeepers or running some other businesses when and where the medieval crafts and trade monopolies became obsolete. Even if Astley's father had a fixed workshop in London, this does not invalidate the hypothesis that the family was from a Gypsy lineage.

Moreover, when and whom Philip Astley married is a murky story. Some have pointed out that most likely more than one Philip Astley lived in London. Historian Steve Ward displays in his 2018 book the relevant archives that appear to settle the question. However, Philip Astley married a young dancer from the entertainment world who was also used to horsemanship. This strongly hints at a commonality of social status and talent.

The hypothesis that Philip Astley was from a Gypsy lineage reduces considerably the gap between the Gypsy tradition and the supposed "birth" of the modern circus, and, at the same time, explains its subsequent developments. Of course, it may be objected that any single one of these arguments does not carry much weight. However, their convergence is rather compelling. One may wonder, then, why the assumed military origin of the circus became so popular among historians as well as among most circus folks. For the former, it is the reassuring feeling that the modern circus is a creation of a respectable member of their own kind who is distinct and distant from the stigmatized Gypsies; for the latter, it is a welcome opportunity to bring some degree of mainstream normalcy to their trade, congruent with their constant claim that their genealogy, five or six degrees down the line, includes a more or less illustrious ancestor who belonged to the nobility or the high end of the business establishment. A typical example is found in the flamboyant autobiography of Ottavio Canestrelli (2016) in which the starting point of the genealogy is claimed to be the illegitimate son of a prominent cardinal and an Italian countess. In other cases, the standard narrative is a romantic story, usually involving a gentleman who fell in love with a female equestrian and joined the circus. This pattern is orchestrated in Gustave Kahn's novel *Le cirque Solaire* [The Solar Circus] (1899), a telling metaphor that begot Ariane Mouchkine's *Theatre du Soleil* [Theater of the Sun], a decade before the name, and the metaphor, were appropriated by the Canadian independent entrepreneurs who claimed to have reinvented the circus under the trade mark *Cirque du Soleil* [Circus of the Sun].

The idea that the circus, as we know it today, sprang from Philip Astley's enterprising mind is simply ludicrous. This view has long been spread in the secondary literature and in the media. Serious historical works do not fail to point out that Astley's permanent setting for his earlier performances was part of a continuous tradition of equestrian schools and trick riders' spectacles. They may not have performed in the now standard circular arena, but the first shabby establishment opened by Astley consisted of a modest grandstand facing the side of an elliptical hippodrome. Years later, after he had secured the necessary resources, a stage was added at one end and the public was seated in the space surrounding the area where equestrian and other acts were displayed. The distance to the stage had to be reduced so that spectators could enjoy both the theatrical and circus parts of the shows. The solution was to shrink the earlier hippodrome shape into a circle, a novelty that proved helpful for the riders doing acrobatics on their horses. The same acrobatics, though, were successfully accomplished before on mounts that moved on straight or elliptic tracks. It is worth noting that after Astley transferred to Paris his Riding School, that was renamed there *Cirque Olympique*, he associated with Antonio Franconi, an Italian acrobat, equestrian, juggler, and occasional wandering physician. Franconi eventually bought Astley's company and successfully ran it for years with his sons through the troubled decades of the French revolution and the Napoleonic empire. As the saying goes, birds of a feather flock together.

The Art of Survival

I clearly remember stealthy long marches into unknown countries, by night. On one such march the horses' hoofs were padded with straw and bound with strips of colored dress material.

Jan Yoors, **The Gypsies**, 1987 [1967]: 117

Whether one accepts or not the hypothesis that Philip Astley was himself from a Gypsy lineage, there is plenty of evidence that he received his early training from men of the trade. The skills of mountebanks, including all forms of acrobatics and animal training, have been well documented in the literature for centuries before 1768. George Strehly, in his reference book on *L'Acrobatie et les Acrobates* [Acrobatics and Acrobats] (1903) underlines the fact that the Gypsies had a crucial impact on the development of the acrobatic arts in Europe during the sixteenth century. We can easily come to the conclusion that the circus under any other name is the ancestral cultural property of Gypsy clans for which performances on the fly were a source of vital income. The probably accidental innovation of the modern standard circular arena is but a variation in a robust tradition that could adapt to whatever physical or social context their proponents would encounter on the paths of their itinerance. The heavy equipment that characterizes modern traveling circuses and some of their acts can easily make us forget that the basis of the spectacular displays produced by traveling Gypsies was eminently portable. Ground acrobatics, either as contortions or hand-to-hand balancing; somersaulting or pyramid building; lifting locally found rocks or logs; sleight of hands and juggling; storytelling and palmistry require only minimal baggage, if any at all. Trained animals, let them be a horse, a bear, and a dog, not only can move on their own but also help transporting light implements and provide protection. The way primal, family-based circuses are still run is an example of an efficient subsistence economy.

The performing specialties themselves are by-products, so to speak, of fundamental survival behaviors. In traditional Gypsy families, the male youngsters are trained very early to develop their muscles and fighting techniques in order to stand their ground when they are attacked or harassed by local men and boys. Some of them often excel in boxing and participate in local matches. Some even became noted boxers in national or international competitions. Clearing high obstacles is also practiced. Leaps and somersaults are classic tactics in martial arts. Jumping over a number of horses has long been a classic of circus acrobatics. In a ring, or in a village square, handstands, hand-to-hand balancing, and fly-and-catch games require strength and coordination that are acquired early in life. Exceptional fitness is indeed the key to a host of circus acts. Three- or four-people-high columns and pyramids make it possible to survey the horizon beyond the limits of someone standing on the ground. Mastering the skill of climbing a vertical, free-standing ladder provides other opportunities than simply astounding naïve spectators. These body-based architectures can also overcome high walls and fences. Contortionists can hide in very small places or containers. Muscular endurance, balancing on a thin edge or across a cable, climbing ropes and developing strong manual grasping and gripping are vital physical assets that can be adapted to spectacular displays when real-life challenges are replaced by stylized acrobatic props. There is a continuum between the successful struggling for life in a hostile environment and the capacity to amaze an audience in an apparently playful context.

However, the circus arts can earn a sufficient subsistence for the performers only as long as they preserve their appearance of novelty. They need to produce information to capture the attention and support of the spectators they attract for the time of an ephemeral show. This is all the more efficient when there is no opportunity for repeat viewings. The dazzling effects run the risk of fading with close, recurring examination of the acrobatic and animal training feats. Familiarity usually breeds contempt. The circus must move on. Nomadism is of the essence of this trade. Acts are remembered as elusive wonders and give rise in the population to embellished narratives that feed the circus legend. From this point of view, the circus is beautifully adapted to the Gypsy culture in the same way as the services they traditionally provided such as repairing metal utensils, sharpening knives, basket weaving, seasonal picking of crops, peddling commodities and good luck trinkets, and predicting the future, for example. These activities would not have been sustainable as sedentary enterprises because the demands are sporadic rather than continuous, and the outcome is far from certain.

For those families that specialized in entertainment, animals were, and still are when they are not prohibited by law, an essential component of this form of subsistence economy. The duration of a show, even in a modest format, must be commensurate with the admission fee or sufficiently exciting for triggering voluntary donations when the hat is passed around. Acts cannot be too long as the interest can quickly wear off. The audience must be dazzled by surprising performances. The members of the group may represent a diversity of spectacular skills, but each act lasts merely a few minutes. Exotic animals, even if they make brief appearances in the arena, and domestic animals that are trained to do unexpected tricks, are the necessary complement for the trade to be cost effective. Animals are not paid artists and can often be fed and sheltered cheaply. Usually, Gypsy families take care of their animals from the time of their birth or have acquired them at a young age. Bonding occurs naturally between humans and their animals across several generations that shared a common destiny. The culture of the circus is a case of multi-species extended families in which some animals such as horses and dogs are closer than others to the core. But all, including predators, are precious assets that require knowledgeable attention. They are all given names to which they respond, thus demonstrating their own sense of belonging in a social environment from which they receive food and life-long care.

Contrapuntal Development 2: What Is a Name?

Monte Carlo, January 19, 2020. The 44th International Circus Festival has attracted once more a large crowd of circus fans and professionals. At the end of the afternoon show I take a stroll to visit the animals that are displayed in large enclosures beside the imposing tent. The public for the evening program has not shown up yet. There is a lull in the usual buzzing activities around the lot. On the way, I pass the fairground booths that offer drinks, sweets, and other snacks. There is a carnival's atmosphere, a blend of music, smell, and loud voices calling the attention of the few people who wander around to the best hot dogs, fries, or mulled wine. *The last booth, at the end of the row, just before the entrance to the stables, is more modest than the others, much less gaudy, not busy at the moment. I decide to stop and order a pancake. The middle-aged lady who prepares my snack is kind and welcomes a chat. We talk about the weather, the festival, the fate of the circus. She asks me if I am connected with the show. I am not, but I mentioned my interest in the circus and, why not, my old association, when I was still a student, with the Cirque Bouglione. I am always happy to evoke that time on the road and, right now, I feel in a comfort zone with these fairground folks. We introduce each other. Her name is Patricia.* "You know, we are from the same family as the Bougliones." *Her husband, who handles the drinks at the other side of the counter, joins the conversation.*

> Yes, our name is Bouillon. We are originally from Northern Italy. But we have been living in the East of France for quite some time. The name was 'Buglione'. It means 'bouillon' in Italian. As we travelled, it was translated into French as 'bouillon' [broth, stock]. One side of the family, when they did the circus, they changed it to Bouglione.

I feel free to ask what her own name was before she got married. "Bouillon also. We are cousins." *As I nibble on my pancake, we come to talk about the discriminations that are still rampant in Europe against Roma people and nomadic travelers.* "We love everybody!" *says Patricia.*

The next day I am back at the circus. There is no show that day but I am curious to attend the ecumenical service that is scheduled in the early evening. This religious event has been taking place for decades. I had seen brief videos online showing an assortment of Catholic bishops, Protestant pastors, Muslim Imams, Jewish Rabbis, and Buddhist priests, all in their colorful officiating gear, saying prayers and celebrating in the ring the great brotherhood, and also, assumedly, sisterhood of the circus. I thought the ceremony was not out of place since I always considered the circus to be more akin to a ritual than a mere spectacle. The admission is free. As I line up to be frisked and checked before entering the tent—a new ritual of our time—I am given a leaflet detailing the program. Obviously, ecumenism has now been restricted to Christian religions—another sign of our time—and the roster of preachers only includes the various denominations that claim a portion of the Christian legacy. The band plays a hymn that has been chosen so that nobody would be offended. Circus hands roll a large wooden cross to the center of the ring and a procession of holy men in drab clothes come in and sit down along the ringside. They will rise in turn to proceed to a microphone and read with solemn intonations brief texts of their choice from the Old Testament or the Gospels. At times, the audience is prompted to sing one of the hymns that have been provided in the program. Three times during the ceremony, some circus hands return to roll back the cross out of the ring to make space for a circus act that is part of the ecumenical event and suddenly brings to the center stage the light, colors, energy, and beauty of lively horses and daring acrobats.

Now, I am back talking with my friends at the pancake stand. The night brings some chilly winds from the sea to the lot. I get closer to the heating pan in which Patricia pours the creamy liquid that soon become a flat, golden disk. She adds some butter and sprinkles white sugar. We talk religion. I wonder if they have ever gone to the pilgrimage at Saintes-Maries-de-la-Mer, in Camargue. "No. We are Evangelicals. We don't do that. We have prayer meetings. We love peace. We love everybody." They look happy. Some customers line up and order pancakes. I step aside, waiting for a moment of calm to take my leave. We are going to hug. Patricia gets her phone: "Let us make a selfie." Her husband joins us. "I will send you the picture." I ask: "May I tell the story of our meeting in my new book?"—"Of course, you may."

Figure 9 The author (center) with Patricia Bouillon and her husband at the Monte Carlo International Circus Festival (January 18, 2020).

The traditional circus is permeated with religious beliefs, some of which are labelled "superstitions" by the mainstream society. Whether Sinti, Kalderash, or other distinct ethnic groups, Gypsies tend to adopt the faith and practices of the countries in which they roam or settle. They also carry with them more ancient ideas of the supernatural and corresponding rituals. Many of those who have embraced Catholicism in Europe worship the three "Saintes Maries," a syncretic trio that paradoxically includes a "Sainte Sarah" also honored as "Sarah-la-Kali," an echo of the powerful dark Hindu goddess Kali [in Romani, *kalo* means "black"]. They periodically gather in the south of France for a pilgrimage that brings together otherwise usually scattered families and clans. My Facebook circus friends occasionally post religious icons portraying Jesus, Marie, and also Saint Sarah. However, other deeper beliefs and customs are perpetuated through their everyday life. Those may appear odd to the outsiders who have their own strange ways of handling the mysteries of human existence, which they take for the norm. The name given to a newborn child is the object of utmost attention, to the extent that it is kept secret in some traditions that have been discussed by Gypsy writers (e.g., Maximoff 1949) or anthropologists (e.g., Cuisenier 1985) who have described the ritual of naming under the gaze of three fairies or fates, the "ursitory" or "ursitoares," who determine the future destiny of the child. Once again these customs show signs of syncretism with local or broader cultures, notably Romania or Spain. Whether these customs are followed or not, all Gypsies have patronyms coined on the model of those they find in the countries they roam. The nation-states demand that each individual be defined unambiguously with respect to their coordinates of space and time. The exact date and place of birth is often unspecified for nomadic people. It has to be credibly invented on the fly when administrative papers are to be established. The chosen patronyms are usually very common names that have been adopted as one of the ways of making oneself relatively invisible. First names are also common and seem to be deliberately in short supply as outsiders get confused by the recurrence of the same first names from generation to generation in direct or cross lines. Thus, it is not uncommon that someone is known in the trade by a moniker that is neither his or her actual first or family name, and additional stage names compound the confusion. True identity, that is one's place in the family or clan, transcends these labels imposed by outside authorities. Knowing and uttering the name of someone is a tool of power or possession. It is better, then, not to disclose one's true name and let others manipulate mere conventional simulacra.

Our Inner Gypsy

> *It was only much later, when revisiting the Balkans extensively, that I realized the extent and intensity of my involvement with the Rom: the depth of my identification with them and my nearly total acceptance of all things Romany, while I lived with them.*
>
> Jan Yoors, **The Gypsies**, 1987 [1967]: 144

> *The Rom played with their casual inquirers, seekers of some exotic titbits of information with which to titillate their friends, and kept them 'out' by ruses, half-lies, and misinformation. In other cases, however, as I discovered, the Rom had no trouble admitting that it was possible to be born a gažo and become a Rom.*
>
> Michael Stewart, **The Time of the Gypsies**, 1997: 59

There is an understandable reluctance in the general sedentary population to endorse the Gypsy ethos and its occasional impact on what we safely take for granted. However, this is not as absolute as it seems. Ambiguity is of the essence of the human experience of life. In some deep sense, Gypsies embody our secret nostalgia of another, primal kind of existence. As Patrick Jasper Lee hints in the passage quoted earlier (cf. page 21–2), the civilization that constrains our existence since Neolithic times is a sad shadow over our destiny. The circus, in its traditional form whether as street performances or elaborate shows, is more than a mere spectacle that displays a range of vital skills for sedentary people's entertainment. It is also, and perhaps above all, a ritualistic contact with our inner Gypsy, a glimpse of a fuller life free of some of the most injurious binds. Like the canary in the mine, the end of the circus might spell more drastic changes to come.

The Gypsy experience is both intimately accessible and almost impossible to grasp from the point of view of the alienated perspectives of humans caught in webs of artificial norms. We can glean interesting details from those who reported about their temporary escape to a life on the road with Gypsies not as a touristic adventure or scientific inquiry but as a spontaneous choice. Probably, the first anecdotal account of this genre was published in French in 1596 in Lyon. The author Pechon de Ruby, a pseudonym meaning "smart kid" in the slang of the time, was a nobleman from Brittany, who had joined in his younger years various troupes of vagrants, thieves, and Bohemians, in which he had been admitted on the assumption that he would not divulge the secrets of their underground rituals and trades, more specially the jargon they used to safely communicate without being understood by outsiders. This short pamphlet includes the descriptions of some of their illicit activities such as a method for keeping the dogs away while they were engaged in robberies, by throwing to them cow horns filled with pork fat. This was meant to keep the dogs busy trying to chew through this hard material in order to reach the tantalizing lard that was packed inside. He added to his report a list of their secret vocabulary. Obviously, for him, a gentleman's word had little value beyond the restricted circle of his peers.

We find hardly less distancing strategies in George Borrow's outwardly sympathetic book, an autobiography, admittedly in part fictional, that recounts his episodic association with a Gypsy man, his family, and their relatives. Although this book, first published in 1851, concerns many aspects of the life and culture of Great Britain in the nineteenth century, its title, **Lavengro**, is the nickname the head of the Petulengro family had given this young man eager to learn their language. It means in Romani: "Lover of language." It was followed by another volume titled **The Romani Ry** [The Gypsy Gentleman or The Gentleman Gypsy]. George Borrow (1803–81) was fascinated by languages since his early years and endeavored to learn Romani when circumstances brought him in friendly contact with British Gypsies. He describes in details, in a non-judgmental manner, the everyday life he shared with them, in the course of which he learnt how to master the art of iron work, notably forging horseshoes on the portable anvil they carried with them. They also taught him how to deal with horses, a knowledge that was a precious resource at a time when horses were the axis of civilization both in peace and in wars. Borrow's inquisitive mind was not welcome by all the members of the troupe among which some resented the disclosure of parts of their language and customs. Although there was some obvious degree of mutual respect and genuine friendship, there is a sense through the book that writing the story was the ulterior motive that vitiated the genuineness of the human interaction.

The third example of this genre of accounts of Gypsy life is undoubtedly more authentic, more primal and sincere but, ultimately, as objectifying as the previous ones, if only because Jan Yoors (1922–77) published it, under the telling title *The Gypsies,* long after the experience he reports, at a time when he had become a celebrated artist and writer. Sure enough, the introduction starts with a declaration from the heart: "This book is written as a protest against oblivion, as a cry of love for this race of strangers who have lived among us for centuries and remained apart" (1987: 5). However, retrospectively, the uncompromising experience of a first love is tainted by its later exploitation as a literary or scientific resource. The expression "race of strangers" is telling. I never considered the Gypsies in my life as "racially" different "strangers." Their ethnicity was irrelevant.

Yoors's story, though, is remarkable in the sense that it allows readers to suspend for a while their prejudices and embrace the experience of a child coming of age among a Gypsy "kumpania" [company], an initiation to life on the road that had a lasting, transformative impact on his whole existence. The only son of an affluent, artistic, and unconventional Belgian family from Antwerp, Jan ran away to join the boys of a Gypsy band at the age of twelve. He was not kidnapped or enticed by devious means but simply became friend with kids of his age, who seamlessly accepted him in their midst and introduced him to their games and ways of life under the mostly benevolent watch of the adults. Tall and typically fair head, he could hardly blend with the rest of the troupe and was the occasional cause of interventions by the police which periodically returned the fugitive to his parents' home. After some episodes of normal schooling, though, Jan would return to what had become his perpetually moving home and lived for ten years on the road with the family he had adopted until he decided to return to the mainstream society and embraced an international artistic career that had become more appealing to him.

It is common, among those who have joined Gypsy families and have espoused their way of life for a significant period of time, to reach a point at which they break the bond and return, often with pangs of regrets and guilt, to the constraints they had once left with glee. The two modes of existence seem to be allergic to compromises. Trying to contemplate the two ways of life and the two worldviews side by side at the same time from the inside of any of them is almost impossible; the experience is akin to looking at the famous Necker cube that spontaneously flips in the eyes of the perceivers from one perspective to its opposite. It is an "either or" situation. In many ways, my own life bears witness to this existential switch.

The traditional circus stands at the ambiguous interface between these two ontologies that depend on each other both materially and symbolically. The meaning produced by the performances is grounded in the coexistence of two narratives and the semiotic systems which sustain their conjoined destinies. Any change in any of these systems is bound to jeopardize the whole sociocultural landscape. We will examine in the successive parts of this book the transformations that impact the integrity of the various aspects of the traditional circus and their capacity to make sense for those who experience them.

Of course, as was mentioned earlier, the circus is only a small aspect, albeit a highly visible one, of the Gypsy culture. Many families have entered mainstream professions through their ability to excel in various disciplines and industries as well as through the opportunities afforded by the financial resources some families were able to accumulate. The resilience they traditionally deployed in numerous survival strategies coupled with the oral mastery of several languages and their experience of a variety of cultures to which they had to adapt at some points in the course of their lives were invaluable assets in the contemporary world that is more open to individual initiatives than was the previous civil order. Often, this new invisibility is a symptom of tradition erasure and cultural integration. However, some powerful voices keep alive the presence of a mode of experiencing life that still haunts modern sedentary societies and offers public resistance to the rampant discriminations that still victimize those who perpetuate their Gypsy heritage.

Let us listen, for example, to Damian Le Bas's gripping account of a year-long pilgrimage along the paths followed by his Romany ancestors in Britain. The title of his book, *The Stopping Places* (2018), refers to the "atchin tans" ["stopping places" in the Romani language] that his great-grandmother, his "nan," had told him about when he was a child. These were the particular areas where travelers used to (and actually still do) temporarily set up camp in the countryside they were crisscrossing all the year round. Damian Le Bas and his wife retrace in a small van the traditional routes followed by his forebears in horse-drawn wagons and attempt to re-experience what it was to be constantly on the move with no permanent place to call home, and how it feels to make one's own full existence fit into those niches on the brink of time. The experience is challenging at times, mainly when he travels alone and encounters rough weather and even rougher other Gypsies who perceive him as an intruder or meddler, and are suspicious of his actual identity. He speaks their language but looks and behaves like a Gorgios. Damian Le Bas is indeed of mixed lineage. His childhood was fully immersed, though, in the Gypsy way of life—the family specialized in selling flowers in markets—but he was sent to school and eventually studied theology in St. John's College at Oxford University. However, his roots remain deeply anchored in his Gypsy culture, perhaps because it is a too fundamentally distinct existential ground. As a writer, film maker, and journalist, Damian Le Bas devotes his life to the defense and illustration of the Gypsy way of life—between 2011 and 2015 he was the Editor of *Travellers Times*, Britain's only national magazine for Gypsies and Travellers—a task he accomplishes with a compelling sort of reflexive empathy, but nevertheless raises the tantalizing issue of whether or not it is possible to be genuinely both in and out of the bonds of a culture. For Le Bas, living in a van and moving from place to place was an experimental choice that could not really replicate the conditions of precarity and the uncertainty of existences totally immersed in the open flow of time running through the mostly hostile landscape of modern civilization, an experience that Dominic Reeve's *Smoke in the Lanes* (2003 [1958]) conveys with compelling, unforgiving authenticity.

An Ode to Resilience: *The Raggedy Rawney*

As this first movement draws to a close, an image will symbolize the epic journey of the Romany people along the paths they trekked for ages through a hostile world. It will strike a note of courage and resilience against the tragic noise of absurd wars and relentless persecutions, and will announce, in symphony-like fashion, the final accord of hope that I will sound in the coda to come at the end of this book. *The Raggedy Rawney* (1988) is a poignant film written and co-directed by Bob Hoskins, a British Gypsy, who also stars in the story as the head of a traveling troupe that tries to escape an unspecified war with their horse-drawn wagons through the fields and forests of nameless countries. The narrative thread is provided by the escape of a young soldier who, shell-shocked after an attack, deserts the army. He is sheltered by a band of Gypsies where he finds cover, dressed in rags and impersonating a mute insane girl. He fits for a while into the Gypsy lore in which a "Rawney" is a madwoman endowed with shamanic power, able to see the future and control animals. The troupe has its own share of inner tensions and conflicts with the local population but manages to stay clear for a while of the warring factions that harass and threaten the Gypsies and their way of life. Across this tumult and chaos, they are driven by the will to survive. The soldier falls in love with the daughter of the band's leader. The caravan goes on. A retarded young boy dies. When he is cremated in the forest, the smoke betrays their stopping place. The army resumes their chase. As they are approaching, the elder ones in the Gypsy troupe decide to make a last, hopeless stand with their old rifles and pistols, just long enough to allow the younger members of the clan, including the soldier and his pregnant girlfriend, a chance to escape a sure death.

Contrapuntal 3: On the Flipside

October 2007. My early plans to attend a conference in Bolzano, in northern Italy, have become a challenge. I am due for surgery to replace my right hip with an artificial joint in December. In the meantime, each of my steps causes a sharp pain that makes me limp. I have nevertheless accepted to give a seminar on circus semiotics at the Fontys Academy for Performance Art in the Dutch city of Tilburg before returning to Canada. I carry in my bag one of the last copies of my early book, Circus and Culture, *that will be the basis for my seminar. On my way to Italy, I decide to stop over in Zurich to meet some colleagues. My friend and former student Duccio Canestrini has decided to meet me there and help me travel by train to Bolzano. I had been warned by my Swiss colleagues of being mindful of the thieves who ride trains. I keep an eye on my bag but Duccio, who is a native of the region, reassures me: "Paul, this is not Napoli or Sicily!"*

On arriving at our final train station, I appreciate Duccio's help because I feel as vulnerable as a limping antelope in the Savanah. Sure enough, I notice some wandering people who do not seem to be going anywhere. We decide to buy right away my return ticket before walking to the hotel. As we are waiting in line, I do not release my grip on the bag that rests on the top of my suitcase. Now Duccio argues at the wicket about the best itinerary. A few yards from me, a young man is standing in front of the automatic vending machine but does not seem to be seriously trying to buy a ticket. "Ha! Ha!," I tell myself ... and secure my hold on my bag. Now, a middle-aged man has replaced him in front of the machine, not attempting either to make a real purchase. He bears a striking resemblance to Bob Hoskins, the Gypsy actor who performs in the film Raggedy Rawney. At least, I know that I am targeted. Duccio hands to me the piece of paper I have to sign to complete the credit card payment of my ticket. I make a step toward the wicket, sign, and reach out for my bag ... which has disappeared.

I do not speak Italian. Duccio takes me to the police station. We are told that there were no police in the hall because they were all celebrating the retirement of one of their colleagues. Duccio fills some papers. We are told to return the next morning. I spend the night phoning my credit cards' companies and other relevant institutions since there were many sensitive documents in that bag. The circus book and all the notes I had prepared for the Tillburg seminar are a pure loss. I feel down, almost betrayed. At nine, the next morning, we are seating in the police station. An officer brings a sheepish looking man, the one who was standing in front of the automatic machine when I was queuing in front of the wicket. Duccio translates the question of the policeman: "Do you recognize this man?"—Spontaneously, without thinking, I answer a firm "No!". The man is let go. I cannot tell my friend what happened. He would not understand the irrationality of the situation.

Later, in the afternoon, we have been asked to come back for news at the police station. On the way, we cross a waiting room. My bag is lying on the floor. "Ah," says Duccio, "is that your bag?"—"No!" and we move on. I notice some eyes in the distance. I will not stoop to pick up that bag. I too have my pride. Nobody could understand that either.

Later, as I go on my trip, I realize that I really did not need what I had lost. I also could walk more easily without the encumbrance of my bag.

The Evolution of Space, Time, and Cultures

Hunter-gatherers tend to be highly migratory.
Daniel Lieberman, The Story of the Human Body, 2013: 183

When I was twenty-five years old, I worked for several seasons at the Cirque Bouglione that was touring France at the hectic pace of a town a day. Firmin Bouglione, one of the three brothers who then owned the circus, welcomed the student who had been introduced to him by his niece Madonna. I had been assigned, at my request, to the menagerie. One of my chores, after I had helped set up the fences and feed the animals in the early morning, was to teach my boss's daughter. Firmin Bouglione was illiterate like most older Gypsies at the time but he wanted his children to receive a regular education. At around ten in the morning, I would go to his caravan and teach his young daughter the basics of the primary curriculum. Some days, the father would quietly come in and sit down across the table. He would listen attentively until he was called to attend some business outside. One day, as I was trying to summarize the successive regimes that governed France from the 1789 revolution on, Firmin Bouglione stopped me: "Don't teach her history. This is not useful to us. Teach her geography and mathematics instead."

Without betraying trust and confidentiality, it is possible to sketch out the nature of the differences that so profoundly separate the Gypsy culture(s) from the mainstream worldviews that are taken for granted by modern Europeans. Some individuals commonly ascribe these differences to racial specificities, an attitude that feeds racist discourse and politics as we have pointed out in a previous section of this volume. We know, though, that all humans share in common their same biological heritage. The only relevant divergences between humans arise from their cultures, that is, their traditional way of interpreting their environment in function of their needs and the habits they developed in order to cope with the challenges of physical and social survival. True enough, cultures impact the physical appearance of human groups over time as mating customs such as endogamy or other traditional ways of arranging marriages may select for particular heritable traits that are considered desirable, irrespective of their physiological consequences. Gypsies think that for a man a matrilineal cousin can safely be chosen as a wife. It suffices for these conservative anatomical features to be relatively neutral and not constitute a long-term handicap. But if we try to find a logical ground that can account for the deep incompatibility of the two cultures beyond the anecdotal and the picturesque, we have to consider their contrasted relationship to space.

Let us recap the overview that has been sketched out earlier in this part of the book. With the advent of agriculture, even in its earliest form, humans became bound to pieces of land that were carved out from the continuum of the earth and stripped of undesirable vegetation that could compete with the needs of the growing crops for sunlight and nutrients. Similarly, the domestication of various animals, even in the pastoralist mode, could not succeed without some means of keeping predators away by setting up fences and breeding dogs that could match other carnivores. The necessity to protect such vital resources required the watchful care of the borders that kept wilderness from encroaching on the staked out territory. Surveying, measuring, and the rise of geometry were the means to legally sustain exclusive property rights, either collective or individual ones. Space became a commodity whose differential accumulation by families or clans generated inequality and created social hierarchies.

By contrast, hunters and gatherers may have territories they roam but these expanses of land are usually too vast for anybody to enforce their exclusive use. Moreover, this space is necessarily shared with other species with which accommodation is sought rather than being targeted for control or eradication. The boundaries of hunter-gatherers' territories are not carved in stone but may fluctuate as demographics require. The contours of niches depend on factors that vary with time. The domestication of wolves as dogs and the taming of horses as mounts, themselves free-ranging species, is not only compatible with nomadism but also brings this mode of survival to a new degree of efficiency when the environment favors mobility rather than impedes it. The Asian-European steppes invite westward exploratory expansion. However, this is also the location of rich alluvial plains and valleys in which Neolithic settlements developed. Nomads and settlers were bound to clash not only in terms of their methods of exploiting land resources but also in their perception and conception of terrestrial space. Gypsies and peasants foster incompatible cosmologies.

In his 1930 comprehensive book on *Les Tsiganes* [The Gypsies], Romanian scholar C. J. Popp Serboianu thus captures the Gypsy attitude: "Their homeland is the whole earth and their abode is their tent. They cannot fathom the existence of borders that separate countries nor the differences between human beings based on their possessions that allow some to oppress others. For them, our civilization is a monstrosity that denies individual freedom and the ability of fully enjoying the present" (p. 60) [translation mine].

The idea that portions of the earth can be exclusively owned by anybody is indeed alien to the nomads' understanding of the world. This claim is considered ludicrous. How much of the soil is owned below the surface? Are not the forces of nature beyond the control of humans? How can the land be divided into separate parcels? Property titles are fictions that only the mutual agreements of some people can sustain as if it were real. In truth, humans belong to the earth, not the reverse. Over the long time, the current "owners" will dissolve in the ground; the fences will move or disappear in the service of new fictitious claims, or simply will collapse and be forgotten; but the land will persist with all its stubborn material resistance made of rocks, mud, dirt, water, mounds, grassy slopes, bushes, and forests teeming with life. The wilderness may be kept at bay for a long while but it will return with a vengeance. The most abusive of all fallacious claims are the political borders, so illusory that they have to be traced on a map and indicated by signs erected in the midst of fields and rivers or guarded with all the military might that a population can muster. They too fluctuate under the winds of history as the outcome of senseless battles or barter and trade-off. The Gypsies dismiss the legitimacy of these boundaries they consider to be a nuisance that must be overcome by force or cunning. They are helped by the fact that property rights cannot be truly enforced when they apply to spaces that greatly exceed the immediate environment of their owners who cannot be everywhere at the same time nor be constantly awake and watchful. Edges, walls, fences, dogs are mostly futile; they are mere obstacles to be cleared by an appropriate method at an opportune moment. What is considered a crime or a sin by Neolithic minds is a heroic act or a virtue from the vantage point of the hunter-gatherers. Self-confidence and pride is a defining trait of the Gypsy ethos.

Farming usually generates a surplus. How to get hold of these disposable resources is a challenge for those who are in need. Several strategies are possible: bartering for some other goods or services, capturing by sheer force, or persuading the owners to part voluntarily from what they have hoarded. Nomadic Gypsies have used opportunistically all the three methods: providing skills that are in demand either because of a lack of knowledge or in view of the absence of the needed material; stealing or other kinds of devious means of appropriation; and, finally, begging with convincing rhetoric, seducing with storytelling and enchanting musical talents, or performing spectacular feats that create awe in the watchers. Ultimately, begging, the proper way, is compatible with the genuine pride that is a defining characteristic of the Gypsy identity.

The aim of the settled communities is to maintain a state of stability and reliable predictability. Sources of uncertainty have to be controlled and kept in check as much as feasible. Long-term planning guarantees security and the system must be immune to the disruption of unexpected novelty through various forms of insurance against unwelcome changes. However, the cost of this way of life is that the villagers have to cope with eventual boredom, that is, the lack of surprise in a redundant environment submitted to the slow cycle of the seasons. Periodic festivities occur at set times for a limited duration. Apart from devastating natural catastrophes that occasionally fall upon communities, information is a rare commodity.

Some distinctions, though, are in order. There are two kinds of information: "bound information," that is, the cases when there is a limited set of possible outcomes such as whether it will rain or not, whether the crop is abundant or meagre, whether the hunt is successful or not. There is also "free or 'unbound' information," that is, the occurrence of something totally unexpected such as the falling of a meteorite close to one's settlement or the arrival of strange, "never-seen before" humans or animals in one's territory. Whatever is not familiar is highly disruptive and rife with potential danger. When such events spring out into a stable environment, out of sync with the periodic return of familiar changes, the whole temporal and spatial frame of expectation is shattered. This is what Karl Friston (2010, 2013) calls "free energy." It triggers efforts to reduce such disruptions or it proves to be the irresistible harbinger of a drastic upset of the state of affairs. New meanings emerge from this chaos.

Human cultures rest upon sets of strong oppositions that determine, usually for a long period of time, the meanings of the diverse forms and events that characterize their social and physical environment, and inspire the institutions regulating a range of distinctive values and normative behaviors. All such systems, however, are subject to entropy, that is, the wearing out of oppositions through the emergence of intermediate values. A case in point is exclusionary gender differences, a powerful matrix of traditional western cultures, that is currently, eroded by the progressive recognition of mixed and transitional forms. Another telling phenomenon is the change of understanding of the differences between humans and animals that sustained for a very long time an antagonistic relationship. We will discuss this issue more fully in the second part of this book but let us remark here that, as wild animals cease to be a lethal menace in the context of modern urban civilizations, they increasingly become endowed with humanlike qualities such as feelings, emotions, and personalities, to the point of erasing any significant differences with humans in the popular imagination. This brings us to the consideration of the circus that traditionally displayed the violent overcoming or dangerous taming of the wild as well as, incidentally, the occasional blurring of genders in the exhibition of freaks such as hermaphrodites and bearded ladies, and transvestites as a component of clowning, domains that we will fully consider in the third and fourth parts of this book. Circus posters from the mid-nineteenth to the mid-twentieth century illustrate in vivid colors these telling icons.

In view of the above, we can understand how Gypsies, through their mode of life, social behavior, claims to the mastery of mysterious forces, and displays of marvelous feats, can be construed as the occasional eruption of free energy in the relatively stable cultures they visited in which transitions from one state to another in a continuous timeline is highly predictable. Expectedly, this sudden relief from the repeatability inherent in the "normal" life of settled populations caused anxiety in the civil and religious authorities which were prompt to counter and reduce as much as possible their disruptive power and the fascination they provoked. The probability of successive states and events in which each new step is largely conditioned by the previous one can be upset by the chance irruption of novelty. Gypsies and their deceptive arts could startle and seduce the population by bringing in their relatively stable world the appearance of radical discontinuity. Time is of the essence in the Gypsy mode of survival as nobody can repeatedly surprise and charm an audience with the same tricks over longer spans of continuous interaction. The circus is ephemeral as the very condition of its existence and resilience.

All the circus artists' spectacular skills, though, have been acquired over long periods of relentless practice but they are displayed with poise and smiles in front of audiences that have no knowledge of the arduous preparation process that made them possible and make their audience believe that they are dreaming with their eyes open. As Ernest Hemingway famously wrote: "The circus is the only spectacle I know that while you watch gives you the quality of a truly happy dream."

In the following parts of this book, we will show that the strong oppositions that sustained the cultural registers that generated the meanings produced by the circus's multimodal discourse are eroding under the force of cultural entropy. New oppositions are emerging, that cause the obsolescence of the previous ones. To wit, a caged lion that was a sign of triumph over lethal wilderness becomes a symbol of injurious violation of natural freedom. Similarly, the opposition between the physical constraints of the settled space and the vast interstitial open space that made free roaming possible is now neutralized by the total grid of virtual spatial representation and the technological advent of absolute monitoring and control on movements within a field that is, at least theoretically, coextensive with the whole planet. Can the impossibility of coming from nowhere and the devaluation of true exoticism ring the death knell of the traditional circus? We will attempt to answer this question in the remaining parts of this book.

3

Second Movement

Vivace Furioso

Animals

"*Tyger Tyger, burning bright*
In the forest of the night:
What immortal hand or eye
Dare frame thy fearful symmetry?"

William Blake, **Songs of Experience**, *1794*

As far as I can remember my earliest childhood, the high point was a visit to a circus and this meant experiencing animals at close range. I was probably four or five years old. My maternal grandfather, born in 1870, was a tinsmith and cauldron maker, who had created his own central-heating enterprise at the turn of the twentieth century in the city of Chateauroux in central France. He never failed to take me to Cirque Bureau when it visited the town. He had installed the new steam-heating system in the mansion of the owners of that circus that was located in the nearby city of Bourges. He always bought the admission tickets in advance, but, as soon as the director, Jules Glassner, identified him in the crowd, he would come to us, shake hand with my grandfather, pat me on the head, and upgrade our seating to a front row lodge. Once, he took us to the backstage, where some horses were kept, ready to enter the ring at the start of the show. Each animal was held by a uniformed groom and some were champing at the bit and stamping the ground in anticipation of the action to come. Later, the family story went that I was shocked and scared. I am not sure whether I cried in terror or excitement. I keep a vivid visual memory of these wonder horses.

This part of the book will focus on animals that are not only central to the circus tradition but also, and more crucially at the primal core of the human

Figure 10 My maternal grandparents in the 1930s. Théophile Eugène Frène, born in 1870, was a tinsmith and cauldron maker who had left his village in his teen years to learn his trade through travelling for several years across France and working for various metal craftsmen as an apprentice. He had rebelled against his father, who was employed as "*régisseur*" [farm supervisor] on the behalf of local landowner nobility. I was told that he reproached his father to "spend his life on his horse watching other people work". Although there was no hint of Gypsy culture in this side of the family, reading about the Kalderash always conveyed to me a sense of affinity as I remembered the many hours I spent as a kid at the bellow of my grandfather's workshop where, after his retirement, he often enjoyed forging some implements for our household or some of his relatives and friends. My grandmother, Marthe Pitard, had worked as a teenager making cigars and cigarettes at the *Manufacture des tabacs* [Tobacco factory], then a state monopoly, in Chateauroux in central France. Although an unpalatable reference, very much at odds with reality as I perceived it, I secretly associated this detail with the notorious Carmen of Charles Bizet's opera.

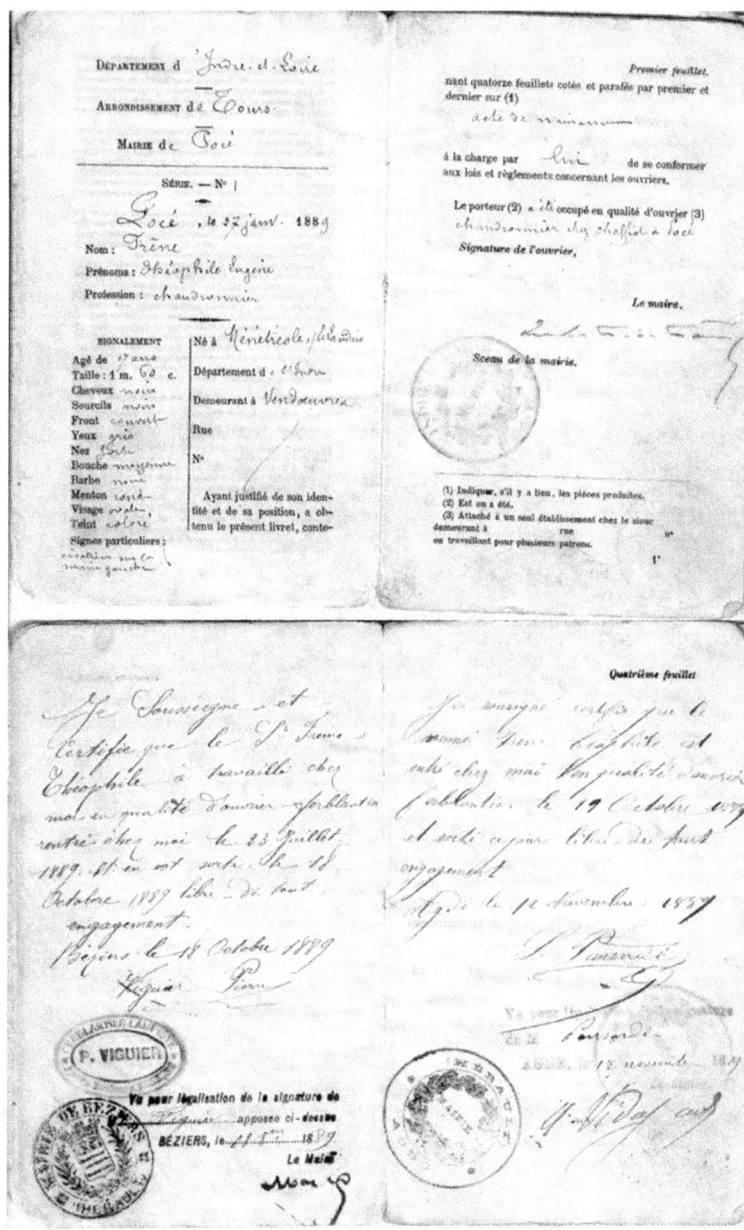

Figure 11 At seventeen, Théophile Frène obtained the legal document that allowed him to travel over the country to learn his trade with the metal craftsmen he would encounter on his way. In this identity kit, he is curiously described as "colored." The workshop owners were supposed to provide written testimonies of his training in the pages of this booklet. However, as literacy was not yet universal in those days, it seems that all the testimonies were written by the same person whose handwriting is similar to my grandfather's as I remember it. The signatures and official stamps, though, look genuine.

Figure 12 This French booklet recounts the well-documented history of Cirque Bureau that was founded in 1854 by Jean Bureau. The poster on the cover is from the late 1940s. We knew that we would actually witness this extraordinary act in the show down to the exact number, color, and trapping of the horses as this circus was famous for its reputation of honest advertisement (Simonet 2009).

experience as far back in time as we can imagine our evolutionary past. Reflecting on animals in the circus will compel us to address complex and controversial issues that must be placed in their biological and cultural contexts. The presentations of trained wild species including predators, involve both natural forces in mutual confrontations, and representations that define the worldview or cosmology of the societies in which these performances are experienced. The meaning of animals framed by the staging of the circus is bound to mesh or clash to lesser or greater extent with the reality of the relentless struggle of all lives on earth. To try to get a hold on this vital entanglement, we will first consider various species that are relevant to both human survival and circus culture. Then, we will take a look at the historical depth of spectacular animal training before considering the current evolution of attitudes toward animals in contemporary societies.

Hunger Rules the World

November 1956. The Bouglione circus is back at its winter quarters near Paris. I spent the full summer working as a barker at the gate of their zoological sideshow and occasional assistant to the lion trainer. The Cirque d'Hiver will soon feature its fall program in the historical building that now belongs to the family. Firmin Bouglione asks me to continue teaching his daughter, a task I had started during the travelling season. I welcome this opportunity as I have to survive on a tight budget while I take some courses at the Sorbonne toward my final degree. My pupil is intelligent and conscientious, but she has to combine my lessons with her training as a juggler and a low wire walker as well as her initiation to the basics of music. The family lives in a comfortable, spacious apartment on Boulevard Richard Lenoir, not far from the Cirque d'Hiver. Several times a week, I climb the two floors, ring the bell, and the maid takes me to the space that had been transformed into a private classroom. I have devised a curriculum that covers the whole spectrum of a primary education. At times, Firmin Bouglione joins us in the room, sits down, and listens to me with interest.

Often, after the lesson, his wife, Violette, whom everybody in the circus calls Madame Firmin, insists that I stay with them for dinner. She routinely apologizes for the state of the window drapes that have been recently torn apart by a couple of tiger cubs that her husband had brought home. As their mother had rejected them, they had to be bottle-fed day and night, and were prone to mess up the place and wreak havoc in the apartment but her husband would not budge: "the tigers first!"

She was from a circus family that had experienced the ups and downs of life on the road. Her elderly mother, who was often present, still practiced fortune telling and palmistry in her home close to Place Pigalle. Her son-in-law never failed to crack the same joke when she was asking what time it was.

I fondly remember these dinners. It was a warm, informal atmosphere, and the copious fare was a welcome change from the student restaurants I had to use daily. One day, she urged me to help myself to a second serving: "Eat, eat, Monsieur Paul, we know what it is to be hungry!" This had been uttered with a deep and genuine intonation that still now brings tears of gratitude to my eyes.

Hunger drives the lives of humans and animals. All organisms need to assimilate some parts of their environment to survive; that is, they have to eat other living things, plants, or other animals, often both. They also crave for other nutrients such as salt or clay that complement their diet. Whether on the tundra, the savannah, the rain forest, or the slopes of high mountains, the animals we see moving are in search of something to eat. They also need water, a necessity that is often hard to get and always risky to enjoy as drinking puts them in a vulnerable position. When the cameras of modern explorers catch animals at rest, it is because, having eaten and drank, they can momentarily relax and digest, although they must remain watchful lest other animals are eyeing them to satisfy their own hunger. There is no lull in this ceaseless game of life and death. It is relentlessly played on all scales on the whole earth. The animal lovers, who are comfortably and securely settled in their urban dwellings, gloss over the messiness of that permanent struggle by invoking the laws of nature that must be serenely accepted. They want to believe that predators do a clean job that does not cause excessive suffering.

No killing is a pretty sight, though. The prey struggles and tries to escape. If they do succeed, they are often impaired and soon become the targets of new hungry animals. Footage of attacks by lions, wolves, or crocodiles, usually filmed from a distance around drinking places, show both failed attempts at catching prey and successful bringing down of herbivores, often young ones or older adults. A limping wildebeest is targeted by a pride of lions: the females start the chase; one of them jumps to the face of the prey and catches its muzzle or lock its throat in her mouth; no energetic shaking from the wildebeest can make the lioness release her hold until the prey collapses because it has been prevented from breathing for a while; then, as the wildebeest lies on the ground, still frantically kicking with its legs from time to time, the other lions undertake to tear apart the softer skin around the anus and the under belly. In his gripping account of wildlife predation in extreme environments, biologist Joel Berger occasionally encounters muskoxen or other large preys that have been eaten in part by bears or wolves but are still alive. Although biologists are not supposed to interfere with the natural dynamics of predation, however traumatic it might be, humans are prone to let their own compassionate drive override their scientific principles and, at times, indulge in using their defensive weapons to shorten these unbearable sufferings. Mercy killing, though, does not belong to the social behavior of animals. Anybody holding a utopian view of wildlife in pristine natural environments should read Joel Berger's *Extreme Conservation: Life at the Edge of the World* (2018) and his earlier *The Better to Eat You With: Fear in the Animal World* (2008). Fear, across the whole spectrum of animal life, is indeed the constant correlate of hunger.

Herbivores need to browse or graze almost constantly. Elephants are ceaselessly on the move chewing on large quantities of leaves and branches. Other species proceed across plains and hills depleting their vegetation. We know that plants have ways of defending themselves by producing toxic substances that are unpalatable to some of their predators, and to release chemical signals that trigger similar reactions in the neighboring foliage. Nomadic herds, though, can go faster than these emergency messages. Some grazers are famous for their long-term devastation of the flora they exploit, even pulling the roots of the grass they eat as older sheep do. As long as these nomads can move unimpeded, and as long as their population is controlled by predators, the food chain is a sustainable dynamic fueled by hunger.

Hominins have long been caught within this unstoppable hunger cycle. There is fossil evidence that the common ancestor of the *Homo* genus, who was much smaller than the apes and the anatomically modern humans, was a common prey for leopards and other felines that were well adapted to hunt their prey in trees. Even tigers, still nowadays, are seen to occasionally chase monkeys from branches to branches. This behavior, though, seems to be observed with young, inexperienced hunters, who usually fail in their daring chase.

Although young carnivores are endowed with all the neuromuscular capabilities that will allow them to stalk and catch their prey, and compete with their rivals, they need time to practice these skills through playing under maternal and avuncular protection. These young are indeed easy prey for other hungry predators even of their own kind. Before they can fend for themselves, it may take several years of learning from their mother what to safely hunt and eat. An immature lion that attacks in earnest a porcupine is already a dead animal since a quill piercing its paw will condemn it to die of starvation.

The Human Animal: The Game of Life and Death

Early people beat themselves a path that was bound to lead them into direct conflict with several well-established, well-adapted, and well-armed predators, all doing the same thing in the same habitat.

Hans Kruuk, **Hunter and Hunted**, 2002: 106

As far as we can imagine human life in the evolutionary past, survival from predators was a daily imperative. Securing their own food, through hunting and gathering, also meant both being hunted and competing with stronger, often even better organized predators. At no point in time, until the advent of modernity, can we conceive of humans independently from a tight, confrontational entanglement with animals. Actually, the organisms we still call "animals" as distinct from birds or insects in folk taxonomies are those that are relatively commensurate with human physical proportions; those that rely on the same resources and can be confronted in more or less equal, albeit often uneven terms. From shrews to elephants, we recognize in them our own organs: eyes, mouths, teeth, ears, limbs, and movements. We all eat and defecate, reproduce and die in very similar ways. Humans, and often female animals, relate to the very young of other species as if they were their own kind because these neonates share the same features of "cuteness". They are perceived as defenseless. They cannot survive without help from adults of their own or other species. For them, seduction is a matter of life or death. They are great semiotic manipulators like some parasitic species. We may think of the hatched cuckoos that fool their host into feeding them better than their own offspring through the strength of their visual and acoustic signaling. Many, though, are eaten before they have a chance to grow up and reproduce. At this critical stage of their development, very young animals are apt to bond and socialize not only within their own species but also with other kinds of animals, including humans, if accidental circumstances have brought them into contact with them.

But those are rare occurrences that are mentioned here because they are relevant in the case of the circus as we will see below. Otherwise, the general dynamics of natural wildlife can be represented as an infinite chessboard on which each individual is an autonomous agent driven primarily by hunger, and secondarily by procreation, that is allowed only a limited number of moves in a perpetual game of life and death. However, the dramatic evolutionary picture evoked by the expression "*nature, red, in tooth and claw,*" is certainly accurate but must be qualified because some states of affiliative equilibrium have emerged, even though temporarily, that bring a modicum of restraints in this reign of fear and all-out war. This does not mean that we should gloss over the inherent cruelty involved in answering by all available paths the hunger imperative.

The last one hundred years or so have witnessed numerous field research, rather than laboratory experiments, that have cast new light on animal behavior in the wild. Longitudinal studies of elephants, lions, hyenas, tigers, wolves, chimpanzees, and meerkats, for instance, have provided robust evidence of the intra- and inter-specific social life of animals. It has thus become obvious beyond doubt that animals have cultures, that is, sets of behavior that are transmitted from generation to generation, through the mothers to their offspring in most cases but also through the general process of integration within the group for the species that are prone to socialization. This includes in particular the recognition of preferred prey as well as those that must be excluded because they present risky defenses. Porcupines, as mentioned earlier, are better to be avoided. In his landmark books, mentioned below, biologist Bernd Heinrich, noted that humans were considered a normal prey for European wolves, while in North America wolves were not considered a prime danger because their preferred prey were the deer and other mammals that could be found in abundance.

Cross-species alliances, driven by self-interest, are a rather common feature observed in nature. In his book, *The Mind of the Raven* (1999), Bernd Heinrich shows how wolves and ravens evolved a culture of cooperation based on mutual interest: ravens are scavengers; they eat meat from dead animals and they scan the landscape from the sky; however, they cannot pierce hides with their beaks; they have been documented to signal the presence of carcasses to wolves, thus saving them foraging time, and taking advantage of the capacity of their strong bites to tear open dead animals; the scene of wolves and ravens feasting more or less together although not without skirmishing, is similar to a familiar sight of the African Savanah showing lions, hyenas, and other predators haggling with each other and with vultures over dead wildebeest or zebras. It is generally accepted that early humans were probably scavengers before developing efficient stone tools enabling them to hunt live prey. They were then competing with powerful predators with which they had to share hunting ranges while avoiding direct confrontation.

Taking the contemporary example of the !Kung, Joel Berger claims that, until modernity disrupted ancestral patterns of behavior, humans and lions were maintaining a kind of *modus vivendi* that greatly reduced the necessity of mutual attacks. The relationship between lions and humans in Africa has been the focus of many scientific inquiries at least since the 1950s. Researchers had noted that lions were not prone to attack humans deliberately. Various causes were considered but Elizabeth Thomas, who did her observations in the Western Kalahari, came to the conclusion that lion culture had changed over a period of approximately half a century. Lions and the !Kung hunters had lived side by side as independent societies feeding on the same prey for thousands of years. After the European colonizers had invaded the coastal areas, they stayed away from the harshness of this unforgiving environment, leaving it undisturbed. Indigenous hunters told Thomas that "the lions around here don't harm people. Where lions are not hunted, they are not dangerous." It was, though, as reports Joel Berger, "an uneasy truce, with both species paying attention to the other" (Berger 2008: 263). This is probably a reliable inkling of the nature of the armed peace between *Homo sapiens* and *Panthera leo* that had endured since Paleolithic times. Prehistoric rock art does not represent aggressive lions nor hunted ones. Lions are bound to have learnt early that humans were using deadly arrows and powerful spears. "With the passing of time, notes Joel Berger, lands [...] fell into private or government hands." In the last century, developments brought drastic changes in the slowly evolving environment. In large stretches of lion territory the familiar sight of the traditional hunters disappeared and the culture of caution that was prevalent among the lions faded away. "When humans strolled from the protection of their car, the emboldened lions did not know how to act ... [they] became aggressive to bipeds [...] and, unlike the !Kung who once walked with lions, the going line was that it was far more dangerous for unarmed biologists to do so. The behavior of lions had changed" (Berger 2008: 264).

The physical, cognitive, and cultural evolution of the genus *Homo* cannot be understood independently from the fauna of which it was a part. Thinking of adaptation only in terms of the challenges of the geographical and climatic environment misses the most crucial sources of vital constraints. For a very long time before humans could think of themselves as radically distinct beings because the advances of their technological cultures gave them a relative power over the animals, they had to cope, day and night, with hungry predators and elusive prey. They were also confronted with a host of invisible enemies such as bacteria and viruses, that could be only explained by the ill-will of supernatural agents imagined on the model of the predators they feared. The archaeological record, from Paleolithic times to the Iron Age and beyond, bears witness to the haunting presence of animals in humans' everyday life as well as in their dreams and fantasies. The emergence of cultures as ways to represent reality and devise explanations of why things are what they are, relied on the observations of, and negotiations with the animals that populated their particular environment. Adaptive ways of behaving transmitted across generations often followed the examples of birds, mammals, reptiles, or fish with which they shared the same survival imperatives. Humans are unthinkable outside their constant interfacing with the other species with which they competed under the same existential challenges. They could not conceive their own nature and existence independently from animals long before they started domesticating some of them.

Bear Power

"Everybody says: 'After you take a bear's coat off, it looks just as a human'. And they act like humans: they fool, they teach their cubs (who are rowdy and curious), and they remember."
Maria Johns, cited in Gary Snyder's **Practice of the Wild**, 1990: 164

Most of the dangerous predators of humans, though, are social species. Their young are prone to bond through playing with the young or even the adults of other species, including humans, if the right situation is created by chance or by design. This opens a window of opportunity for whoever wants to assert control upon some of these animals. The individuals who could bring up the cubs of predators, let them be lions, bears, or wolves, and socialize them to some extent until they reach adult size but before the onset of sexual maturity, could claim to possess magic power over dangerous animals and thus assert for themselves a special status in their own society. Short of breeding predators, something that would have required complex infrastructures, the most obvious option was to steal neonates from the mothers, a risky strategy that had the advantage of sparing reproductive females. For instance, in the Pyrenean region, those who made a living through exhibiting dancing bears, the *orsalheres*, had devised a daring method once they had located a bear den with young cubs: while the mother was away foraging for food, they would snatch the cubs and place them in a container hanging from a cable down the sharp slope toward the valley; thanks to a pulley system, their catch would quickly slide down away from the female bear's reach to the point that she could not even hear their alarm calls. A film was produced in the Pyrenees region to demonstrate this hunting technique in the context of traditional bear training.

The raising and training of bears for ritual purposes in the mountainous regions of the Eurasian peninsula from the Caucasus to the Pyrenean chain is well documented. The most complete ethnographic research on this ancestral tradition in the Basque country, whose last manifestations could still be observed in the early twentieth century, has been conducted by Rozlyn Frank (e.g., 2008, 2015). Many very early photographs show men with their muzzled animals. The bear trainers were often Gypsies but also local people who claimed to have inherited from their ancestors the knowledge and the status of medicine men, a social function that was then considered strictly relevant to folkloric oddities by mainstream society. Shamanism may sound exotic and belonging to distant times and places, but we can assume that this distinct religious behavior has been present, under any other name, in traditional European cultures since immemorial times. It appears to be consistently associated with a bear cult.

At least since the Paleolithic, humans had to share their living space with bears that were formidable predators. Humans and bears are both omnivorous species that competed for live prey and vegetal food. Like the prehistoric hunter-gatherers, the bears killed animals to eat their flesh, and picked berries and roots. They gave evidence of being exceptionally smart. They took shelter in caves. Many features of their morphology and behavior made them stand apart in the fauna, if only because they were commonly seen standing up or even walking on their hind legs. Actually, as noted above, once a bear is skinned, its body looks uncannily human.

It is very plausible that bears were not considered to be just another kind of animal in the early cosmology of prehistoric Europeans. Still recently, in the Basque country, former bear trainers have been reported to tell researchers, in a confidential tone of voice, that in the old days bears were considered to be the ancestors of humans. In the Christianized folk tradition of this region, they are said to be the "dogs of Saint Peter," that keep guard at the gates of Heaven and vet the newcomers while the wolves are all in Hell. The survival of these contrastive values between bears and wolves undoubtedly opens a window on the relationship of Stone Age humans with predators that were ever present in their environment. This vital interface of humans and the wild animals did not disappear with the advent of Neolithic civilizations. Pastoralists, still nowadays, have to cope with the frequent loss of sheep to bears and wolves in areas where urbanized conservationists have succeeded in re-introducing traditional species for the sake of preserving their idealized vision of nature, oblivious of the countless millennia during which these predators were a constant menace to the lives of humans and their stock.

We can understand the respect that a man or a woman, who could demonstrate their absolute control over powerful predators, could command.

This is the litmus test of supernatural mastery that may entail other powers such as curing diseases or knowing the future. Later in this part of the book, we will note that before the nineteenth-century expansion of the European colonial empires and the emerging trade of exotic species, bears and wolves were the main animals exhibited by nomadic trainers. This was taking place in a context in which villagers had to cope daily with possible encounters with these predators. Moreover, they were living in oral cultures suffused with narratives staging personal memories and credible legends that, when told by the elders at night in the light of candles or in front of the hearth, would create goosebumps in their audience. Of course, this is not a purely European phenomenon. All over the planet, hungry humans lived side by side with hungry predators. The men and women who apparently could overcome the divide between the hunters and the hunted, and demonstrate their mastery of the wild by controlling some of the most feared animals, would acquire heroic, if not supernatural status.

The Hyena Men of Nigeria

A white taxi van swerves from the stream of traffic and stops at a street corner in Abuja. From the side door emerge some brightly dressed men dragging three muzzled hyenas tied to long ropes, a couple of costumed baboons, and bags of snakes. The passing crowd makes space around them as they proceed toward a wider area, beating their drums and stomping the ground. The rhythmic clinking of the metal beads wrapped around their ankles signal the start of a performance. Onlookers soon form a circle. It is the dry season and the Gadawan Kura, the hyena handlers, are back. They claim to be immune to the venom of snakes and to have power on wild animals. They soon engage in mock fights with the hyenas, prompting them to attack and embracing them when they reach for their throat. They lift them from the ground, and carry them on their back while whirling around. They take off their muzzles and open their jaws with bare hands for all to see the teeth that can crush bones. They briefly trust their arms or face to these killing machines. At times, the crowd withdraws in fear as the hyenas rush toward them, held by mere ropes. The baboons are also on leash, all dressed up like little people. They do backward somersaults on command and other circus tricks. The hyena men are here to sell their secret medicines that protect from snake bites, cure diseases, and boost virility. Transactions go fast. When someone in the crowd waves a banknote, a baboon rushes to get the money and bring it to its trainer in exchange for the goods. The performers do not linger. They soon gather their drums, bags, and animals. The white taxi van drives them to the next crossroad where they will again attract an audience and peddle their miracle medicines.

Half of the year they live in the mostly Muslim Northern city of Kano where they lead traditional family lives, grow some crops, and train their children and animals until they can resume their nomadic life, hopping from town to town in Southern Nigeria once the dry season starts. They are well off. Their public performances are only a part of their trade. They are rumored to be hired as debt collectors and to engage in underground activities such as trafficking wild animals they sell to circuses and zoos. They are indeed reputed experts in catching hyena pups in their inaccessible dens, snatching baby baboons from their mothers, and hunting for bush meat.

The lives and deeds of the hyena men have been featured in several documentaries that make it possible to witness their public performances and follow their daily life in their settlements in Kano. The men, their wives, and children are well fed and groomed. The hyenas and baboons are tied to poles in a covered yard next to the families' living quarters. Every other day, the hyenas are given a big chunk of meat and bone, an antelope's head or leg. They have been raised from pups and are half-domesticated but they have not lost their aggressive instincts. They growl and bite at times even if they let the men scratch their back. The trainers sport many scars inflicted by hyenas and baboons. South African photographer Pieter Hugo temporarily joined their group to take shots of their ways and deeds. His stunning collection, *The Hyena & Other Men* was published in 2008 by Prestel in Munich. He was struck by their relationship to the hyenas: "There was something very strange going on between the guys and the hyenas, bordering on sadomasochism. These animals had been taken out of the wild as pups. They couldn't return." They were entirely dependent on these guys for food. And these men were dependent on these animals for their livelihoods. They needed each other, embedded in a grey zone where culture and nature interfaced. Obviously, the deep-rooted fear of the hyenas still haunted the tamers and their mesmerized audience.

The skills and trade of the hyena men have been transmitted from fathers to sons over many centuries if not millennia. In one of the documentaries made in 2005, we can see a toddler being broken into the art of manipulating snakes without fear and another young child straddling the back of a hyena. The Gadawan Kura are proud of their traditions and ways of securing their livelihood through their versatile skills but their identity is indelibly stamped with the sign of the hyena. As good Muslim men, they go to pray at the mosque every Friday but they foster more ancient beliefs in magic which comfort their self-confidence and project a sense of invulnerability. The hyena is a powerful African symbol rife with immemorial legends and superstitions that are sustained by the troubling biological and ecological characteristics of these animals. The hyena men, as well as other similar clans in Ethiopia, deal with the spotted hyena, *Crocuta crocuta*, the more massive and fierce looking species.

Figure 13 Spotted hyena (*Crocuta crocuta*). Abdullahi Mohammad with the hyena Mainassara by photographer Pieter Hugo who has vividly documented the street performances of Nigerian nomads exhibiting trained hyenas. These predators remain a serious threat for humans in some African countries. *The Guardian* of November 20, 2020, provides details about the death of an old man in Zimbabwe, who was dragged from his hut during the night by a pack of hyenas. Only the upper half of his body was recovered the next day in the bush. Published with the kind permission of Pieter Hugo.

Wolves

Not long ago, my friend the globe trotter, who is an ardent ecologist, took a bus ride in Java on his way to trekking around Mount Merapi. He soon struck up a conversation with an older man who was sitting next to him and wanted to practice his English. As they passed a large river, my friend asked: "Are there crocodiles in Java?"—"No! We killed them all! Thanks God! We killed them all a long time ago." My friend is still in shock. He lives in Western Poland, close to a river where he can safely fish and swim, and a forest where he takes long, leisurely walks.

In the 1940s, during my childhood and teen years, the wolves had mostly disappeared from the forests of France. However, the family conversations, the tales I read, and the occasional news that wolves might have killed a sheep somewhere on the national territory, kept feeding a deep-rooted anxiety: the fear of the wolf. On the paternal side, my grandfather who was born in the early 1880s, recounted that as a child he had to cross a wooden area with his brothers and neighbors on their way home from school as the family lived in the outskirt of the village. In the winter evenings, on their way back, they used to take off their clogs and banged them against one another to make noises that were supposed to scare off the wolves which might have been roaming around in the bushes. The mere thought of it was making my spine shiver. The forests of the backward province of Perigord remained one of the last strongholds of these feared predators. On my mother's side, my grandfather, who was born in 1870, liked to remind us that his own grandfather had decapitated a wolf that had attacked him as he was busy splitting logs to make a fire. This was in the central province of Berry, famed for its forests, farmlands, and wild swamps. When I was on vacation in his house, I was reading the works of George Sand, the notorious female writer from the nineteenth century, who had become a local hero in Berry when she retired and settled in Nohant, the village of her grandmother's estate. I was not told about her earlier scandalous Parisian career but most of her novels which were set in the region were a part of the small family library. I was devouring her haunting stories of wolfmen and wolf handlers who roamed the countryside at night. The deadly presence of the wolves in Europe was then woven into the fabric of popular imagination long after they had been decimated and did not represent the lethal danger they once were.

Wolves remained alive, though, in literature, principally in children books. This was probably an echo of a time when toddlers who escaped the watchful eyes of their caretakers and wandered away were easy prey for hungry animals.

There were also stories of wolf-children like the founders of Rome who had been raised by a she-wolf. However, children were more often the victims in the folk narratives. A happy ending, staging a last-minute rescue, would have been counterproductive since, obviously, these frightening tales were meant to equip the youngsters with a life-saving fear of the wolves.

Among the earliest travelling animal exhibits that have been documented in France, caged wolves were one of the main attractions. There is also visual evidence that trained wolves were a hit with the public both on stage and in the circus as late as the end of the nineteenth century. Posters from Paris's *Folies Bergère* and *Cirque d'hiver* advertise the German "dompteur" Rudesindo Roche presenting his fourteen-wolf act in a central circular cage. The drawings, made by artist Louis Charles Bombled (1862–1927), show bare-teeth animals rushing toward the man who appears to wrestle with one of them and, besides, an outsized wolf is portrayed in a self-assured, threatening pose. In the center of the poster, as a stunning contrast, the trainer stands with two wolves balancing on his shoulders while the rest of the pack forms a pyramid on specially built chairs. The trainer wears a military-like costume, thus emphasizing the heroic nature of the performance. This act was also featured in some of the most important traveling circuses of the time as it was attracting the fascinated attention of a wide public. Wolves had still, by then, quite a reputation as ever-present dangerous predators that lived in the immediate environment of farmers and villagers and in the memory of city dwellers. Earlier animal showmen such as Jean Pezon and François Bidel, who became famous through their daring confrontation with lions, had also demonstrated their power by training wolves (Tait 2016). Obviously, these wolves had been raised under the care of the trainers and were actually behaving like dogs but, for the audience, the word "wolf" carried enough symbolic baggage and actual memories for endowing the act with an aura of fear that created awe. Rudesindo Roche's animals were featured as being Russian, undoubtedly in order to add an exotic touch of wild ferocity to his otherwise docile charges.

Nowadays, in Europe, the wolves, like the crocodiles in Java, "have all been killed" and it would be difficult to stir people's imagination by showing some in a staged confrontational situation in a circus ring. They belong to a species considered to be threatened with extinction, that is quasi absent from the environment except in some remote regions of Spain, Italy, and Romania. It is noteworthy, though, that the deliberate reintroduction of wolves in mountains and forests in the name of ecological balance periodically reawakens ancestral obsessions and the discovery of a lone wolf wandering beyond its expected

Figure 14 "Traveller Attacked by Wolves" by Richard Ansdell (1815–85), Royal Academy 1854. In nineteenth-century urbanized Europe, the fear of the wolves is kept alive by rumors, tales, and popular imagery. Courtesy of the Victorian Web and the Hathi Trust.

range immediately makes the news. This does not trigger, though, a call to arms; *The Guardian* reported, with excitement, on April 27, 2020, that a couple of wolves that had settled in the north of Belgium were expecting cubs, and quoted the post of an ecologist that had appeared in Facebook: "I am proud to announce that she-wolf Noëlla and wolf August are expecting wolf cubs." Of course, breeders of sheep and other domestic animals do not share this enthusiasm but governments compensate them for any loss that can be attributed to wolves' attacks.

We can note the tendency to give familiar names to the animals that are identified and monitored as a way to integrate them symbolically into the social milieu that claims them as their own and henceforth "protects" them. The same ambivalent attitude is noticeable in North America where we also find evidence of the moral bond that may develop between humans and wild animals in the context of the contemporary approaches to nature. Consider, for instance, the sorrow expressed and shared on Facebook in November 2018 when a female wolf was shot by a trophy hunter in the state of Montana (USA). She was a seven-year-old black wolf that happened to become popular among the wardens at the

Figure 15 Before photography became the main source of visual information, newspapers and magazines used drawings to illustrate their contents. Louis Bombled (1862–1927), a celebrated French artist, provided the press with realistic renderings of contemporary events. This composition appeared in Le Monde Illustré [The Illustrated World] of December 1, 1888, to document the circus act of the wolf trainer Rudesindo Roche at the Paris Cirque d'Hiver. Source: Bibliothèque Nationale de France.

Yellowstone Park and a favorite of visiting tourists. She was easily identifiable from a distance and had been dubbed Spitfire, an admirative nickname congruent with a culture that worships weapons of all sorts. She was the alpha female of a successful pack, the daughter of an alpha female from Canada which had been introduced in Yellowstone Park when it was decided that the eradication of wolves in this vast wildlife reserve was detrimental to the ecological balance of this territory. Spitfire had made the fatal mistake of wandering beyond the border into the neighboring state of Montana in which wolves are still fair game. Nobody had ever hugged Spitfire but her demise nevertheless caused bursts of genuine sadness as would the loss of a relative.

How can humans empathize with predators that could well have killed and devoured them had they crossed their path in the wild at a time when they were hungry? The case of wolves is particularly relevant in this context. As we saw earlier, they have been most feared in Europe as far back in time as collective memory can go. Now that they have been practically eradicated at great costs over the last two centuries, they have become for some an object of fascination. Pictures taken in reserves and friendly encounters between cubs and their

Figure 16 A poster advertising Rudesindo Roche's fifteen-wolf act on the stage of the Folies Bergères theater in Paris by lithographer Tom Merry (1852–1902). Alamy Stock Photo.

keepers quickly turn into memes on the Internet. Their assumed "nobility" and the smart tactics of their pack hunting raise their profile among animal lovers. Biologists commend their functions in the food chain and their role in maintaining an optimal balance in their natural milieu. Logical reasoning leads to their re-introduction in the fauna of regions from which they disappeared. Now they are returning to haunt western Europe, in part through deliberate policies, in part driven by their own dynamics that make them extend their territories under demographic pressure. Wolves have been reinserted in the French Alps but when suddenly an individual is identified prowling Belgian forests, this makes headlines and raises concerns. The wolves in statistics are not the same as the wolves on one's doorstep.

The ecological ideology that permeates the cosmology of the urban North American population is all the more wolf-friendly as the low density and prey-richness of this vast geographic area makes serious encounters with these predators rare and mostly innocuous when people venture for vacations in the wilderness. There are, however, circumstances in which the imaginary wolf brutally clashes with the real thing. CNN reported on August 14, 2019, that Matthew Rispolis, his wife Elisa and their two sons, a New Jersey family on a camping trip in the Banff National Park in Canada, were fiercely attacked by a wolf while they were sleeping in their tent. This news item was qualified as an "unthinkable" event. The wolf tore through the tent, grabbed the man arm with its jaws and started dragging him out. All woke up in sheer terror. The frantic screams of the wife and the two boys alerted a man who was camping nearby and immediately came to the rescue. In his own words: "The screams were so intense that I knew it was obviously a terrible situation. I kind of kept running at [the wolf] and just kicked it sort of in the back hip area." Eventually, the wolf released its grasp. Now, quite significantly, the rescuer, Russ Fee, added in the interview that he "immediately regretted kicking the wolf, but it did make the animal release Matthew and pop out of the tent." They then all shouted and threw stones at the wolf. The man was treated in a nearby hospital. The fact that, in a life-threatening situation, someone feels compelled to apologize for hitting an animal betrays the reach of the ethos of political correctness applied to the treatment of animals.

Predators are predators. Defenseless, nature-loving humans are often easy-to-catch prey. Their utopian view of wild animals entails unguarded approaches and careless roaming in unknown areas. Every summer in Canada, events similar to the close encounter of the Rispolis family are chronicled. They do not always end well. On August 20, 2019, *The Guardian* reported that Julien

Gauthier, a French artist who was travelling with a biologist in order to record sounds of nature in the Northwest Territories was dragged from the camp and killed during the night by a wild bear. This predator had no name. It surged from the wild, unannounced, and killed to eat. It tore apart the veil of representations that humans cast over the natural world. It was for its victim a pure and sudden presence, death itself.

The Death of a Tigress

Tyger Tyger, burning bright
In the forest of the night:
What immortal hand or eye
Dare frame thy fearful symmetry?

William Blake

Whoever regularly reads the Indian press in print or online is often informed of events concerning the wild tigers that still live in fair numbers in the forest of the country. For the purpose of conservation, they are monitored as closely as possible through periodic censuses and direct observations by wardens. Tigers are secretive and exquisitely camouflaged to the point that most data come from the recording of their tracks on damp soil or in mud. These imprints, though, yield much information on their sex, age, and health status. Some camera traps also provide visual evidence of their movements within their territories. Over the years, a few animals have come to the attention of the media through the reports of the wardens who refer to them by the names they bestow upon them for the sake of identification. Like humans, these names or nicknames pick up a physical feature or a personality trait. A one-way bond thus develops between foresters and the animals they monitor and protect from poachers and defensive farmers. The tigers that roam free in wildlife sanctuaries are thus woven into a narrative featuring their assumed personality and characteristic look. As they are not hunted, they have lost some of their natural shyness and they can often be observed from the safety of the wardens' jeeps or the tourists' buses. Social media are flooded with esthetically pleasing images that make us forget their serial killer instinct. Some individual animals reach stardom in the realm of representation.

The death of tigress Machli, the "queen" of Ranthambore National Park, was greeted with deep sorrow in *The Times of India* of August 19, 2016. Her carcass "was cremated following a guard of honour."

https://www.facebook.com/groups/571266496406061/permalink/1384670261732343?sfns=mo

For the bureaucrats who keep track of the wild tiger population, she was T-16. For those who monitored the whereabouts and behavior of the registered tigers, she was Machli, "fish" in Hindi, an affectionate nickname due to a pattern in the markings on her face. During most of her adult life she was admired for her poise and self-assurance. Humans had never hurt her and she was not afraid of their presence. She became celebrated as the most photographed tiger in India as she was not wary of the tourists who remained in the park minibuses at a distance and clicked their cameras when she was cooling down in the forest lake she regularly visited. She was also known as the Queen of the ruined fort that stood at the center of her territory. She raised many litters which survived and prospered. However, as she was aging, the wardens encountered her less often in the areas where she used to hunt. They noticed she was losing weight and they now were finding her tracks mainly in peripheral regions. One of her daughters, Sundari, had taken over the prey-rich forest around the lake and had become the new Queen. Machli had to contend with other tigers that were prowling the borders of her former territory. There were signs of fighting that she did not win. This tigress had become a ghost at the margins of her lost kingdom until it was announced with great sadness that she had not been seen for too long a time to have any hope of encountering her alive again.

Her last years, though, bear witness to the one-way bond that can develop between humans and wild tigers. The wardens are familiar with the laws of nature and their duty is to preserve the normal course of things, not to interfere with its unfolding. They had noticed that Machli had been injured in a fight and that her two canines had fallen off. Empathy can submerge dutiful indifference and override the passive recording of events. The wardens started providing her with baits they deposited on her new paths. It was a struggle because other tigers could come first or steal her meal. She was no match for them any longer. Machli was starving. Toward the end, the wardens could hear her roaring close to the spot where the wardens' jeep would stop to deposit some meat. Machli was hungry but could not kill any longer.

The Ranthambore National Park is a Bengal tiger reserve in the Sawai Madhopur District located in Eastern Rajasthan. The Indian government takes very seriously the protection of the tiger population that was threatened with extinction through intense poaching and conflicts with developments encroaching on their traditional forest range. The rangers who reported about the life of the tigress Machli also keep monitoring the whole population under their watch at Ranthambore. Cameras are posted in various strategic spots that enable them to keep track of the demographic dynamics at play within each tiger's territory. The wardens also roam the forest in their vehicles to catch occasional sights of everyday life in the deciduous tree forest. Mahuya Acharia posted on Facebook on April 23, 2020, a YouTube film documenting the history of the population within the old fort territory over the last thirteen years under the title "Tigers attack own family" (tiger vs tiger). The early euphoric visions of "Queen Machli" were in fact but snapshots of a brief period of apparent bliss in the life of this predator, that was taken out of a context in which we usually have no access. The data over more than a decade deliver a different picture that reminds us of the realities of animal lives in nature.

Although each tiger in the sanctuary bears an administrative identity code such as T-16 or T-23—Machli was T-16—the wardens bestow less impersonal names on each individual animal as it is easier for them to communicate about their whereabouts and behaviors. Indeed, no two tigers are alike. First, they have ways to identify each other—something all the more crucial as relationships among individuals can be problematic in this non-social species—through both proximal and distal signs. The former are visual marks formed by the stripes, notably on the face that function like a bar code since the black marks are symmetrical above the eyes but dissymmetrical on the lower face, and each individual has its own patterns. This makes it possible to know who is who from a distance as the contrast between the various colors is enhanced by the presence of black and white combined with the orange hues of the rest of the fur. Tigers also leave physical marks, both visual and olfactory, that can be deciphered in their absence on the places they visit when they patrol their territories. Humans use mostly visual semiotic resources to identify individual tigers since both species share at least this means of face recognition. Regular observers of tigers, either in nature or in captivity, also process information coming from their character and typical behavior. This is what allows the wardens of wildlife sanctuaries to keep track of individual tigers through encapsulating their characteristics into a nickname that reflects their perceived personality.

Longitudinal observations, such as the ones reported in the narrative by Mahuya Acharia can accurately document the population dynamics in the form of life stories. Its arbitrary point of departure is the tenure of Machli as the dominant tigress of the Fort territory. Her last litter consisted of three daughters that she raised successfully. Several years passed during which she taught her offspring how to hunt and manage their lives in the wild. Young tigers are indeed very vulnerable because they can mindlessly expose themselves to deadly encounters, including with other intruding tigers. Predators also happen to eat other predators including their own species as cannibalism has been often witnessed. Machli's three daughters reached adulthood but then the family structure became stressed. One daughter, Sundari (T-17), turned out to be a dominant female and started attacking in earnest her shy sister Baghani who eventually had no choice but to move away. Then it was the turn of the third daughter, Krishna. Machli remained in control of her territory for a while until Sundari took aim at her mother and forced her out of the Fort domain and its rich prey resources. We saw above how her demise was monitored by the wardens and her eventual death was honored by a religious cremation. In the meantime, Sundari proved not to be a productive breeder. The local resident male, Star, failed to father any litter with her. She eloped to meet the neighbor male Zalim, a dangerous liaison that brought up some cubs but forced her to abandon the Fort, to seek a new territory after a fight with Star. She met her death in the hands of farmers at the periphery of the wildlife reserve. Baghani had a short reign as the queen of the Fort. Currently, Krishna holds the title and is raising her new litter.

Hunger Never Stops

"In the Bangladesh part [of the Sundarbans], *a total of 392 people were killed by the tigers between 1956 and 1970, an annual average of 26, or 0.6 deaths per 100 km² [square kilometers] per year. In some areas the killing rate was as high as 1.8 per 100 km² per year.*

Hans Kruuk, **Hunter and Hunted**, 2002: 57

The literate population that reads the Indian press mostly shares the contemporary officials' concern for preserving tigers in their natural environment. The farmers and other workers, though, who toil in the fields and tend to their cattle on the edges of, or within tiger territories hold a different perspective. They often lose family members to the sneak attacks of hungry tigers. The two attitudes are profoundly incommensurable. When there is a loss of life or cattle, the Indian government usually pays a compensation meant to prevent people from retaliating by indiscriminately poisoning or otherwise eliminating these predators for which humans are an easy meal. Traditionally, when farmers and foresters would come across a den with new cubs while the mother was away hunting, they did what other people do when they find a nest of rats or other vermin in their home. Nowadays, it is a punishable offense in India to kill a tiger whatever its gastronomic taste might be. A man-eater can get away with murder. The blame is put on people who have encroached on its territory and the animal is usually sedated and flown to another, distant forest where, hopefully, it will find enough to eat to stay away from humans.

On July 26, 2019, *The Guardian* featured an article titled "Indian villagers beat tiger to death after attacks on locals." The animal had strayed out of a tiger reserve in the Northern state of Uttar Pradesh. Its attack triggered a defensive mob reaction and nine people were injured in the commotion, one of them fatally. The villagers beat the tiger to death with their wooden sticks and spears. Someone filmed the fight with their mobile phone and the footage showing the motionless animal being battered while lying on the ground went viral. "Thirty-three people were wanted over the killing of the tiger and four had been arrested so far, the magistrate [said], [adding] that the villagers were scared and angry after the attacks on humans." The same article reports that in the previous month a female and two cubs had been poisoned. *The Guardian*'s article contextualized this information by reminding its readership that "[a]bout 30 people were killed by tigers in India in 2018, and more than 60 tigers have died or been killed so far this year [2019] across the country."

Bombay [Mumbai], November 1984. As I stopped over in that bustling city on my way to a conference in Mysore [Mysuru], I notice that a big circus has pitched its enormous tent at Church Gate, a walking distance from my hotel in the Kolaba district. Circus Apollo displays large banners above the entrance, some showing fierce lions and tigers leaping through hoops or rearing in front of the trainers. My first experience of an Indian circus is truly puzzling as the cage act that starts the show falls short of the expectations of a spectator used to the decorum and drama of the traditional European circus. I decide to return to the circus for the evening performance with my notebook in order to record differences I find interesting from an ethnographic point of view. In that second show, the cage act is the last one in the program because they obviously alternate the order with the flying trapeze act, which also requires some lengthy setting up. This way, the cage will remain ready for the beginning of the next performance.

The trainer enters the ring with three helpers while the animals, four tigers and seven lions, are driven to their stools, some being collared with a rope held by an assistant. Two male lions are made to take their place on the left of the cage entrance, and the other five, apparently females or castrated males, are lined up on the right, some being tied up by a rope to the bars behind their pedestals. The four tigers then reach nonchalantly their stools opposite the lions. The men perform their task in a subdued, perfunctory manner, paying more attention to the animals than to the audience, in a marked difference with the showmanship of American and European "dompteurs." There are higher pedestals in front of the animals' stools and the first routine consists of having all of them put their front paws on these pedestals. Then, three lions take place on a pyramidal construction while one of the helpers sits on the back of the lion that stands at the top. The next figure consists of another of the helpers standing with his feet resting on the backs of two lions. The lions are made to roar and do a bit of a mock fight when they are driven back to their stools. Then comes the turn of the tigers. They take place on a higher pyramid that has been pushed in the center of the ring. The next routine is a leap from one pedestal to another over the head of one of the helpers, followed by a jump through a paper hoop in the appearance of a lotus leaf. Finally, the four tigers are made to clear a fiery hoop held by the trainer but the last one refuses to comply and rushes from the ring through the cage exit. This last episode triggers some laughter in the audience. Interestingly, the show of the Venus Circus that I saw a few days later, November 30, in Cannanore (Kerala), followed exactly the same pattern using, though, a different combination of animals: a tiger and nine lions, plus three lion cubs that remained seated on their stools during the act.

In both cases, the pace was slow but the spectators, as far as I could assess, were attentive. Even though they were city dwellers, a large percentage of them had moved to the city not so long ago. Tigers were not for them exotic animals. Like for the bears and wolves in traditional Europe, their folk culture is replete with memories of events involving the ever presence of these predators. Man-eaters, as the daily press in India still reminds everybody, is a not so rare an occurrence in the lives of villagers.

January 1992, Delhi. The presence of Circus Gemini near Chandni Chowk prompts me to skip a session in the conference on masks I am attending at the Indira Gandhi National Centre for the Arts. I manage to secure a front row seat close to the elevated ring. Among the outside banners, I had noticed the tantalizing painting of a tiger riding a bicycle. Sure enough, in the middle of the show, some tigers on leash were featured without the usual steel arena and one of them was led around the ring straddling a tricycle. For the local audience this feat was a hit: the ritualistic humanization of a serial killer; the delusional submission of the wild predator and its integration into the technological realm of modernity.

Trying to make sense of the fascination of the audience for the demonstration of absolute mastery over these predators, we have to keep in mind that, even if urban spectators are not threatened on a daily basis by them, the Indian press serves as an echo chamber for such attacks. The following titles bear witness to the commonality of deadly encounters: "Tiger attacks in Sundarbans wake-up call"; "Squads formed to kill man-eater in Faizabad" (*The Times of India*, January 14, 2009); "West UP [Uttar Pradesh] maneater strikes again" (*The Times of India*, February 8, 2014); "Tiger snatches man off boat, leaps back into Sundarbans jungle" (*The Times of India*, June 27, 2014); "Man-eating tigers on prowl in Madhya Pradesh" (*The Times of India*, July 25, 2014); "Tiger snatches woman off boat" (*The Times of India*, August 9, 2014); "Tiger kills fisherman in Sundarbans" (*The Times of India*, August 10, 2014); "The hunt is on for the man-eater of Maharashtra" (*The Times of India*, September 12, 2018). In other parts of Asia in which there are still some declining tiger populations, we note the same kind of reports: "Tiger mauls Indonesian palm oil plantation worker to death" (*The Jakarta Post*, January 5, 2018); "Sumatran tiger kills a man in Riau" (*The Jakarta Post*, March 11, 2018); and, closer to home, "Keeper killed by Siberian tiger in Zurich zoo" (*The Guardian*, July 4, 2020).

However, in all these journalistic reports, the blame is nowadays consistently put on the victims who did not respect the law by breaking into protected tiger territories—a fine line drawn by bureaucrats on a map and sparsely indicated by signage on the ground—or assigned collectively to the general encroachment of agriculture, pasture, and other developments on the edges of the forests. In the case of zoo accidents, the cause is found to be a human error that exonerates the killer. The empathy is implicitly redirected from the humans to the tigers, a discourse strategy aimed at prioritizing the survival of the species, now construed as a national emblem in India and commanding substantial support from international agencies.

As a consequence of this policy, tigers have now disappeared from Indian circuses. The central government banned the use of wild animals for entertainment in 1998 and added elephants to the list of the species concerned in 2013. Around the same time there were alarming reports that the tiger population in the wild was fast declining and inching toward extinction as a result of their shrinking range under the pressure of developments and increasing poaching aimed at fueling a lucrative trade in skins and body parts. The dreaded predator of Indian villagers became the threatened glorious emblem of India. Self-defense was hardly justified and, as we mentioned above, farmers are arrested for harming wild tigers.

It is interesting to trace the transformation of the meaning of the tiger from an indiscriminate sneaky killer which, traditionally, was hunted and slaughtered by the hundreds, into a cultural emblem embodying esthetic and, implicitly, moral values. It is symptomatic that, around the time when tigers were banned from circuses, the southern India writer R.K. Narayan (1906–2001) published a short novel whose hero is a tiger. In *A Tiger for Malgudi* (1983), the tiger itself recounts the story of his life in definitely anthropomorphic terms and, expectedly, it includes a circus-bashing episode. "Malgudi" is a fictitious place invented by Narayan on the model of a south Indian village. The author tells in his introduction that the idea that gave rise to this novel was a photograph of a hermit attending a religious festival in Allahabad with a tame tiger that followed him. The man claimed that this bond was due to the fact that they were brothers in a previous life. Why not write a book from the point of view of a tiger, a being obviously endowed with feelings? The fictional leap from feeling to reflexivity led Narayan to imagine a tale that would be told by the tiger himself.

The narrative starts with the idyllic depiction of the life of his hero as the head of a family enjoying the jungle with his "wife and children," notwithstanding the fact that male tigers are not monogamous and do not take part in raising the cubs, a task exclusively performed by the female who is prompt to aggressively chase the male away after copulation. The narrative, though, requires this delusional touch of humanity as its starting point. Alas! This happy "family" that has plenty of deer and other prey to eat in the forest comes under attack from hunters who kill the "mother and the children." Understandably, the "father" is angry and seeks revenge by killing humans. This leads to the tiger being captured and given to a circus in which a trainer, called the Captain, forces him through starvation and harsh treatment to perform tricks.

Thus, the novel substantiates the myth that circus animals are captured in the wild and tortured in order to entertain an audience whereas, in reality, training always starts with young animals usually born in the circus or in zoos. True enough, they are often introduced by their trainers as "forest-bred" or "recently captured" in order to enhance their assumed courage. In the public imagination to which the circus caters, the heroic image of the wild animal trainer must be built through metaphors and deceptive narratives. The tiger recounts that he is further exploited by a film maker who makes him perform with a Tarzan actor. Enough is enough. The tiger decides to put an end to his ordeals and mauls the Captain to death. The readers cannot fail to be in sympathy with this outcome. Having liberated himself from the predicaments of circus life, the tiger goes on a rampage in the village and wreaks havoc among the population, eventually taking refuge in the local school where he finds himself cornered. Then comes a monk, a holy man, to the rescue, who convinces the tiger to abandon violence and follow him in his life of errancy and meditation until, feeling that he was soon to die, he brings the tiger to a zoo where he will be taken care of. The tiger, who has then become quite a Buddhist himself, accepts his destiny with philosophy.

The media are saturated with representations of predators as lovely anthropomorphized characters. From feline and canine heroes to cuddly carnivores, there seems to be no limit to building up the meaning of animals as inoffensive companions, at times even saviors of their masters. Hollywood films such as the popular *Lion King*, whose plot owes more to Shakespeare than to the biology and ethology of actual African and Indian lions, biases the perception of their audience to the point that tourists, spreading videos taken from the safety of their vehicles, trivialize the idea that humans are the villains on the great stage of nature.

Narayan's novel is symptomatic of the radical shift that has occurred in the twentieth century in the popular image of wild animals that no longer constitute a serious threat to the life of the global population with the exception, of course, of rural Asian and African communities which have to cope daily with the risks entailed by working close to nature reserves or within the remnants of predator-rich wilderness in the world. Their fears of, and struggles with hungry animals there remain a constant issue, and the sight of a human demonstrating actual power upon a predator can cause awe and admiration. European audiences in the nineteenth century were similarly impressed because the abundant colonial narratives reported stories of man-eating tigers and terrifying lions. Circus trainers, then, were making sure that their charges would conform to this image. They selected animals that were prone to roar at the least provocation, a sign of fear rather than aggression, and they trained them to mount mock attacks. These spectacular interactions were not risk free, of course, and circus men and women occasionally lost their lives during the shows or while practicing. This still happens nowadays in spite of the emergence of a style of presentation that attempts to comply with the new perception of predators as partners if not accomplices playing together in the steel arena. For instance, Ettore Weber, a sixty-year-old experienced Italian trainer, was mauled to death by a male tiger named Sultan during a practice session before the circus show was due to start near Bari on July 4, 2019. The tiger slashed his throat. He collapsed and it was reported that the other three tigers that were in the steel arena joined the onslaught and cavorted with his lifeless body around the cage. It took time for the helpers, including his wife, to recover his corpse.

From Non-Animal Humans to Non-Human Animals

The more we learn of the true nature of non-human animals, especially those with complex brains and correspondingly complex social behaviour, the more ethical concerns are raised regarding their use in the service of man – whether this be in entertainment, as 'pets', for food, in research laboratories or any of the other uses to which we subject them.

Jane Goodall, **Through a Window**, 2000: 145

Ever since humans expressed themselves through art and narratives, the animals they could observe in their environment and which they confronted in their daily life have been for them a topic of utmost interest. These animals have generated vivid metaphors, for instance in fables in which they represented human types or in circus performances in which they were made to act as humans. In many ancient religions of the world, they manifested divine power and embodied transcendence, or they served as messengers and mediators between the gods and humans. All these functions presuppose, though, an ontological divide as animals are conceived as radically different from humans to the point that humans commonly self-define as non-animals. This entails several consequences, the most drastic of them having been formulated in the seventeenth century at the dawn of the Enlightenment by philosopher René Descartes who contended that animals are machines deprived of emotions and consciousness, faculties that are the exclusive properties of humans. Although this attitude is still somewhat pervasive in contemporary society as the industrial breeding and slaughtering of animals for food or other commodities demonstrate, a sea change has occurred over the last few decades. Modern mentalities have increasingly become sensitive to the commonalities that can be observed in social animals and humans, thus giving rise to the progressive erasure of the ontological divide through the generalization of anthropomorphism, that is, the interpretation of animal behavior in human terms.

Influential, media-savvy scientists, such as Frans de Waal and Jane Goodall, greatly contributed to the semiotic neutralization of the culturally fundamental opposition of the wild and the tame, and ultimately of the mutually exclusive categories of human and animal. The memory of eons of vital struggle between humans and their predators was progressively erased to be replaced by a flattening of the differences. Both scientists, riding the hippy wave of the mid-twentieth century, published best-selling books that promoted a view of animals as so close to humans that they appeared at times even morally superior to our own war-prone species. In *Chimpanzee Politics* (1982), de Waal showed how similar the social process in a group of *Pan troglodytes* was to human intrigues and occasional tragedies but the observers overlooked the fact that this group was kept in an enclosure that was deemed sufficiently large by their human keepers but did not allow any individual to escape and migrate beyond their clan's territory as they are known to do in their natural environment. For the sake of tracking who was doing what, Waal's research team had given Dutch first names to the actors involved in the narrative. Later on, in his landmark *Peacemaking among Primates* (1989), he set the stage for a complete reversal of values with the idealization of Bonobos (*Pan paniscus*) that appeared to have invented, through their sexual social behavior, long before humans, the "make love, not war" slogan. At least, this is the gist of this scientific study as it was amplified and interpreted in the popular press.

Jane Goodall had acquired earlier a hero status by being the first woman to confront the harsh life in African jungles in order to study chimpanzees in their natural milieu rather than in a laboratory. It helped her high visibility to have conducted her research with her partner photographer who recorded episodes in which she appears alone in interactions with some friendly primates. Her method that consisted in provisioning the animals with bananas and other food in order to establish contact with some individuals was questioned by other scientists but the media took at face value her conclusions that tended to gloss over the differences between chimpanzees and humans. The confusion was helped by the fact that she too had given English first names to the few individuals that had captured her attention and honored her baits. She soon became a high-profile advocate of the discontinuation of using chimpanzees in medical research as well as in circuses, promoting the idea that these primates were persons with their own rights. Carefully staged interactions in which she was shown comforting young chimpanzees or "liberating" some adults, from a safe distance, into fenced parks still occasionally flood social media with pleas to support her foundation.

The creeping notion of personhood and civil rights attributed to animals in the cosmology of the contemporary urban population is a profound re-categorization of the human environment in which predators are but a remote memory. It leads to the belief that using animals is a form of unethical abuse or slavery that should be criminalized and sanctioned by appropriate laws. This dangerous analogy with human situations has the perverse effect of not only trivializing the violations of civil rights in contemporary societies by hinting that it is worse to victimize defenseless animals than fellow humans—on the assumption that humans can defend themselves while captive animals cannot fight for their rights as they are deprived of speech—but also giving precedence to animal victims that are themselves exempt of duties. It glosses over the fact that rights and duties are the two inseparable faces of the social contract, and the fundamental basis of civil society. This animal liberation ideology rests on the fallacy of the natural goodness of nature as opposed to the corrupting forces of culture and civilization, a philosophical view that gained prominence in the late eighteenth century with the writings of Jean-Jacques Rousseau (1755), and was orchestrated in the following century by Henry David Thoreau (2016 [1854]; 1994 [1862]) and Ralph Waldo Emerson (1985 [1836]). The latter, symptomatically, reported a life-changing experience when he suddenly felt essential kinship with all the organisms he discovered during a visit to the *Jardin des Plantes* (Botanical Garden) in Paris that was holding rich zoological exhibits.

The ideological dynamics that drives the erasing of the modern theoretical and practical gap that sets humans apart from animals, has an impact on the legislative discourse and its constraints on the lives of citizens. On July 4, 2018, NDTV (All India/Press Trust of India) reported that the High Court of the Uttarakhand had ruled that all the animals in this northern state have the status of "legal person or entity" on the ground that "they have a distinct persona with corresponding rights, duties, and liabilities of a living person." This ruling was followed by "directions" specifying that "the entire animal kingdom, including avian and aquatic ones, are declared as legal entities […] All the citizens throughout the state of Uttarakhand are hereby declared persons *in loco parentis* as the human face for the welfare/protection of animals." Puzzlingly, though, all the precise instructions entailed by this ruling exclusively concern the welfare of domestic animals. A similar ruling by the High Court of Punjab and Haryana was reported on June 3, 2019, by the journal *Jurist* published in collaboration with the University of Pittsburgh. This ruling declared that "citizens have legal responsibilities and functions similar to those of a parent vis-à-vis minor children for the welfare and protection of animals." The underlying metaphor—"animals are the children of humans"—betrays the inconsistency of this view since the test of legal universalism should lead to the obligation of taking care of the predators as well as the prey. Such a ruling implicitly excludes many animals from its application and proves to be merely an *ad hoc* move ultimately designed to ensure the good maintenance of enslaved animals with a touch of humanity.

This legalistic approach is global and equally inconsistent in all its local forms. In 2010, Swiss voters were asked in a referendum if they would approve the obligation for each canton to appoint lawyers on behalf of the animals on the ground that their lack of speech prevented them from suing the perpetrators of wrongs and obtaining redress. This, of course, applied primarily to cattle and horses rather than wolves and foxes. It all boils down to the tacit cosmology of the populations concerned: what is meant by "animals" in general is a limited segment of the whole spectrum of non-human organisms that reflects folk cultural categorizations such as domestic vs. wild, indigenous vs. exotic, and useful vs. harmful, but other subjective qualifications may interfere with this nomenclature such as cute vs. repulsive, or symbolic vs. insignificant. Furthermore, should animals that inflict pain on members of their own or of other species be condemned under these laws?

From the planetary obsession with the preservation of exotic fauna to the relentless advocacy of associations aimed at protecting animals, a global discourse has emerged and succeeded in redefining predators as victims of human violence. The few cage acts that still form parts of circus programs omit the whip-cracking and occasional (blank) gun fire that were the trademark of their art and they foreground instead, as much as feasible, close contacts and apparent harmony between mostly sub-adult animals and their keepers. The multimodal discourses they display gloss over the fact that the animals they drive through their paces are still, fundamentally, formidable killer machines. However, the men and women who perform in front of appreciative audiences must create through their acting an atmosphere of playful engagement. Trainers, though, are fully aware of the biological rules of the game. Thomas Chipperfield, the scion of a legendary dynasty of wild animal keepers (McPherson 2014), who bills himself as the last lion trainer of England, in spite of being prevented from performing by government regulations, reminds us, in an article he published in 2015 in *The Telegraph*, that whenever he is practicing or performing with his lions, his father and mother are standing behind the cage, paying utmost attention to the behavior of the animals. Predators, like all other organisms, have evolved what the early ethologists (e.g., Cooke 2017; Lorenz 1966 [1963]; Tinbergen 1953) called "innate releasing mechanisms", that is, an automatic neurological response triggering a fixed action pattern in presence of a specific elicitor. In plays and in earnest attacks, as Thomas Chipperfield explains, a feline will crouch and pounce whenever a playmate or a prey is not paying attention to it. It is crucial that the trainer be warned by an outside observer whenever one of his charges exhibits this typical behavior while he is busy working with others. When they are not going through their paces, lions and tigers must be kept in place, seated on their stools, a position that makes their occasional crouching very noticeable. Being called to attention, meaning that they are being watched, defuses the beginning of a chain of events that is difficult to stop once it has gone beyond the preparatory movement. It is interesting to see how Chipperfield comments in this interview on an accident that happened to a female lion trainer in Egypt, Ms. El-Helw, that was recorded and widely spread through social media:

> Having watched the video taken from ringside, it was immediately clear to me from the lion's body language that it never intended to harm Ms. El-Helw. The fact that she was back on her feet within seconds confirms that. Obviously, she was hurt and reportedly suffered a hairline fracture to her pelvis, just from an animal of that weight jumping on her. But if it had meant to do serious damage, it could have. […] judging from the lion's behaviour, the only mistake she seems to have made is a split-second lapse of concentration. […] You see [the lion] crouched for about three seconds, looking before he leaves the pedestal. […] From the way the lion grabbed her, I think he was probably trying to play with something on her costume – or just play with his trainer.
>
> (Thomas Chipperfield)

The Cage Acts of Yesteryears

Female tamers increased the appeal of the cage act through the fear of attacks because of their feminine vulnerability.
Peta Tait, Fighting Nature: Travelling Menageries, Animal, and War Shows, 2016: 28

A personal example of the rhetoric that sustained then the audience's reception of the "wild" is in order, even if it may be judged self-incriminating and ethically dubious.

> When, in my early twenties, I was working at the French Cirque Bouglione during the summers, one of my jobs was to entice people to visit the circus's traveling zoo when there was no performance going on under the big top. I had developed a certain oratory skill that mixed reality and fantasy, something that the circus's owners appreciated. Occasionally, I was called up to stand up for the speaker whose task was to introduce the artists during the show. One of the major attractions was the lion act of Henri Dantès, a presentation in the heroic style with plenty of roaring and mock attacks that played on the spectators' nerves and emotions. It was the first act on the program. One evening, shortly before the show

was scheduled to start, the news spread on the lot that the trainer was nowhere to be found. We heard that he had celebrated that day his twenty-seventh birthday and was probably drunk and sound asleep somewhere. There was no alternative cage act that could be substituted on short notice. A clear sense of panic seized the circus. Some spectators were still lining up to reach their seats. The music had started. The steel arena was standing in the ring, with all the stools ready for the lions. Firmin Bouglione, the famed wild animal trainers who owned the circus with his two brothers, had to make a decision. In his sixties, he had retired from active duties and had not presented wild animals for some years. Although he was familiar with the trainer's act, he could not simply enter the cage. The spotlight was on him, though. I overheard his wife begging him not to do anything and just have the steel arena taken down. But he decided otherwise. There was in the menagerie an older, massive tiger, Prince, that was a part of an act he had presented in the recent past. Prince had lost an eye in a fight with another male. Firmin Bouglione gave a few orders. The stools were rearranged. The show should have started ten minutes ago. He called me: "Paul, go to the mike and say something!". He then turn to the back stage and shouted; "Send in Prince!". It was my turn: "Ladies and gentlemen, for the first time in circus history, you will witness tonight a unique event: Firmin Bouglione will confront for the first time a wild tiger recently captured in the jungle of India. Please keep silent. Any movement could have tragic consequences." With due caution, Firmin Bouglione drove the tiger through its former routine in a way that my introduction had made credible.

This was more than fifty years ago, another age of the traditional circus. Wild animal trainers were concerned that their charges would not seem wild enough and they would prod them to roar and aggressively swipe their paws and show their claws. Henri Dantès was then a heroic figure in the French circus world. His fighting act with five lions punctuated by brief close contact with one of his animals who had been bottled fed as a cub and had remained rather tame, was dramatically staged. His boldness—some were saying recklessness—led to occasional bloody episodes caused by clawing that were making the headlines in the local press. This was spectacular, potentially life-threatening. Other lion trainers, though, were not as lucky. Some of his contemporaries were killed or seriously maimed during their cage acts or training practice. The recording of Henri Dantès presenting a six-tiger act from the Bouglione circus for the French television broadcast "*La piste aux étoiles*" [The Ring of Stars] (1967), offers a striking example of this genre. It is available on the website *Circopedia*. The man is elegantly dressed but pays scant attention to the audience because the animals are obviously stressed and aggressive, and must be kept under strict control. He occasionally cracks his whip but the rather long and strong stick he holds alternatively in his right and left hand is more prominent and is constantly used to maintain a safe distance with the tigers, even at times hitting them on the head to prompt them to advance toward him as the tricks require. The occasional close-ups of the camera reveal the animals' facial expressions that show readiness to attack if they were not held back by the obvious determination of the trainer who provokes them to snarl and roar by thrusting himself and the stick he holds at closer range. This act displays a confrontation between a group of dangerous predators which are forced to go through their paces by a daring individual who demonstrates human courage and skill. At the end, the trainer chases the tigers in circle along the ring until they rush out through the tunnel that leads to their cages as soon as the gate is open.

This act is completed in approximately six minutes. Its fast pace was a hallmark of this trainer. It includes seven segments which form the canon of the tiger acts produced by this particular circus's tradition. First, once the animals have reached their assigned stools, they are prompted to rise on their hind legs, some getting support from the bars of the cage. The music changes from the heroic mode to an oriental sounding melody and two tigers are made to jump in succession through a rather small self-standing metal hoop that has been placed between two high pedestals on a stand. Then, the trainer is handed from the outside a larger hoop with fire burning on its upper half and he holds it between the two pedestals while prompting the tigers to jump through it. The hoop is quickly removed from the ring through the cage bars and attendants extinguish it by putting it in a metal container. In the meantime, the trainer rearranges the pedestals so that they form a symmetrical pattern with a low pedestal at the center, two higher ones on each side, and two lower ones at each end. Five tigers are prodded to take their place and they are made first to sit down, then raise their body with their paws vertically extended. This "pyramid" is quickly dismantled by the trainer who clears up the central area of the cage and calls in two animals which are provoked to roll over five times synchronously. The final tricks consist of bringing five tigers lying down in a row in front of the man and, after a brief pause, forcing them backward to face the opposite direction, in front of the exit. The sixth tiger that was not involved in this last segment is let go. The remaining animals are chased around and eventually rush frantically toward the exit gate through the tunnel. The trainer takes a short bow by lowering his head with an expression of modesty. The public's applause indicates a genuine appreciation for the performance.

Reflecting upon my own experience of this act live—it was indeed, that year, the opening number of the regular spring program at the Cirque d'Hiver in Paris—I can assume that the spectators' attention is focused on the man and closely follows his movements in relation to the tigers. This is obvious when we watch the recorded performance: the cameraman strives to keep the trainer in the center of the visual field as much as possible to the extent that we miss at times the full context of a trick. This is noticeable when the tigers are prodded to jump on the pedestals to form the "pyramid." During the act, only for two very brief moments does the camera zoom on a tiger's face in order to emphasize the wild character of the animal, hence the courage of the man. Obviously, this is the result of the editing of the footage, but it is nevertheless reliable information regarding the reception of this animal act. We should keep in mind, though, that in a live performance the audience for the most part does not focus at length on individual animals but on the action and its meaning: the goal, the resistance, and the result. "Wild" is the overpowering concept that qualifies the animals as a kind of abstract category for which token images and acoustic events provide evidence.

The same group of tigers was presented by Joseph van Been in 1966 at the Hippodrome in Yarmouth. A video recording of this act can be found in the website *Circopedia*. It is interesting to compare the two performances, both in the confrontational mode but with variations in the style: the man demonstrates his control over the predators by kneeling in front of them at the end of two of the segments when the tigers are lying in front of him. Moreover, the sixth tiger which is kept apart of the others on the left of the circular cage and was hardly involved in the presentation of the act by Henri Dantès, is petted by Joseph van Been at the conclusion of the act in a display of remarkable tameness, indicating a special relationship with this trainer.

This act, though, had been initially trained and presented by Firmin Bouglione. It was recorded in 1961 during a televised performance at a time when the celebrated wild animal trainer was edging toward sixty and prepared his retirement from the central cage. It is a masterly presentation of the cage act of yesteryears. It is performed without bravado but with a serious, determined style. The trainer is obviously focusing on each step of the routine with due caution. The recording of this performance is available on Facebook through the link: "La France dit STOP aux cirques avec animaux—Firmin Bouglione [France says STOP to circuses with animals]." It shows other members of the family anxiously monitoring the unfolding of the act from the outside, at times prodding some tigers to make their move, and otherwise showing readiness to intervene should anything go wrong. Compared to the later versions of this act by Joseph van Been

Figure 17 The posters and banners of the traditional circuses and menageries enticed their audience with hyperbolic representations of wild predators, showing a single diminutive but bold human outnumbered by raging oversized carnivorous animals such as aggressive polar bears …Circo Orlando Orfei (Italy). The comment reads [in Italian]: "White bears from the North Pole: Fantastic !!!" (Courtesy of Jovan Andric). https://www.circus-collectibles.com/poster/detail/805

and Henri Dantès that were described above, in which the editing foregrounded the trainer in action rather than focusing on the tigers' reactions and demeanor, the footage used for the editing of the 1961 performance as an incriminating example of cruelty to animals underlines the stress and fearful expression of the animals, the reliance of the trainer on targeted whiplashes and hard sticks, and the confrontation that pitches the man against nine predators reluctant to obey. This way of processing the information flowing from the arena is at odds with the reception of this act as a heroic performance in the eyes of the beholders. The dynamics of its narrative, the actual risk involved in molding wild behavior into an esthetic composition, and its ritualistic power are offset by the selective attention to "irrelevant" details that transform this performance into a senseless, absurd exercise grounded in human cruelty.

More than five decades later, there has been a sea change in the style of feline presentations which had not varied for the last two hundred years. First, the

Figure 18 … or reluctant lions that are forcefully driven through their pace while the whole pride menacingly encircles the trainer armed with a mere whip. Italia stock poster from the late 1960s, Artwork by Marcello Colizzi. (Courtesy of Jovan Andric). https://www.circus-collectibles.com/poster/detail/1307

number of extant wild animal acts has drastically declined and those which are still in business underline playfulness and cooperation with their charges rather than emphasizing confrontation and coercion. Hynek Navratil and Alex Lacey, for instance, whose acts can be viewed online through YouTube or Vimeo recordings, insert brief episodes of staged wild outbursts as nostalgic quotations from a style long gone and, also, as a reminder that their animals are potentially dangerous even if they are not any longer billed as "jungle-bred." Before the shows and during the intermissions, the public can admire their lions and tigers in spacious enclosures connected to their transportation trucks.

By contrast, the tigers presented by Henri Dantès and Joseph van Been, for instance, were permanently kept in small individual cages in reinforced wagons which they left only for practice and performance in the steel arena. The predators had to be restrained like criminals. This was a part of the cultural landscape that only a very small minority of individuals were finding objectionable. On the symbolic level, the "wild" was the absolute antagonist, the lethal danger embodied by the presence at close range of predators often

Figure 19 Feared predators, crocodiles are featured here being subdued by the magic power of a master who has donned the outfit of an Indian fakir. Circus Krone (Germany): poster from 1987 featuring Karah Khavac with crocodiles. Artwork by Marcello Colizzi. (Courtesy of Jovan Andric). https://www.circus-collectibles.com/poster/detail/335

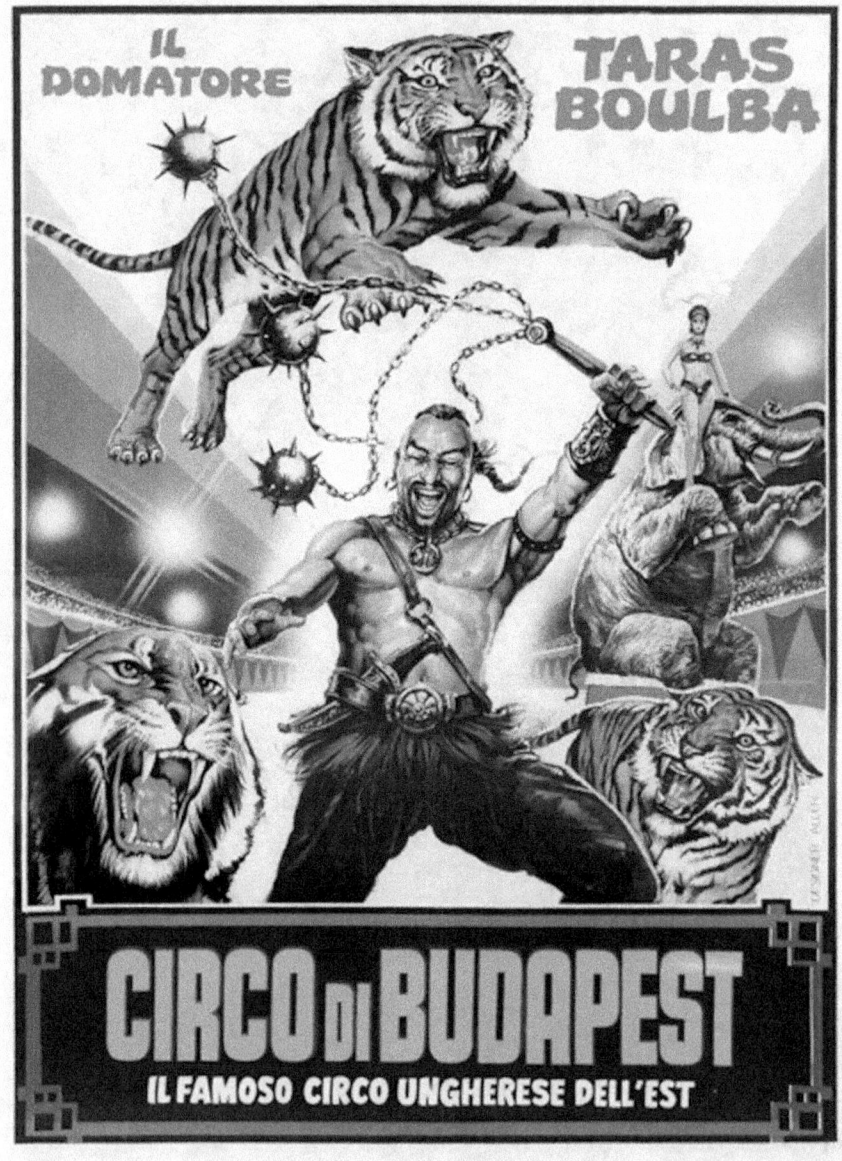

Figure 20 Another genre of posters represents man as the wild master of the beasts. Here, the trainer impersonates the Cossack hero of Gogol's novella, Taras Bulba, popularized by the 1962 Hollywood movie starring Yul Brynner. It conveys the idea that one has to share the predators' wildness in order to subdue them. Circo di Budapest TARAS BULBA—Italian circus poster from the mid-1980s featuring Emilien Beautour a.k.a. Taras Bulba, a French tiger trainer. Artwork by Aller. (Courtesy of Jovan Andric). https://www.circus-collectibles.com/poster/detail/1397

Figure 21 In a totally different mode, an elegant and poised trainer demonstrates his dominance by controlling a grossly oversized tiger. In spite of the unrealistic rendering of this scene, the audience will be influenced not only in their perception but also in their memory of this act. Circus Knie (Switzerland) poster from 1960 featuring the animal trainer Gilbert Houcke. Artwork by Marcus Campbell. (Courtesy of Jovan Andric). https://www.circus-collectibles.com/poster/detail/1482

Figures 22 and 23 Female dominance over male lions or black jaguar is a powerful icon in the traditional promotion of animal acts that suggests complicit wildness. These symbolic compositions combine raw eroticism with the dramatic staging of a circus background. Note the leopard skin patterns of the minimal outfit of the trainers.
Figure 22 Circo Braun—Italian poster from 1978. (Courtesy of Jovan Andric). https://www.circus-collectibles.com/poster/detail/1388
Photo 23 Circo Medrano (Italy) poster from 1974. Artwork by Renato Casaro. (Courtesy of Jovan Andric). https://www.circus-collectibles.com/poster/detail/1686

labelled "man-eaters" in countless episodes of the colonial epics. The tamer, or the "dompteur," a French word that did not imply the technical process of training but rather the action of dominating hostile forces, was standing as a civilizing hero. The conquest of the "wild" in its most terrifying form was re-enacted through a ritual that was accomplished with the seriousness of a priest. The total absorption of the man or the woman in this task was not faked since it actually required their utmost attention to every detail: the changing moods of the animals, their moves and positions with respect to each other, the placing of the pedestals, the threshold distance that should be safely maintained lest it would trigger an attack in earnest, mindful of the constant possibility that the whole process could derail and lead to chaos.

Figure 24 Overcoming the fear of snakes with charm and authority is a powerful image of human supremacy that is commonly displayed in the traditional circus. The comment on the poster reads (in Italian): "Miss Chantal in a mortal hug with giant python, boa constrictor, and anaconda." Crazy Cobra Show—Italian poster from 1997 featuring Miss Chantal, snake charmer. (Courtesy of Jovan Andric). https://www.circus-collectibles.com/poster/detail/418

Figure 25 The precondition for the emergence of civilization is the effective control of predators that are more powerful than humans. These images illustrate the mastering of the wild through skill and courage, and celebrate the triumph of the wild animal trainer as a cultural hero. Circo Rinaldo Orfei. Italian poster from 1978. (Courtesy of Jovan Andric). https://www.circus-collectibles.com/poster/detail/621

Figure 26 The ultimate triumph of the manly hero riding the wildest of animals. Such representations feed the symbolic capital of the imaginary circus by embodying the victory over the erstwhile challenge of predators. This image extracts from a relatively common act with tame animals the ritualistic significance of the performance it advertises. Circo Medrano (Italy) poster from the mid-1980s promoting Davio Casartelli's tiger and elephant act. Artwork by Franco Picchioni. (Courtesy of Jovan Andric). https://www.circus-collectibles.com/poster/detail/997

We can notice, for instance, that, during one version of the recorded performance with Firmin Bouglione, the last tiger which is prompted to take its place in the "pyramid" gets confused and agitated. There is a risk that its momentary panic will spread to the other animals. The trainer does not try to correct its course but first sends it back to its stool, then, starts again from scratch and repeats the step by step routine that drives this animal to its assigned pedestal. Adult tigers are live biological ammunition. Improvisation is not a part of the circus game.

What Is a Wild Animal?

> *In recent years political parties advocating animal rights and animal interests have sprang up in several countries and seem to constitute a new party family. At first sight, they appear to be single-issue parties, but a closer look at their party programmes suggests that they are developing a new ideology based on the core concept of compassion and adjacent concepts of equality, intrinsic value and interdependence.*
>
> Paul Lucardie, "Animalism: a nascent ideology? Exploring the ideas of animal advocacy parties". ***Journal of Political Ideologies*** (2020) 25 (2): 212

Circus folks have dubbed "animalists" a loose coalition of associations and individuals devoted to the eradication of the traditional circus for the sake of animal welfare and freedom from exploitation. These self-appointed defenders of animals have taken upon themselves to fight the traditional circus not only on the basis that training animals is cruel and detrimental to their health, but also that it is wrong to exploit animals for the purpose of entertainment, mainly wild animals that belong to specific environments. There are degrees, though, in the scope of their arguments. Some embrace the radical view that any use of animals in the broadest sense of the term is immoral, including domesticated species that provide meat and eggs as well as work and company. Consequently, they advocate "veganism" and condemn the use of equids and bovids for work and transportation. They also proclaim that no animals should be used as pets, and still less as service animals such as police and seeing dogs, functions they equate with slavery. Their extreme attitude is not very popular among the population at large, but their campaigns targeting circus animal training have been influential.

Most anti-circus militants set as a target of their attacks the use of "wild animals" in exhibitions and spectacles as being abusive and reprehensible to the point that any action aimed at liberating them and harming their keepers and trainers is permissible, including drastic legislation prohibiting the presence of wild animals in circuses. Their propaganda, supported by constant posting of alleged "visual evidence" in the social media, the press, and in television's advertising and broadcasts, generate a flow of donations, some of which have been shown to be diverted to the wellbeing of the organizers and their close associates (e.g., Julliard and Nobili 2015). These "animalists" find indeed a receptive audience among a large constituency of well-meaning people who are impressed by the documents they spread: photos and videos purporting to show animals being confined in cramped cages and forced to perform under violence or the threat of violence. As such proof is not so easy to find nowadays, animal defense organizations have been denounced for offering attractive prices for photos and videos that support their cause. The *Washington Post* published a report documenting the commissioning by PETA of a fake video showing a cat being brutalized in order to "teach" it a trick and attempting to launch this "evidence" in social media as a meme (Ohlheiser 2017).

As a result, the financial incentives offered by animalist associations created in some countries a profitable market to the point that the Australian government, for instance, had to make illegal the abuse of animals for the purpose of providing evidence of mistreatments. This is, unfortunately, a widespread practice as it was reported in a publication of the National Animal Interest Alliance titled "Deception in the name of animal rights": http://www.naiaonline.org/articles/article/deception-in-the-name-of-animal-rights#sthash.BCIEdyBR.dpbs

Other means used to undermine the cause of circus trainers is to spread irrelevant photos or videos. In the summer of 2020, a small French circus that had a license to keep four lionesses was prosecuted when inspectors discovered that they had also a male lion that was a recent addition. This "illegal" animal was seized and entrusted to a wildlife refuge. Soon appeared on the Internet the photo of an emaciated lion, allegedly showing how poorly this animal was cared for in that circus. The circus owner protested that this image was a fraud and pointed out that this was not his animal but the photo of a lion that had been seized some time ago from a private zoo in the United States.

Since there are no signs of widespread abuses in the displays of trained animals and since countless expert reports (e.g., Kiley-Worthington 1990; Wilson 2015) have concluded that circuses in general take adequate care of the welfare of their charges, these prohibitionists have come to claim that these animals are nevertheless wrongly subjected to humiliations through being forced to act in ways considered to be contrary to their nature outside their natural milieu. England offers a striking example of this shift from animal welfare concerns to ethical issues. In the course of 2019, the UK government considered a bill to forbid the use of wild animals in circuses on ethical rather than welfare grounds. This has now become the law of the land and all animals classified as "wild" have disappeared from traveling and stable circuses, thus sentencing the traditional circus to death. Wales followed suit a year later, thus extending the ban to the entire UK.

The ideological and legal discourses that sustain the success of the campaigns to prevent traditional circuses from using animals indeed focuses on "wild" or "exotic" species such as lions, tigers, leopards, zebras and elephants, but may cover an open-ended list including birds, rodents, and reptiles. It is taken for granted that the meaning of the category "wild" that is applied to these circus animals is obvious in this context. If we carefully consider such a characterization, we can soon discover that it is far from being so simple. What is a wild animal? Perhaps, it is understood as opposed to a tame or a domestic animal. It may also be conceived as the contrary of an autochthonous species and therefore be the equivalent of "exotic." If we switch from the domain of abstract categories to observable behavior, a wild animal is an individual which either flees humans or attacks them as a way of defending itself or capturing a prey. Can an animal that responds to its name and willfully comes toward its keeper be considered "wild" whether it is a lion or an elephant? Tameness does not imply domestication but does referring to a "tame wild animal" make sense? This oxymoron points to a fundamental inconsistency in the arguments of the activists. After all, domestic species were first wild and still have original wild populations as well as feral populations in various parts of the world. Furthermore, some cattle and horses are both domesticated and more dangerous to handle than circus lions and tigers which have been selectively bred in captivity for countless generations. "Wild" is too hard to define for providing a robust legal category based on semantic features.

Let us now examine another meaning of "wild" as characterizing an animal that is usually found in a natural environment different from the one in which European circuses and zoos operate. The notion of "exotic" carries the idea that there exists a proper geographic area for some species. Their transportation from Africa, for instance, and their installation in the British countryside or in traveling circuses are stigmatized as "unnatural," a transgression of an assumed transcendent order. Is there any value in the belief that lions and tigers "belong" by some kind of natural necessity to tropical or sub-tropical regions of the planet earth? This is a strikingly ill-informed position that reflects the worldview of the recent colonial past of the European cultures in which "animalists" are the most virulent. Tigers are indeed perfectly adapted to the Siberian climate or, actually, to any other part of the world, and lions have disappeared from Eurasia because they have been hunted to extinction, not because Africa is for them a kind of home country. The archaeological record, both historical and prehistorical, provides ample evidence of this. The idea that there is a "natural" environment assigned to each animal species by some natural or supernatural order is a delusion. Evolution and adaptation have no frontiers. It is true that some organisms happened to be so narrowly adapted to a constraining environment that any significant changes may indeed spell their demise. But felines and canids, like the genus *Homo*, are not of this kind. They can successfully breed and prosper anywhere on the planet earth and feed on anything fleshy that moves, including humans for which they are the erstwhile competitors for vital resources. Their young may be cute and playful but, ultimately, as grown-up, they are killing machines, driven by hunger, sex, and territorial imperatives.

Although they are not predators, elephants must be included in the category of dangerous animals. In today's India and Africa, more people are killed by wild elephants than by tigers, and, even those that have been submitted into domestication are reputed to be unpredictable. The circus annals feature a long list of elephant trainers who were killed by their charges. The elephants' destructive force was exploited in warfare very early in the rise of military powers in North Africa, Asia, and the Mediterranean Basin although they often turned out to be a liability as they were prone to direct their rage toward their handlers as well as against the enemies they were meant to scare and destroy (Armandi 1843). The Romans were long traumatized by their first encounters with these *belua* [monstrous creature] in the Punic wars. As we will see below, once this fear was exorcized by appropriating for a while these live weapons themselves, the spectacle of trained elephants remained a powerful ritual of dominance during the Empire.

The conflictual interface with predators and other dangerous animals forms the background experience of life written in the cultural memory of humans. Once they had settled in permanent dwellings, holding wilderness at bay, predators and raiders remained a permanent threat and a haunting presence that had to be constantly contained lest they bring death and devastation—as they still do in some areas of the natural world that have not yet been fully covered by the wasteland of technology. Once the menace, real or imagined, of the predators is defused, the ritualistic domination by force or magic of these animals loses its capacity to make sense. For long, staged performances demonstrating the power of humans over merciless beasts provided existential reassurance and collective self-confidence. This semiotic scaffolding has now mostly collapsed and the traditional wild animal circus acts have become meaningless, if not reprehensible, for a majority of our contemporaries. Before developing further this argument, let us turn back to the historical deep past of Western culture in order to take the measure of the robustness and resilience of the spectacular training of wild animals in the midst of the settled environment, both rural and urban, at a time when predators and other untamed beasts were not merely represented in cultural productions but actually constituted an existential threat for humans.

The Antiquity of the Animal Circus: The Elephants

Bundu (Jharkhand): Wild elephants went on rampage in Bundu killing at least two people and leaving over a dozen injured on Monday. The wild pachyderms also destroyed several houses, leaving several villagers homeless, spreading fear and panic among the locals. Locals say this was not an isolated incident and they are regularly at the receiving end of elephants' wrath – especially during the paddy season.

The Times of India, May 5, 2014

Over two millennia ago, the epicenter of literate western civilization was in Rome. Let us take a look at the city during the first century of the empire. There is no dearth of written accounts that vividly document the everyday life of its diverse population. The center of a sprawling empire, Rome is teeming with commercial and social activities. Its streets and squares are jammed with horse-drawn chariots and donkeys, litters carried by slaves, riders and pedestrians, loafers and loiterers, hawkers and prostitutes. It is mid-morning in the spring. Suddenly, the crowd clears the way: the elephants are approaching. They are taken by their handlers to the amphitheater for the show that is scheduled for the afternoon. This is a scene that would also become familiar to modern Europeans and Americans who, during the last two centuries, could witness similar processions in cities where a circus had pitched its tent. Today, we can see such herds of over twenty animals only in vintage photographs. All major circuses have discontinued their keeping of trained elephants and only a few families maintain a small number as part of their spectacles although it is for them a constant struggle to resist prosecution and seizure by the authorities.

We will note that the presence of these elephants in Rome was reported by no less an authority than Plutarch, the celebrated Greek philosopher and historian of the first century of the current era, whose fame as writer and lecturer earned him Roman citizenship. The animals Plutarch mentions in his *De sollertia animalium* [About the cleverness of animals] (1957) were performing animals. The Romans had been dealing for over two centuries with war elephants, first as formidable weapons of their enemies, then as their own war assets once they themselves adopted this means of warfare (Armandi 1843). By the time of Plutarch, though, they had become obsolete in this capacity because they proved to be too unpredictable on the battlefields. However, by the first century of this era, there still existed breeding and training centers in the vicinity of Rome that produced a quantity of elephants to be used in triumphal parades and amphitheater spectacles. Elephants were a daily part of the life in Rome, in a way comparable to today's Indian cities. But the people of Rome remained always fascinated by elephants and they stopped whatever they were doing to watch their column proceed along the road when they were led to the amphitheater. Some dogs barked and some spooked horses had to be restrained. The handlers were keeping a close watch as they were walking along the animals, ready to bring them back to order should they show a hint of panic or insubordination.

Plutarch reports a telling incident: A group of youngsters carrying the wax tablets on which they learnt how to write by etching letters on the soft surface stretched their hands toward the inquisitive trunks of the elephants always expecting gifts of sweet food. Instead, a mischievous kid poked the tip of a trunk with the pointed end of his stylus. In no time, he was lifted high above the ground. People shouted in terror. The worst was feared but they were relieved when the boy was gently brought down by the animal. A scare but no harm.

Plutarch's aim was to illustrate, through this snapshot of a dramatic street event, the intelligence and moral nobility of this animal that just wanted, in Plutarch's opinion, to give a lesson to the boy. Of course, it is more than likely that the handler quickly reacted and shouted an order while prompting the animal with his hook.

There is an abundance of testimonies in the Roman literature concerning the tricks performed by elephants in the amphitheater. For instance, in the early third century, Aelian (*Claudius Aelianus*), a writer and rhetorician who emulated Plutarch, authored a series of books on "The Characteristics of Animals." The second book features a long development concerning the trained elephants that could be admired in the amphitheater:

Now this troupe was twelve in number, and they advanced in two groups from the right and the left sides of the theatre. They entered with a mincing gait, swaying their whole body in a delicate manner, and they were clothed in the flowered garments of dancers. And at no more than a word from the conductor they formed into line (so we are told)—supposing that to have been their teacher's order. Then again they wheeled into a circle when he so ordered them, and if they had to deploy, that also they did. And then they sprinkled flowers to deck the floor, but with moderation and economy, and now and again they stamped, keeping time in a rhythmical dance.

That [some gifted humans] should be experts in music is certainly matter for wonder but by no means incredible or absurd. The reason is that man is a rational animal capable of understanding and logical thought. But that an inarticulate animal should comprehend rhythm and melody, should follow the movements of a tragic dance without a false step, fulfilling all that its lessons required of it—these are gifts bestowed by Nature, and each one is a singularity that fills one with amazement.

But what followed was enough to send the spectator wild with delight. On the sand of the theatre were placed mattresses of low couches, and on these in turn cushions, and over them embroidered coverlets, clear evidence of a house of great prosperity and ancestral wealth. And close at hand were set costly goblets and bowls of gold and of silver, and in them a large quantity of water; and beside them were placed tables of citrus wood and of ivory, of great magnificence, and they were laden with meat and bread enough to satisfy the stomachs of the most voracious animals. So as soon as the preparations were completed in all their abundance, the banqueters came on, six males and an equal number of females; the former were clad in masculine garb, the latter in feminine; and they took their places in orderly fashion in pairs, a male and a female. And at a signal they reached forward their trunks modestly, as though they were hands, and ate with great decorum. And not one of them gave the impression of being a glutton nor yet of trying to forestall others or of being inclined to snatch too large a portion, [...] And when they wanted to drink, a bowl was placed by each one, from which they sucked up the water with their trunks and drank it in an orderly manner, and then proceeded to squirt *the attendants* [bottoms] in fun, not by way of insult.

Many similar stories have been recorded showing the astounding ingenuity of these animals. And I myself have seen one actually with its trunk writing Roman letters on a tablet in a straight line without any deviation. The only thing was that the instructor's hand was laid upon it, directing it to the shape of the letters until the animal had finished writing; and it looked intently down. You would have said that the animal's eyes had been taught and knew the letters.

There are numerous descriptions that, like the examples given by Aelian, evoke with precision the tricks performed by elephants in the modern circuses such as acrobatic poses, throwing and catching objects, impersonating dramatic actors, imitating human, and even walking on tight ropes high above the ground. The latter was apparently a common trick since it was mentioned by Pliny the Elder, a navy commander from the earlier decades of the Empire, who had authored a monumental encyclopedia titled *Naturalis Historia* in which a part of the second chapter is devoted to elephants:

> The first harnessed elephants that were seen at Rome, were in the triumph of Pompeius Magnus over Africa, when they drew his chariot; a thing that is said to have been done long before, at the triumph of Father Liber on the conquest of India. Procilius says, that those which were used at the triumph of Pompeius, were unable to go in harness through the gate of the city. In the exhibition of gladiators which was given by Germanicus, the elephants performed a sort of dance with their uncouth and irregular movements. It was a common thing to see them throw arrows with such strength, that the wind was unable to turn them from their course, to imitate among themselves the combats of the gladiators, and to frolic through the steps of the Pyrrhic dance. After this, too, they walked upon the tight-rope, and four of them would carry a litter in which lay a fifth, which represented a woman lying-in. They afterwards took their place; and so nicely did they manage their steps, that they did not so much as touch any of those who were drinking there.

Other historians, chroniclers, and poets such as Seneca, Suetonius, and Dion Cassius have documented the performances of elephants they had witnessed in the amphitheater. The full references to these texts can be found in Bouissac (1958: 24–52). These authors often refer to the trainers as being from India or Ethiopia, countries in which the husbandry and training of elephants harked back centuries if not millennia.

The point to be made through demonstrating the remarkable continuity of the staging of these elephant performances over at least two thousands years is to emphasize that, while cultures evolve over time, not every stream of semiotic systems changes at the same pace. Languages are fast movers although, as Saussure pointed out in his first public lecture at the University of Geneva in 1891, nobody ever noticed that they stopped speaking popular Latin and started using the forms of the old Romanic tongues because the changes were minimal but cumulative. Technological innovations, though, may create precipitous transformations and occasional accelerations in the performance of some vital tasks, such as transportations or communications, but other meaning-making processes remain unchanged or undergo much slower modifications with merely superficial effects. The Roman imperial culture, that itself was a mosaic of chaotic systems and influences, has remained active to the point that modern political rhetoric, public architecture, and references to the significant legacy of the past still invoke the memory of Latin institutions and cultural values. The rise of the European empires and the progress of their colonial conquests were conceptualized on the historical model of the Roman Republic and Empire, and so was the foundation of the United States of America. The traditional circus—starting with its very name—is replete with Roman references. Lions, for instance, are commonly called Cesar, Brutus, or Nero. Trainers are billed as modern gladiators, and Rome has often been the explicit theme of spectacular staging. From the eighteenth century on, with the rise of the British Empire and its global reach, the circus has symbolically merged references to both Rome and India, a discourse in which elephants were the common denominators. Furthermore, in the conflict of symbols, the elephant was chosen as the icon representing the ideology of a political party that often makes explicit references to its Roman legacy. Elephants were such a powerful component of the meaning of the American circus that once they were permanently removed from the show, many proclaimed that this loss signaled the end of the circus. Elephants, in many countries, have now practically disappeared from the circus through prohibition, attrition, or decision of their owners. In spite of some regrets expressed by a few spectators, this change has not caused massive popular protests.

Two questions naturally come to mind: First, why did the training and presentation of performing elephants show such powerful conservation dynamics over millennia to the point that the methods and the tricks themselves did not substantially change? And, secondly, why did this cultural stream come to an end? To answer the first question, we can note that the constant basis of this tradition were the elephants themselves that did not change during such a short window of evolutionary time. The makeup of their physical and behavioral characteristics commanded a stable set of practical knowledge and habitus on the part of the trainers, whose skill was transmitted across generations without notable modifications. To answer the second question, we can adduce the argument sustaining this whole book by invoking the radical cultural shift that is occurring in the current century with respect to the conceptualization and interpretation of the animal world, and the blurring of previous categories through the post-modern discourse that defines the new ethos of the Anthropocene, a vision that rests on the delusion of total control of the environment. We can identify the same evolution with respect to the treatment of predators.

The Antiquity of the Animal Circus: The Predators

For our contemporaries, Tarzan and Mowgli are familiar icons that inspired the outfits and demeanors of circus wild animal trainers. On a different key, these artists also readily borrowed their costumes and styles of action from military uniforms, including those associated with the colonial era. In the Greco-Roman popular culture, more than twenty centuries ago, two heroic figures were playing similar roles: Heracles and Orpheus. Heracles, or Hercules in the Latin version, was, according to the legend, a half-god who had overcome fierce monsters and predators; Orpheus, by contrast, was a sublime poet who had tamed wild animals with his melodious voice and the music of his Lyra. Both were represented in the abundant iconography of the time: Heracles with his club dragging the carcass of a giant lion; Orpheus leading a procession of peaceful tigers, leopard, lions mixed with sheep and doves, and even boulders and stones that could not resist his charm and followed the animals. These narratives and the corresponding imagery provided productive metaphors for the staging of trained predators in the spectacles of the Roman amphitheater.

There is ample textual and iconographic evidence that the people of Rome were given to enjoy violent spectacles of men fighting for their life against other men or predators, and the staging of animals killing each other or being hunted to death within the confines of the arena. It is less known, though, that the Greeks and the Romans had also opportunities to admire trained wild animals that performed in ways very similar to those observed in the later traditional circuses of Europe, thus providing a supplementary proof of the cultural continuity of this trade and art.

The Athenian Isocrates (436–338 BCE), a rhetorician, alluded in one of his pleadings, *Antidosis*, to:

> [T]he shows which are held year after year [showing] lions which are more gentle toward their trainers than some people are toward their benefactors, and bears which dance about and wrestle and imitate our skill.
>
> (Isocrates 1980)

Through his casual allusion to a common experience of everyday life in ancient Greece, Isocrates meant to convince the court that training and education can achieve unexpected results. We find in Greco-Roman art and literature, over the following centuries, countless mentions of such traveling entertainers who exhibited trained animals. The Romans called them *circulatores*, a word derived from *circulus* [small circle], and ultimately from *circus* [circle, ring] (Ernout and Meillet 1967: 122). The *circulatores* were people performing acrobatic tricks and showing their trained animals in the center of a small circular space formed by the spectators who surrounded them like a wheel to watch their shows. From these small street spectacles to the gigantic displays of imperial Rome's Colosseum, the Flavian amphitheater that was completed under Titus in 79 CE, there was merely a difference of scale with respect to the trained animal acts they presented. Indeed, gory fights and staged hunting scenes were not the only items in their daily program of entertainment. For centuries historians, philosophers, and poets have alluded to these true circus performances (Bouissac 1958: 59–86). As we have seen earlier concerning the role of the elephants, predators were trained according to two opposite modes: one emphasizing their wilderness, the other demonstrating their peaceful submissiveness to their master. The latter, expectedly, was not immune to accidents like in the modern history of cage acts. The poet Martial (Marcus Valerius Martialis ca 36 to ca104 CE) wrote a series of brief poems (epigrams) in 80 CE under the general title *De spectaculis* [about spectacles], in which he celebrated in concise form notable events from the amphitheater. Epigram 21 is particularly informative in spite of its brevity as it refers to a trainer impersonating Orpheus who was leading a group of mixed predators and herbivores accompanied by animated boulders and plants in order to re-enact the legend. The show, however, had a tragic ending when a bear attacked the trainer. As was pointed out above, the tradition of wild animal training shows a remarkable continuity over at least two millennia. In the late nineteenth century, French poet Stéphane Mallarmé reports a similar event he witnessed in Paris. During a pantomime that included a trained bear, the animal rushed toward a clown and attacked him. The animal was brought under control by some helpers but the show was interrupted and cancelled. As we pointed out earlier, neither did ursine behavior evolve over the last two millennia, nor did the methods of training bears vary. What has drastically changed during the last century, though, is that there are not many bears left in our environment because they have been eradicated in most European countries.

A Roman amphitheater lion act has been memorialized to these days thanks to several accounts found in the writings of the time. The story is reported in *Attics Nights* by Aulu-Gelle (Aulus-Gellius), a Roman rhetorician of the second century CE, who quoted an earlier Greek author of the first century CE, Apion, who claimed to have personally witnessed the event in Rome. As a part of the amphitheater spectacles, a slave was going to be fed to a lion as a punishment. The animal appeared to be wild and ferocious but as soon as it saw the man, it approached him peacefully and licked his hands. The emperor and the audience were then told that the man was a former slave of a Roman consul in Africa, who had escaped and encountered a lion that was wounded by a large thorn piercing its paw. The man had removed the thorn and the lion had not attacked him. Three years later, both the man and the lion had been separately caught by suppliers to the amphitheater. It just happened that it was precisely this lion that was scheduled to kill the fugitive slave but that it had recognized his savior and spared him in gratitude. The crowd loved the story and the Emperor was moved and pardoned the man who was henceforth reunited with the lion. The man's Latin name was Androclus. The chronicler added that, afterwards, people in Rome could see the man holding the lion on a leash "making the round of the taverns in the city," and, undoubtedly telling the story of this extraordinary friendship in exchange for some coins.

Other authors, such as Aelian in his *On the Nature of Animals*, reported the same story with a few added details such as the fact that after the event that had occurred in the arena, the audience were handed tablets providing the narrative that was also verbally explained by announcers. Rather than a moral example of human compassion and animal gratitude, this arena event that found such an echo in the literature obviously was a well-staged circus trick. This is all the more likely since the tale of Androclus (or Androclès in Greek) and his lion can be traced back to Aesop, a storyteller of the sixth century BCE, whose fables inspired a long tradition of using animals to express moral principles and political philosophy.

Animal acts with predators are frequently presented, or are spontaneously interpreted as re-enactments of mythical heroes of the local cultures, let it be the Orphic procession of mixed species, the biblical evocation of Daniel in the lions' den, or the Armenian saga of the heroic warrior Sasunti Davit (Bouissac 2015: 180–1). Whether the performances are staged with a deliberately violent acting out such as the vintage tiger acts of the French trainer Tarass Bulba (Emilien Beautour) that is available in the website Circopedia.org, or in the opposite, but no less risky style of a trainer claiming to be endowed with the gift of mystical control over deadly predators, the basic assumption is the irreducible ferocity of the predators that legitimizes the exceptional status of the man or woman who displays their power in the confine of the arena.

The Wild Utopia

"All good things are wild and free."
Henry David Thoreau, **Walking**, 1994

An ethnocentric colonial mind persists in the popular worldview of most European countries. Typically, the current British definition of "wild animals" is "any species not 'commonly' domesticated in the United Kingdom." This is an *ad hoc* definition that specifically and discriminately targets circuses. It implies that today's domestic species fall outside the ethical imperative by virtue of belonging to the farming economics or traditions of the nation. These species may be subject to animal welfare requirements and, potentially, be accepted as trained circus animals. Ethical considerations do not apply to them to the same extent as "wild" species even though bovids, equids, and their subspecies have "wild" or "feral" representatives in many parts of the planet earth.

The concept of wilderness deserves further consideration. This term is ambiguous: on the one hand it conveys the negative notions of danger, unruliness, and strangeness that challenge the civil order and security of sedentary cultures; on the other hand, it also means pristine purity and innocence; it embodies the "natural" as opposed to the artificiality and inauthenticity of modern civilizations. This latter value emerged in the West during the eighteenth century, in the context of a cultural revolution that celebrated the fundamental goodness of nature, emancipated from the biblical curse that had persuaded countless generations that they were lost souls which had to be redeemed. A utopian vision of absolute otherness endowed with natural virtue was elaborated through travelers' chronicles and philosophical speculations. Jean-Jacques Rousseau's legacy still pervades our lives when we pay a higher price for "wild mushrooms" than for cultured ones, and choose "natural" produces over processed ones. The "wild" is a modern construct that carries a load of positive emotions in contemporary societies. The ghost of the "noble savage" still haunts western post-modernity. "Wild animals" are worshipped as icons of freedom and purity, and the media usually represent perfect specimens slowly walking or resting in exotic landscapes. When confronted to the visual reality of predators stalking and killing their prey, their admirers dismiss these violent and gory pictures as simply demonstrating the ultimately rightful laws of "mother" nature.

This attitude is relatively recent in western cultures. The harmonious life of humans and animals in the state of nature is a fiction of the modern imagination grounded in edited films, animation movies, children's literature, and all other media from toys to games. Historically, this vision is grounded in the utopian myth of the Garden of Eden and other similar depictions of an original Golden Age. Such narratives obfuscate the permanent battle ground that is life on earth since its inception. As it has been pointed out at the beginning of this movement, the tragic chord keeps resonating in many parts of the world. Predators are still a major threat in countries in which they have not been eradicated. Under the aegis of ecology, conservationists can protect threatened species such as tigers, bears, or wolves only through ruthless coercion that involve political liability. It is not easy to convince farmers in many parts of India, for instance, that predators which routinely kill some of their family members and their cattle should be immune to retribution. If, in the absence of forest wardens, they come across a den with newborn tiger cubs when the mother is away hunting, they destroy them as, undoubtedly, the "animalists" treat rat and mouse pups they discover in their household. Of course, the latter may afford to hire professional "exterminators" and look away while the job is done. No western government has yet prohibited the elimination of live pests. Many insect species are gleefully zapped from existence through industrial means that carry a host of collateral damage to other species, including humans. However, if crops are destroyed by elephants or other wild herbivores, their owners are entitled to financial compensations so that physical retaliation can be avoided.

The fracture zone between two epochs of animal perception still can be vividly sensed in the Indian media. Stories of man-eaters that haunted colonial tales of the nineteenth century are echoed in today's frequent press reports in which the two modes collide. As we have seen earlier in this part of the book, villagers, farmers, and foresters are exposed daily to the danger of falling prey to tigers when they till their fields, gather wood, or keep their cattle.

It is in the context of the colonial discourse that circus exhibitions of wild animals became popular. Showmen foregrounded the ferocity of their lions, tigers, and leopards in the banners and posters advertising their spectacles as well as in the verbal presentations introducing their acts. The staging itself was making sure that there would be no doubt in the mind of their audience that, indeed, these animals were aggressive and blood thirsty. Some lions were selected because they were prone to roar loudly at the slightest provocations. This characteristic is considered in the circus trade as a valuable asset since it also indicates an animal more likely to make noise than cause harm. It is a part of the bluffing behavior of males. Those who are actually prepared to attack in earnest are believed to be less vocal. This does not mean that cage acts did not carry some risks. Occasional accidents, including lethal ones, occurred and were widely publicized. They were rare, though, and trainers of both genders were skilled professionals rather than candidates to martyrdom. Their animals had been born and brought up in the circus, and those who were deemed to be manageable had been patiently trained from a young age. In the course of the cage acts' dramatic unfolding, there often was a rare moment of physical contact with one of the charges, such as kissing an animal or entrusting one's head within its open jaws. This would bring the mastery of the trainers to a superior level with a hint of magical power. Some were credited to possess a "sixth sense" that allowed them to communicate with, and control the wild forces that were embodied in these beasts.

Ethos, Ethics, and the Peterson Effect

The Dr. Jordan Peterson way is a hard way, but it is an idealistic way – and for millions of young men, it turns out to be the perfect antidote to the cocktail of coddling and accusations in which they are raised.

David Brooks @nytdavidbrooks, Twitter,
January 26, 2018

Birmingham, UK. May 20, 2019. I am due to meet Thomas Chipperfield, "Britain's last lion trainer" as he heralds himself with resentful irony. We have become friends on Facebook through the friend of friends algorithm that often expands one's networks in felicitous directions. Ever since, I have been impressed by the texts he posts on his wall. Thomas is articulate, intellectually sophisticate, and self-confident. He submitted firmly argued "written evidence" to the House of Lords when the legislation to prohibit the use of wild animal in circuses was to be examined. On my way to Birmingham, I recall having seen him at the Duffy Circus that was performing in Dublin in July 2008. He was still in his late teens but presented a lion and tiger act. I was moved then by his relative lack of assurance and the way in which his father, the seasoned trainer Tommy Chipperfield, was monitoring his moves while his mother was standing to attention behind the steel arena. At the time, I reflected on how the circus skills were transmitted along the generational lines with obvious rigor and fervor. I am now going to meet Thomas as a grown-up man, close to his quarters where he keeps two lions and a tiger that often appear on his Facebook page.

I present him with one of my books on circus ethnography. His critical feedback would be precious to me. I had inserted my business card showing my academic affiliation and personal email address for further contact. "Ah! University of Toronto! You must know Professor Jordan Peterson! How is he?"

I am taken aback. The controversy about this colleague of mine is raging on the campus and the last thing I was expecting was Thomas's question. "Yes, I know him although I have not seen him in recent years. Long time ago, I wrote a review of his book on meaning." Thomas wants to hear more: "I do not agree with all that he says. He is often on TV here to debate his ideas. But he makes some good points. When you see him, tell him that you met a fan of his who is Britain's last lion trainer."—"I certainly will!"

Thomas has been brought up in the traditional circus ethos, a demanding way of life in close contact with animals of all sorts, more precisely in his case, with predators that you learn early to understand and respect. To control their wild instinct and train them to perform, one has to work out a common code with them, mindful of the risks. To be accused of mistreatment and torture is hurtful to Thomas. He feels victimized by an ideology that is driven to eradicate his honorable trade and the ancestral tradition of which he is proud. As a man of his generation, Thomas relates to the liberal culture of the twenty-first century that collides with the most extreme tenets of Jordan Peterson's manifesto. However, Peterson's culture war finds a responsive echo in the midst of his existential struggle.

Humans, in technologically advanced, urban societies, have mostly lost their instinctual fear of wild animals. They experience their actual presence at a safe distance in zoos or virtually through various media. Wild felines are perceived through the lens of esthetically pleasing images and the rhetoric of conservation. Tigers are indeed threatened by extinction in the Indian subcontinent and have already disappeared from Southern China, Vietnam, and Java. There are still isolated populations in Sumatra and Siberia. African lions are not yet on the critical list but some biologists are sounding the alarm in view of the constant encroachment on their habitat by farming and cattle breeding. Asian lions have survived in northwestern India only through strict conservation laws. In areas where they survive, both tigers and lions still prey on people and their domestic animals but, in developed, industrial Western societies, their cultural status has switched from feared predators to protected species toward which humans have legal and moral duties.

It is in this context that the ethical issue has emerged in the twenty-first century with respect to the presence of wild animals in circuses. In the second part of the previous century, the keeping of these animals and their training for the purpose of entertainment was scrutinized by government experts under the pressure of humanitarian associations that were claiming that these animals were abusively treated by their nomadic keepers. Their confinement in small cages and their constant transportations from cities to cities were deemed to be detrimental to their physical and psychological well-being. In addition, their training was claimed to be based on violence and cruelty, amounting to torture. The human propension to empathy toward species that possess humanlike morphological and behavioral characteristics kept feeding effective campaigns of support for prohibiting circuses from using animals. In response to these accusations, many governments developed legislation aimed at ensuring that some minimal conditions would be met for the keeping of animals in traveling shows. Most circuses quickly adapted to these requirements and commissions of experts repeatedly certified that basic animal welfare was generally respected in circuses like in other institutions legally dealing with animals, and that prohibiting the use of circus animals in these circumstances was a matter of politics and ideology rather than biology and psychology.

However, a new front was open, notably in England for banning wild animals from circuses on ethical rather than welfare grounds, a move that was inconclusively opposed by circus representatives on the basis of technical and philosophical arguments. It is indeed extremely difficult to counter ethical premises through scientific or logical arguments. Ethics is the domain of social norms that are demonstrably conventional and arbitrary. It is the part of any cultural system to which we happen to belong that impacts the most on our lives in the form of constraints imposed on our behavior. Questioning these imperatives amounts indeed to undoing the tacit foundations of the moral and legal apparatus that structures and organizes our daily lives as part of a binding social net. Shifting from an "exclusive ethics" that restricts the application of behavioral norms to a specified domain, to an "inclusive ethics" that applies the same norms indiscriminately to an open-ended variety of domains, is a major existential move that shatters the cultural system we were taking for granted. Ron Beadle, a professor of Organization and Business Ethics at Northumbria University, has clearly articulated the issues raised by the ethical turn as a basis for prohibiting the use of wild animals in circuses (Beadle 2019). The rise of such legislations is a global phenomenon. Let us recall that a recent ruling by the Indian High Court asserted that animals are legal persons: "The entire animal kingdom, including avian and aquatic, are declared legal entities having a distinct persona with corresponding rights, duties, and liabilities of a living person." As it is difficult to figure out what kind of civic duties wild animals are supposed to respect beyond the blind implementation of their biological programs, the legislators classify them as "minors" which humans have the responsibility to protect. Lest we consider this ruling as an oddity arising from the peculiarities of Hinduism or Buddhism, let us recall that Swiss citizens were asked in 2010 to vote in a referendum whether all counties in the country should appoint a special lawyer whose task would be to represent animals in courts of law in order to plead on their behalf in cases of mistreatment or other injuries. The motion lost but the fact that it was supported by a sizeable portion of citizens to the point of being accepted as a legitimate question is significant. In the same vein, *The New York Times* reported on December 2, 2013, that an animal rights group sued to have a chimpanzee recognized as a legal person (Gorman 2013).

It appears that the shift toward endowing animals with full-fledged civil identities rather than treating them as biological entities or mere commodities for food, work, or entertainment, is global and has consequences far beyond the local horizon of the prohibition of wild animals in circuses in various countries of the world. However, we should not zoom in on the tree and ignore the forest. The area of contention in which fans of the traditional circus, that features wild animals, confront the attacks of those who fight with passion for their abolition is part of a more extensive fracture zone in contemporary western cultures. The zone should be considered as a broadly defined whole crisscrossed by the constant ebb and flow of social media.

The advocates of the termination of the circuses that use animals on ethical grounds flood Facebook and Twitter with mostly fabricated visual arguments wrapped in the rhetoric of extermination against those whom they accuse of torturing animals for their own profit. In some countries such as France and Italy, as we pointed out in the first section of this book, the explicit target of their hatred is the traveling Gypsies and other itinerant communities. The exhibition of trained wild animals was one of the traditional trades of these ethnic minorities. The animal circus, though, involved a much wider constituency of producers and artists. It was a major component of popular culture long before it reached a high degree of visibility in the industrial age. The accumulation of legal prohibitions and the spread of public hostility are now bringing about the perception that the traditional circus is coming to an end. This rising trend is compounded by the opportunistic self-censoring of major circus companies that, over the last few decades, have progressively removed wild animal acts from their programs. This is not an accidental phenomenon, a temporary setback for a tradition that has experienced ups and downs over its millenary existence. As we documented, the powerful meaning-making of wild animal acts was grounded in a context, both real and imaginary, in which wild animals were a formidable force to contend with. Those men and women who demonstrated their capacity to control this threat could claim heroic status or the possession of magic power. The prestige and success of this art was sustained by cultural patterns and values that reached far back in time and transcended the vagaries of history. The radical changes we witness in the twenty-first century call for an inquiry into the fundamental cultural evolution that is currently taking place and undermines the meaningfulness of the traditional circus among many other aspects of the forms and values of human existence.

A Self-Defeating Strategy

> *Things that are bitter, feared, and avoided must nonetheless be approached and conquered, or life finds itself increasingly restricted and miserable. [...] It is in the voluntary embodiment of the heroic pattern, therefore, that the most fundamental form of meaning is to be found.*
>
> Jordan Peterson, **The Pragmatics of Meaning,** 1999: 11

The individuals and associations that have set for themselves the mission of eradicating animals from the circus on the ground that their training involve violence amounting to torture and that they are forced to perform demeaning, unnatural behavior, have flooded for decades all social media with videos purporting to prove their point. It has been shown that most of these visual proofs were contrived as it was demonstrated in a staff report of the National Animal Interest Alliance (2000) and other journalistic investigations (e.g., Ohlheiser 2017). However, it kept generating a demand for this kind of video that created an industry of production of such evidence to the point that the Australian Government, for instance, had to outlaw the deliberate abuse of animals in response to the financial incentive offered by the animal rights associations. A media statement issued by the Department of Agriculture on July 26, 2019, reported it was investigating allegations of "payment for animal cruelty footage."

Circus folks have been slow to react and eventually realized that it was not sufficient to protest and simply suggest that people should come and see for themselves how they treat their animals. They also were prompt to mention that their profession was one of the most heavily monitored by inspectors in charge of checking the respect of the many animal welfare laws that have been voted by parliaments in numerous countries throughout the world. During the last decade, some animal trainers have regularly posted in social media samples of their interactions with their tigers, lions, camels, elephants, and horses, for instance, showing that these animals enjoy enough space and voluntarily come to them when they are called, a behavior that could not be expected if they were routinely mistreated. The training process has been thoroughly observed and explained a long time ago by psychologists and zoologists such as Pierre Hachet-Souplet (1895) and Heini Hediger (1961, 1962), who had direct, unimpeded access to the absorbing creation of the wild animal circus acts of their time. The principal target of the animal defenders has always been the felines and the elephants, species that enjoy a special symbolic status among the population at large, an attitude that is greatly influenced by the popularity of their iconic representations in the form of plush toys and characters in animation movie. Circus trainers know too well that the management and training of these animals in the circus context demand controlling skills commensurate with the strength and instinctual reflexes of these wild species that are intrinsically dangerous at close range. Even if the training methods are humane in the sense that they do not rely on excessive, unnecessary violence, animals must learn to respect consistently their trainers lest encounters turn chaotic and unmanageable in the ring or backstage. In the traditional circus, the presentation of lions and tigers usually endeavored to achieve a balance between the demonstration of two kinds of control: force through mock-fighting episodes—that, incidentally, turned out to be lethal at times—and close, friendly contacts with at least one of their animals. The last tiger act presented by Firmin Bouglione is a striking example of this performance pattern as seven of the tigers were driven though their pace with lots of whip cracking and roaring while a few episodes involved a young tigress that repeatedly would jumps through the hoop without any hint of resistance and that the trainer would occasionally pet.

In the contemporary version of the traditional circus, the ratio between force and charm is usually reversed: most tricks are performed in the soft mode and one or two tricks involve mock fighting as a sort of (nostalgic?) quotation from the past and a reminder that these animals are not subdued pets. Some acts even totally eschew any sign of violent confrontation with the predators, thus ushering in the utopian vision of interspecific reconciliation.

This trend has inspired two young Frenchmen, not born to circus families, who are anachronistically fascinated by wild animal training to the point of having seriously considered a career in this specialty, to make a contribution to the defense of the profession by creating a Face Book page they call "Animal Complicity." They post a stream of photos of men and women trainers in very close contact with one of their animals, usually in the portrait format with the two faces side by side, or with the human hugging the lion or tiger. This is on their part a genuine attempt to counter the negative publicity of the anti-circus propaganda. However, it is likely to turn out to be in the long term a self-defeating strategy as it undermines the very meaning of wild animal training in a world in which controlling predators is irrelevant, at least in modern urban cultures.

All circus animals belong to social species. As soon as their young can move around, they are instinctively driven to play in the form of mock-chasing, catching, and wrestling with each other and with things they come across. They test each other's strength and learn their rank in the group. They also constantly engage their mother and other adults, and take cues from them. They are also prone to play with the young of other species and often form lifelong bonds with them when they are brought up together. This happens even across the divide that separates predator and prey. For tiger and lion cubs, until they reach sexual maturity—and sometimes beyond—humans are just members of another playful species and it can be fun to live with them. At the same time, they take behavioral cues from their reactions which they observe with the same intense attention shown to their own mother in the wild. They thus become socially integrated in a cross-species social group that develops a mutually understood repertory of gestures, sounds, and routine interactions, and is ruled by a hierarchy that is constantly in need of being tested and negotiated. Wild animal trainers are fully engaged in this dynamic which is based on the convergence of shared lives, emotions, and memories. However, they must remain mindful that things can get out of hand on the spur of the moment. Firmin Bouglione used to say: "Never play with young tigers or lions because they will quickly learn that they are stronger than you!"

The relationship between humans and animals is based on a mutual capacity to establish social partnership (Hediger 1964) but is also rife with mutual misunderstanding and anthropomorphic delusions. Seasoned trainers know that the kind of honeymoon they enjoy with young and sub-adult animals cannot last beyond the coming of age of the lions and tigers, principally the males once they reach full sexual maturity. Of course, there are variations among animals regarding their genetic makeup and level of claim to dominance as well as individual character. The idea of "complicity" may be a good public relations slogan but this concept presupposes a reciprocity of intention that cannot exist between people and predators. Even when there is a modicum of mutual trust, the trainers that make selfies with their tame lions or tigers are not alone in open space. There are within the confines of a high-fenced enclosure, assisted by a helper who does not appear in the photos, and, more than likely, they keep a stick in their spare hand or within easy reach should it be necessary to reassert their control. By spreading in the social media well-staged posts illustrating examples of assumed complicity between humans and their animals in close contact, these circus fans feed the same illusions that are conveyed by animation movies and plush toys.

But there is more, if the power of these images generalizes in the public the vision of wild animals as inoffensive and "complicit" actors, then the very basis of the relevance of the circus wild animal acts collapses as it blurs by implication a fundamental distinction that organizes the Western perception of the environment as it emerged in modern times. The semantic opposition between the notions of tame, domestic, and indigenous on one side and the notions of wild, savage, and exotic on the other, determined a whole range of specific values that commanded not only the cognitive mappings of reality but also the feelings and emotions that were correlated with these categories. The particular forms that this overarching structure has taken in modern times largely derived from the exploring and colonizing that expanded the reach of Europeans from the sixteenth century on, and generated a flood of textual and visual discourses illustrating the challenges of conquering exotic wilderness and savagery. The circus offered a ritual staging of this process through representing actions that matched the rhetoric associated with the ideology of Western superiority (Carmeli 2003; Tait 2012, 2016). The trainers that confronted "jungle-born" lions and tigers fitted well into the same conceptual frame that produced performances re-enacting scenes from colonial and American history. The conquest of the West with its iconic cowboy outfits and the vintage garments of the explorers of African wilderness still inspire the style of some circus costumes. One of the most successful circuses in France rose to prominence in early twentieth century by exploiting both the iconic Buffalo Bill legend while featuring at the same time their skills as wild animal trainers foregrounding the ferocity of the predators and the heroism of the presenter.

It should be clear that, in spite of their intrinsic dramatic, esthetic, and symbolic qualities, wild animal, as well as American Western-themed acts are not any longer sustained by the cultural background that inspired them in the first place. Wherever they live, humans are immersed in a system of values and cognitive structures that enable them to make sense of the daily experience of the world they inhabit. While the constitutive oppositions that characterize these semiotic systems are not as consistent in today's multicultural societies as structuralist anthropologists used to claim in the previous century, children nevertheless acquire as they grow up sets of cognitive constraints through which they perceive their environment and interpret the events of their lives in the social context in which they were born. In a relatively stable state of their world, the semiotic landscape provides the resources needed to make sense of things and events. Minor variations may occur as new information enters the cultural horizon but the conjoined cognitive strategies of adaptation and accommodation secure the stability of the semiotic system that defines a particular cultural area over a number of generations. As Jordan Peterson remarked, two decades ago: "The world is too complex to manage without radical functional simplification. Meaning appears to exist as the basis for such simplifications" (Peterson 1999: 1).

However, any living system is prone to undergo variations and social structures are not immune to slow and cumulative changes. In addition, technological innovations and contacts with alien cultures may bring drastic upsets to semiotic systems by offering divergent values and shattering accepted cognitive categories. The contemporary global culture that is defined by emerging values and expanding cognition is at odds with the popular culture within which the traditional circus flourished, only rarely questioned, until the late twentieth century, although strains were perceptible from the mid-century on in the West. Animals, predators in particular, progressively changed from being feared as perpetrators of wrongs to being considered victims of abuse either in the general context of the destruction of their natural environment or as unjustly exploited for work, food, and entertainment (Bouissac 2013). Cultural evolution does not proceed, of course, as a sudden monolithic revolution. New and previous systems overlap and create tensions in the social fabric of a particular cultural area. Current cosmological interpretations concerning, for instance, the geometrical form of the earth or the meaning of diseases and earthquakes bear witness to the heterogeneity of the mental universe of coexisting segments of a population. Some members in our social environment exclusively rely on scientific knowledge while others unconditionally trust their religious faith. No society is perfectly homogenous as all cultures comprise both elite and marginal members, central and peripheral constituencies. Each holds a variety of beliefs even if they are all under the umbrella of an official doctrine or religion. Moreover, in modern complex societies, this diversity is compounded by multiethnic and multicultural components that contribute to introducing variations in the semiotic landscape. Forces of both dissipation and integration are relentlessly at work.

In the mid twentieth century, a French circus featured Martha la Corse, a female trainer who "controlled her man-eating tigers by the sole power of her gaze." The act, indeed, consisted of a woman who was driving a group of six tigers without holding a stick or a whip, using only words and hand gestures. The audience was thrilled by the performance but not everybody shared the same interpretation: those who believed in the supernatural gift of the psychic Gypsies they would occasionally consult over their love or business affairs had little problem trusting the claim made by the circus. On the other end of the sociocultural spectrum, those who were versed in Pavlovian psychology had a different interpretation of what they were seeing without being less impressed by the skill of the trainer. They noticed, for instance, that sticks and whips were discretely placed on a pedestal on the side of the cage within easy reach of the trainer, and that helpers holding fire extinguishers were unobtrusively standing behind the bars ready to intervene should anything go wrong. Both kinds of spectators, though, shared the same notion of "the wild" as a negative value to be controlled and neutralized. Around the same time, another trainer, the Indian Damoo Dhotre, presented his panthers and tigers dressed as a Hindu prince or a fakir, in congruence with the exotic imagery produced by the colonial era. He was credited in the circus promotional material as endowed with all the mystical power that could be expected from his magical country of origin. The meaning produced by this celebrated act derived from both the mutually exclusive categories of "domestic" versus "exotic", and "tame" versus "wild." Of course, not all trainers costumed as Tarzan or Fakir were from Asia or Africa but they were efficiently playing on the same semiotic register.

Progressively, through the popularization of scientific evidence concerning the social life of exotic species and their capacity to experience a range of emotions similar to ours, the hitherto unquestioned opposition between people and other mammals has eroded. Those that were predators in distant times have lost their negative value for modern urban dwellers. The commonality of human defining features such as identity, feelings, and civil rights have become generalized to a select group of species in the public discourse of the media. Powerful propaganda in the service of various causes has amplified this cultural shifting of attitude. As a result, the heroic triumph over "the wild," principally the deadly predators, has lost its cultural relevance. Some trainers have drastically changed their tack and, like the Byelorussian Sergei Nestorov who presented his five white tigers at the 44th International Circus Festival of Monte Carlo, perform with these predators as if they were large but mostly inoffensive animals. They stage acts that convey the impression that their charges are complicit and engage in playful interactions, roaring from time to time in order to perform their role to "represent" the former, now obsolete "wild." Then, one may wonder, why the wire net arena? Why the obvious precautions taken by the trainer who never discards his stick? Why are these animals kept in strong cages and deprived of their "civil" liberties? The ground upon which circus acts with predators rested and illustrated a glorious past has collapsed in the mind of the population at large, and efforts to "reform" the genre by denying the radical, lethal antagonism between ancestral predators and their prey are bound to falter in a self-defeating spiral.

Naturally, this evolution occurs merely on the imaginary level in the realm of the semiotic constructs that orient and govern our capacity to make sense of our experience of our physical and social environment. Humans have now appointed themselves keepers and guardians of "the wild" that for many of us must be saved at any cost. In the previous two centuries the press was carrying a flow of news about treacherous attacks by tigers in India and elsewhere, and horror stories of lions preying on pastoralists and construction workers in Africa. The notorious man-eaters of Tsavo in Kenya, for instance, were making the headlines of news from Africa in 1898 and left a legacy of deadly encounters' narratives both in the press and in fiction. Now, as we advance in the twenty-first century, the media reports data indicating that tiger and lion populations are declining to the point that these species might soon go extinct in their respective geographic areas. As we repeatedly pointed out earlier, this anxiety does not reflect the point of view of the local people who still have to cope on a daily basis with these redoubtable predators. European audiences, though, dismiss these considerations as the necessary price to pay for saving the species. They blame the humans who encroach on the animals' territories. Their experience of the wild comes from utopian zoological displays and occasional safaris during which lion prides are admired from the safety of tourist buses. Facebook and other social media constantly feed the illusion of the beautiful, and even cute, "good predator" echoing the eighteenth-century doctrine of the inherent goodness of nature as opposed to the perversion brought about by modern civilization. This approach stigmatizes the traditional wild animal acts of the circus as inhuman and barbaric, if not simply criminal. The broader framework of twenty-first-century global culture undermines and destabilizes the predictable meaning-making narratives that have been for millennia the backbone of ritualized confrontations with predators. We must keep in mind that for eons, hominins then humans have lived in fear of being eaten by ever-hungry felines, ursids, and canids that were stronger and often smarter than themselves. Civilizations could not emerge unless these permanent threats were brought under control by matching force and cunning. Stone weaponry and fire were instrumental but would have not sufficed without daring individuals violently confronting predators. The traditional cage act symbolically re-enacted the foundational triumph over fear of the civilizing hero.

Cultural Entropy and Semiotic Panic

"Adaptive agents must occupy a limited repertoire of states and therefore minimize the long-term average of surprise associated with sensory exchanges with the world. Minimizing surprise enables them to resist a natural tendency to disorder."
Karl Friston, The free-energy principle: a unified brain theory?
Nature Reviews Neuroscience 11: Key Points, 2010

As we noted in the previous sections, the notion of cultures as coherent wholes both cognitively and ethically is a structuralist delusion. Cultural areas that can be broadly identified on the basis of a shared language, history, and mode of life are in fact patchworks of different sets of beliefs, values, and symbols brought together by the hazards of history and bound within political entities and languages that strive to reduce diversity through the imposition of a single ideology and legal system. However, all the local meaning-making traditions keep changing at various paces as does the overall unifying legal and moral apparatus in which they are embedded. The flow of cultural evolution is a relentless process during which minimal variations constantly occur at many levels without, generally, the full awareness of the individuals that form a population or a sub-group. Some salient changes may, at times, be met with resistance on the part of the more conservative members of the mainstream social constituency, but progressive assimilation eventually defines new cultural norms. Meanwhile, some elements such as toponyms and archaisms survive from long-past cultural contexts. This phenomenon can be readily observed with respect to language changes bearing on the accentuation, lexicon, and even syntax, or concerning other semiotic domains such as clothing, hairstyle, and music. Those are changes, though, that happen on a continuum and do not question the fundamental infrastructure of a culture.

However, some changes are more consequential than others. Cultures are grounded in deep systems of tacit oppositions that account for, and legitimize the legal and moral norms embodied in institutions, customs, and discourse.

The fluid heterogeneity suggested by the patchwork metaphor is kept under control, albeit in a constant state of tension. The wholeness of a culture needs indeed to be sustained through persistent sanctions of deviances lest it dissolve into anomie and anarchy as a prelude to the emergence of an entirely different culture. A degree of variations and inconsistencies is manageable but only in as much as it does not threaten the tacit foundations. For instance, the loose set of what is commonly referred to as western cultures has rested for long on strong oppositions between, males and females, individuals and society, and humans and animals, to name only the most relevant to the issues addressed in this chapter. These mutually exclusive categories are redundantly asserted not only in the foundational Biblical myths but also in cumulative cultural productions irrespective of their language and local traditions. The process of homeostasis has ensured relative cultural stability over a very long period of time, at least with respect to the human scale. Evolution, though, whether biological or cultural, never stops. Inclusive fitness rules the emergence of new phenotypes and social imitation fuels novel cultural norms. These two dynamics operate on different timescales at various speeds but are bound to interact as they are necessarily entangled.

Like all dynamic systems, cultures are subject to entropy, the ineluctable increase of disorder. The polarities that define a particular cultural order are cognitive artefacts extracted from a continuum. For example, the topological oppositions between center and periphery, sacred and profane places, or home and foreign territories are superimposed on spatial continuity and relevant only to the members of the cultures that foster them. They are ignored by other organisms that freely exploit the spatial affordances of their environment or structure it differently. Among humans, nomadic cultures deny the validity of these oppositions in the confrontational or deceptive modes. Gender is another case in point. The natural variety of sexual morphologies and orientations forms a biological continuum that is overridden by the mutually exclusive categories of "male" versus "female," with differences regarding which pole is marked to define patriarchal and matriarchal cultures. Similar patterns apply to the categories of mind and body, or the unbridgeable ontological divide between humans and animals. On the epistemic level, the classical distinction between *doxa* [common sense opinion] and *dogma* [normative doctrine] is illustrative of two conceptions of knowledge on the scale going from heuristic ignorance to absolute certainty. Modernity, and, more specifically, post-modernity can be experienced as an entropic process that dissolves these cultural polarities for the sake of restoring a fair distribution of legitimacy in the name of political correctness. *Dogma* tends to be recast as mere *doxa* supported by the power of temporarily dominating paradigms (Bourdieu 1977). The binary conception of sexual roles is displaced by a rainbow of possibilities equally acceptable and conforms to the natural diversity of the human sexual anatomy and gender fluidity. The "monstrous" status of hermaphroditism disappears as polysexuality and transsexuality tend to erase the duality that was inscribed in the institutions and material cultures of the recent past. Language follows suit and the gender distinctions conveyed by the pronouns in English and other idioms are eradicated through new conventions and neologisms.

Inclusiveness becomes the new norm. Animals cease to be defined as lacking human attributes. *Homo sapiens* is construed by evolutionary psychology primarily as a social mammal whose behavior can be best understood through comparisons with other social species of the same family. Conversely, animals are recognized as persons endowed with rights and civil status that command respect and entail duties. The Cartesian dualism that contended that they were mere machines is replaced by a legal and ethical continuum. The result is a flattened landscape of previously sharp distinctions.

It is easy to understand that cultural entropy creates a semiotic panic among those whose identities are anchored in the status quo. As the twenty-first century unfolds, middle-aged white males launch calls to arms as they perceive themselves as the main victims of this cultural revolution they construe as a systemic attack on their dominating position. Karl Friston's theory interestingly grasps this process in formal terms, using Bayesian statistics and the algorithms of the Markovian chain to describe the stability and relative predictability of dynamic cultural systems. However, drastic and catastrophic changes happen to occur that modify the local and global balance, neutralizing some fundamental oppositions and raising new ones, wreaking havoc in the semiotic landscape and triggering a frantic search for restored or novel stability. Friston called such emerging, unpredictable disturbances "free energy."

Provocative resistance is spearheaded by savvy media gurus who denounce the dictatorship of political correctness in life, online, and in books. They invoke freedom of speech as a right that should transcend any form of censorship. As we indicated above, the best known is probably Canadian psychologist Jordan Peterson who gained visibility and international attention when he uncompromisingly refused to comply with the new inclusive norms for the use of personal pronouns in dealing with his students that was prescribed by his university. Pronominal systems form indeed a very sensitive interface between language and society as they indicate as well as regulate the dynamics of social interactions (Bouissac 2019). However, the de-gendering of address and anaphoric pronouns in English is only the tip of the iceberg that signals deeper transformations involving sexism, machoism, and other forms of exclusion and oppression. Peterson also forcefully attacked the Canadian legislative context that was meant to support the enforcement of the new norms in society promoting equality and inclusiveness. His pervasive presence on mainstream and social media exposed his ideas beyond the academic sphere. Some animal trainers have become sensitive, albeit with some reservations, to his attack against political correctness in as much as they identify the animalists with this global cultural evolution. I have dubbed this circumstantial leaning among circus folks toward conservative ideologies: "the Peterson effect." We will return to this phenomenon when we discuss the plight of clowns in the next part of this book.

Animalism, as an ideology that denies the cultural and ontological divide between humans and animals, and consequently deactivates the opposition between prey and predators, is a constitutive part of this movement. In August 2020, activists were petitioning the French government for the organization of a popular initiative referendum on animal rights that included the prohibition of animals in circuses in addition to other measures aimed at promoting the wellbeing of animals such as the discontinuation of industrial breeding, factory farming, hunting, and ultimately any aspect of the exploitation of other species by humans. The anti-speciesism movement advocates the reintroduction in the environment of predators that have been eradicated in recent centuries. The animalist ideology is comforted through its interface with various ecological parties to the point of becoming a decisive political force.

The traditional circus is a collateral victim of this cultural revolution because it is an easier target than the food industry or hunters' associations for being used as a scapegoat. Preventing circuses with animals from performing allows the animalists to score victories that gratify their financial supporters. Since the traditional circus is squarely embedded in a patriarchal culture, it is also vulnerable to the accusation of sexism and child exploitation. Naturally, it does not escape circus folks' attention that countries run by authoritarian, nationalist regimes are more friendly to their traditional artistic trade than democracies in which the conjunction of animalist and environmentalist forces may carry a critical electoral weight. It is, though, a double-edged bliss because these ultra-conservative powers are prone to restrict transnational freedom of movement and, at times, to repress ethnic diversity that may lead to systemic or selective persecution of the circus culture.

It is difficult to anticipate the unimpeded continuation of the traditional circus with animals in the countries in which it still prospers under strict regulations. It has already disappeared from the cultural landscape in vast areas of Europe and the Americas. The efforts made by individuals and associations to counter the aggressive propaganda of the animalists through posting videos showing men and women, and even children engaged in playful interaction with wild animals including predators cannot sway the tide because they are confronted with an ideology rather than a rational or scientific position. Experts have certified again and again that animals kept in circuses are healthier than in nature, usually well taken care of, and enjoy some modicum of positive adaptation to the mixed human–animal culture of the circus. However, facts are irrelevant when dealing with ideological dogmas. Only major upsetting such as environmental cataclysms, political revolutions, or civilization collapse, and the subsequent return of the wild with a vengeance, could bring about the conditions necessary for the renaissance of rituals of the traditional circus under any other name. This would be, of course, a hefty price to pay but this is the way the world goes as people keep screaming on the fast rollercoaster of cultural evolution on which they have hardly any control.

In the fog of cultural wars it is difficult to identify determining causes among the multiple factors of change that are at play, and to anticipate forthcoming stages in the interrelated evolving strands of semiotic systems and their meaning-making affordances. It is always possible to outline a virtual roadmap with diverging exit roads. It all depends, though, on the cosmic environment within which this evolutionary saga is embedded. Will the subset of life forms that humans call "animals" vanish as a casualty of the Anthropocene age? Or will they reclaim the space and resources that humans appropriated and transformed to suit their needs and fantasies. Free animal energy is always lurking in the margins, ready to seize any opportunity that an unexpected turn of events may offer and to stake out new hunting and grazing grounds. During the 2020 pandemic, as the lockdown was enforced in many cities, wildlife soon reappeared within the confines of mostly empty and silent cities, slowly creeping in to expand their niches. Was this an adumbration of things to come? Will humans, once again, fiercely compete with other predators for their dear life and scarce resources in a world they will have mindlessly altered?

4

Third Movement

Adagio Lamentendo

Clowns

Wikipedia: *"Clowns is a 2014 American horror movie by John Watts."*

The fall of an icon

As the cover of this book suggests, something is amiss in the kingdom of the circus, and this crisis is symbolized, as a dramatic symptom, by this frightful congregation of clowns ganging up on a circus dog. Do they intend to commit a murder or have they come together for a wake? Or, are they simply perplexed by the ways the world changes and pulls them on the side of the road. Indeed, circus clowns increasingly voice their anguish as they are confronted not only with a marked decline in their popularity but also with various forms of sheer hostility. This general despondency negatively impacts their creativity and, in spite of some exceptions due to individual charisma, the genre seems to irrevocably become culturally irrelevant. This part of the book will address the issues raised by this semiotic undoing in which the external signs of the trade such as stereotypical makeup, slapstick, gags, and narratives persist through the force of inertia but keep losing their capacity to produce meaning (or meaningful nonsense) that can engage people and make them laugh. The clown community is experiencing exacting soul searching, a moment that is symptomatic of the current predicaments of the traditional circus.

Clowns can be considered from two main points of view: first, in the narrow context that makes it possible to retrace their modern emergence in the circus from the late eighteenth century to their heyday in the twentieth century. Their history has been as thoroughly documented as possible from Joseph Grimaldi to Charlie Cairoli, for instance, through the compiling of sporadic biographical information and anecdotes (e.g., Disher 1925; Rémy 1945; Towsen 1976).

Secondly, clowns can be understood in the much wider framework of the transgressive rituals that have been described and discussed across many diverse cultures in which, under any other name, they seem to perform similar functions. They are universally characterized by their manipulation of the rules that defined local norms and by their affinity with the primordial chaos that is assumed to have preceded the foundation of the legal and moral standards that regulate social life. In all the cultures in which they have been observed, they hide or transform their face to protect their identity in more or less conventional manners, ranging from masks to makeup.

Masks

"The horrible, ugly face of the archaic masks found at the sanctuary of Arthemis Orthia at Sparta and at Tiryns of Argolid suggests that these rituals masks (prosopeia) were to create to the spectator a violent surprise which immediately yielded to real fear."

Ioannis Loucas, "Ritual, Surprise, and Terror in Ancient Greek Possession-*dromena*," **Kernos**, 2 (1989), 97–104

Masks have been ubiquitous, or at least widespread across the cultures of the world for as long as the archaeological record allows us to peer into the past. These artifacts are always altered versions of human or animal faces. They are produced by a range of techniques: some are heavy wooden or other material constructions that are fixed to the head of people (Lévi-Strauss 1988); at the other end of the spectrum, simple modifications of the natural face are achieved through the application of colors directly upon the skin, thus creating a variety of designs along the distinct facial lines and natural protuberances (Bouissac 2015: 19–48). The addition of a simple spherical red nose can be considered to be a minimal mask as it actually reconfigures the whole facial pattern around that focal point.

The face of animals, including humans, is a kind of social signature indicating individuality and current mood and attitude. This domain of visual communication has been extensively studied by psychologists and neuroscientists. The neuromuscular versatility of the primate face is a crucial interactive resource that signals affects and intentions through various configurations. Research by Paul Ekman (e.g., 1979) and Alan Fridlund (e.g., 1994) for instance has provided detailed correlates between facial expressions and emotions or intentions. Systematic studies of non-human primates have yielded similar results (e.g., Zeller 1981). Quite recently, an investigation of the neuromuscular facial substrate in rodents has shown that mice themselves have a range of distinct facial signaling resources to manage their social life (Dolensek et al. 2020).

Tampering with this biological and behavioral information—and the conventional grooming that characterizes various cultures—is a serious interference with the social process that requires continuous mutual visual control with definite values and functions that are conveyed in humans. On the one hand, there are distinct semantics of the gaze, the glance, and the stare, and, on the other hand, patterns formed by the range of opening and retracting of the eyes and lips, and the ensuing uncovering of the sclera and teeth.

In response to the more or less insisting visual intrusions into someone's sense of privacy during social interactions, several strategies can be observed among individuals such as eye contact avoidance, protective hand gestures, or challenging stares. Similarly, the neuromuscular variations of the mouth and lips produce important signals that trigger adaptive responses to the affiliative or aggressive intentions that are thus indicated either deliberately or spontaneously.

The complex neuromuscular system of the human face that is, at least in part, under voluntary control makes it possible to purposefully transform one's facial configuration by "making faces." For instance, a range of grimacing can emphatically play out submissiveness, displeasure, arrogance, mockery, sarcasm, disgust, or insult. It can also produce a frightful configuration by creating an animal-like impression through retracting the lips to show the teeth and protruding the eyes as much as possible. Some individuals have the capability of extending their eyeballs from their sockets to the point of appearing unhuman. In Greek mythology, the monster Gorgon or Medusa is a prototype of this facial pattern (e.g., Loucas 1989: 99). In Northern England there is a long tradition of this grotesque face called "gurning." Many other cultures have their own frightening facial icons that are displayed in graphic forms or described in their folk narratives.

Modifying one's natural face by physical substitution or permanent transformation entails an altered identity in as much as it determines a markedly different attitude from others. Our personalities are indeed largely influenced by the ways our fellow humans treat us. Identities are mutually constructed during lifelong social processes. Thus, to a lesser or greater extent, masks can create altered states of consciousness in as much as the bearer of a mask escapes the most basic social constraints. Masks, indeed, hide both identities and intentions, and freeze expressive patterns that do not respond to feedback. By stepping outside the expected mutual harmony generated by the gaze and the register of its interactional modulations, the bearers of a mask or a distorting makeup literally tear up the visual ground of the social fabric and join the realm of the wild and its transcendent forces that humans fear because they are unpredictable and entail unbearable uncertainty. By the same token, masked individuals, for instance shamans, are credited with some measure of access to, and control of unknown agencies. Masks may embody or empower invisible monsters or hostile divinities. Those who craft and wear them are bent on exploiting more or less temporarily the immunity they confer to them in order to exploit others through stealing, destroying, or raping. Sexual license is indeed associated with masks even in sophisticated cultures in which deviance is codified. In conclusion, masks are intrinsically terrifying through both their appearance and the disorderly actions they make possible by hiding the identity of the perpetrators and invoking evil, uncontrollable agencies.

During the last two centuries, ethnographers have documented a separate class of individuals they have observed in many different traditional cultures. They have referred to these men and women by generalizing the names they are given locally, such as "shaman" in Siberia (e.g., Beffa and Even 1995; Singh 2018; Toffin 2018). In the Americas, cultural anthropologists have usually used the term "tricksters" and some have proposed to name them "sacred clowns," the circus metaphor being modified by a ritualistic qualification. The ethnocentrism of this categorization is obvious: the observers could not fail to notice that there are similarities between what characterizes these individuals and the clowns with which they were familiar in the circus but since they considered the latter trivial and purely secular, the mask-bearers of the Pueblo Indians, for instance, had to be made distinct by the word "sacred." This is a clear case of cultural bias or even cultural blindness. In this part of the book, we will explore the idea that "shaman," "sacred clowns," and "clowns," as well as other denominations referring to similar classes of individuals, embody a transcultural function whose differences are relatively superficial (Kirby 1974).

Even those who transform themselves temporarily through masks and disguises at the time of the solstices or other ritualistic events participate in this self-alienating and liberating process that causes fear and awe in the rest of the population. In many parts of rural Europe, as well as in other parts of the world, ancient celebrations are still periodically revived probably because they never were totally discontinued in spite of the opposition of Christian or other official religious authorities which have tried to substitute their own celebrations to these ancient rituals. The latter, nevertheless, persisted in the supposedly devalued form of folkloric festivals. These resilient rituals hark back indeed to the immemorial past of hunter-gatherer and early agricultural cultures.

We can assume that there is only a difference of degree between the various kinds of masks and makeup that are documented in the archaeological record of past cultures and those that are observed in a range of contemporary societies. The basic functions of the masks remain constant along a scale going, on the one hand, from the ritualistic celebrations of the solstices and other cyclical occasions to, on the other hand, the conventional makeup of circus clowns. The key function is to provide norm transgressors with some form of social immunity and, at the same time, to discourage their unmasking either through causing awe and fear, or establishing a separate performing, off-limit identity as is the case for circus clowns. Both are ways to embody a transcending power.

In today's Germanic countryside, pre-Christmas festivities perpetuate ancient traditions in which gangs of young men—sometimes called the Krampus or Anif Krampus demons—don frightful goat-horned masks and scraggy coats of fur and rampage through villages and towns often drunken; they are driven to scare and hit people with branches, and to commit other licentious abuses. As one of them declared to journalist Philip Oltermann (2019): "In an anonymous collective, we are always more likely to overstep our boundaries." This practice shows remarkable continuity and resilience (e.g., Christinger and Borgeaud 1963).

Figure 27 Krampus mask celebrating the winter solstice, also known as "devils of Christmas." Photo credit: Nicola Simeoni/Alamy Stock Photo.

What Is a Clown?

Clowns aren't masked figures, but their painted faces come close. With face and neck covered in white or pink or tan makeup, and exaggerated features drawn in red and black, these characters are instantly recognizable as troublesome. The fluidity of their dress may actually contribute to why they make so many people uneasy.

Krystal D'Costa. Why Are We Afraid of Clowns?
Scientific American, October 31, 2011.
https://blogs.scientificamerican.com/anthropology-in-practice/cant-sleepclown-will-eat-me-why-are-we-afraid-of-clowns/

"Clown" is a term that has come to exclusively designate a comic performing role on the stage and in the circus in eighteenth-century England. Like the standard characters of the Commedia dell'arte that can be played by different actors, "Clown" refers to a man of "coarse nature and manners" who behaves in an awkward way at odds with the norms of urban, civilized people. It was, before becoming semantically specialized in the nomenclature of popular entertainment, a word denoting a peasant with the derogatory connotations that can be expected from city dwellers. Joseph Grimaldi (1778–1837), who was heir to a family of traveling mountebanks, is credited for having given prominence to the term, and the corresponding character, through his brilliant interpretations of this role in various pantomimes. Naturally, comic performers have always been a part of public celebrations and the fact that "clown" reached a kind of universal socio-semantic value beyond the realm of the English language is purely circumstantial. In fact, it competed for a while with the term "Joe" (that is, Joseph as a reference to Grimaldi). In North America, a "joe" still means a clown in the slang of the circus.

"Clown" appears to have ridden the wave of Anglomania in Europe where some performers from England set the standards of circus comedy in the nineteenth century. In some other countries such as India, "joker" is the common word for the same role in modern circus spectacles. In Southern Europe, the Italian *pagliaccio* generated various versions such as the Spanish *payaso* and the French *paillasse*. The origin of this term in Italian is the word *paglia* [straw] and refers to the traditional costume of the comic character that was made of the same fabric as the one used for straw mattresses, a marked breaking with clothing norms.

We can note that the "clowns" under any other name are designated indirectly through a range of metaphors and metonymies as if their hidden identities, well protected by the masks of their painted makeup, were not to be uttered. Similarly, in societies that live in close proximity with dangerous predators, it is taboo to refer explicitly to their actual names and mention them only indirectly. This is well attested in Africa with respect to the lions and in Asia concerning the tigers. In Europe, mentioning the wolf was equally avoided. A French saying claims that: "*Quand on parle du loup, on en voit la queue*" [as soon as you mention the wolf, you see its tail]. Uttering the word was believed to provoke the animal's threatening presence and, therefore, was better avoided.

All the avatars of this type of norm-breaking character that is found in many countries and cultures as far in the past as the archaeological and historical record goes have in common that their natural face is drastically modified either by masks or heavy makeup with the result that their native social identity is replaced by a distorted pattern. The masks in general follow the contours of the human face, unless they are representing animals, and conserve, even in this latter case, the mammalian organs of ingestion and communication: the mouth, the nose, the eyes, and the ears. There is, however, systematic modifications of the appearance of these facial elements. Masks are profoundly unsettling because they disrupt the constant reading of emotions and intentions that regulated social interactions. They are primarily designed to frighten rather than entertain and ultimately to protect those who wear them from retribution for their unruly behavior. They also liberate those who wear them from the shame that their actions should cause as this prevents them from "losing face." An application of this principle is found in the traditional apparatus devised by the Catholic Church for the confession of one's sins to a priest. This piece of furniture provides a hiding screen between the faithful and the confessor. On the one hand, the priest is invisible as if he were masked, and, on the other hand, the penitent is equally "masked" since only a few holes in the partition allow verbal communication.

Obviously, circus clowns belong to a vast paradigm generated by the powerful technology of the mask as a tool of social distancing and ontological separation that affords both means of oppression and shields of protection. It is important to note that, in the case of circus clowns, it is not the mask or the makeup *per se* that causes laughter but the actions they perform in the ring or on the stage. A look at the prototypical makeup of Joseph Grimaldi compared to his natural face shows how drastically the latter is transformed by the former (McConnell Stott 2009: 116). This key to switching identities from a reassuring human presence to disfiguring unnatural geometric patterns explains the ambiguity inherent in a clown's persona.

However, not all clown makeup is alike in spite of fundamentally fulfilling the same functions. At one extreme of the scale, the basic features of the human face are radically transformed by adding black and crude color patterns that override the subtle effects of the muscular contractions that convey feedback in face-to-face interactions, or by a totally unnatural whitening that produces the same effect, thus achieving results close to a solid mask; at the opposite extreme, only some parts of the face are physically and chromatically modified in order to enhance selectively significant organs and their communicative potential: the white patches of the sclera and the teeth, the roundness of the face, the dimension of the nasal protuberance that can be reduced to a less aggressive spherical red bulb.

As we noted above, "clown" is a recent addition to the vocabulary that designates comic characters in the context of the modern circus. It evokes awkwardness, ill-manners, body deformation such as hunchback or other forms of crippling, limping or abnormal walk, all features that are found in many other cultures to identify mythological tricksters and comedians performing transgressive actions.

Figure 28 The Chickys, an iconic traditional duo in the circus of the twentieth century. The elegant, arrogant, and sumptuously dressed white-face clown interacts with the ill-kept, downtrodden auguste. Photo credit: Serge Fleury.

A Detour to India: The Vidûshaka

The Vidûshaka is dwarfish, having protruding teeth, a hunch-back, lame, with bald head and red eyes; his face is deformed; in short,[he] is ugly and deformed in appearance.

G.K. Bhat, ***The Vidûshaka,*** 1959: 48

Cultural evolution does not know any physical or temporal borders. We saw in the first part of this volume how the Gypsies and their Indian legacy permeated the social fabric and imagination of the Middle East and European mosaic of kingdoms and empires for about a millennium, possibly more. We also saw that, much earlier, in the Greco-Roman world, Indians were mentioned in relation to circuslike activities such as elephant training. Nomadism is an obvious tool of cultural diffusion. The clowns of the circus have not appeared suddenly as a spectacular innovation. Historians, though, relish the apparent evidence of absolute beginnings, hence the propping up of Joseph Grimaldi as the origin of the name and the function at a time when urbanization and the rise of the press served as echo chambers to competitive popular entertainments and, thus, started to create both accidental and deliberate archives. Evolution proceeds through variations in the reproduction of pre-existing forms. The idea of "hopeful monsters" is a delusion fed by the human craving for magic. Gypsy magicians, for instance, have preyed on this weakness of our psyche and have mastered from immemorial times the art of making things appear and disappear to cause awe and exploit the credulity of the populations they visited. As in the case of technological changes (e.g., Basalla 1988), cultural evolution is based on a continuous stream of variations, some more drastic than others. Nothing emerges from nothing. The case of the bicycle is a good illustration of this technological evolutionary process that led to its use as an acrobatic prop in the circus (Bouissac 1992: 69–99). Even willful oppositions to a state of affairs that motivate improvements or innovations depend on something to be bettered or opposed. Only the artificial fragmentation of historical periods and domains, and the reluctance or inability to consider phenomena through their transformations over very long stretches of space and time, create the illusion of the emergence of totally new cultural forms.

As a celebrated acrobatic comedian, Joseph Grimaldi was heir to a long lineage of nomadic artists hailing from Italy, who had been trained by his father, himself famous in his own time, before the London theatres and their pantomimes became the talk of the town in a pleasure-seeking era of British urban society. The Commedia dell'arte, often mistakenly construed as a well-defined, albeit multifarious performing institution, has fuzzy boundaries at both ends of its historical existence.

It might sound preposterous to invoke the *Vidûshaka*, a comic character in the Sanskrit classical drama that was a productive form of Indian culture approximately from 200 BCE to 700 CE, as an attempt to elucidate the nature and meaning of the circus clown. However, as the early Greek comedies emerged from rituals performed in honor of the god Dionysos, there is evidence that, similarly, the Sanskrit drama finds its origin in Vedic and Hindu cults, notably in relation to the god Bhairava, who, in the cosmogonies of the Asian subcontinent can be characterized as the supreme transgressor (Chalier-Visuvalingam 2003; Visuvalingam 1989).

Hephaistos, the limping god of the blacksmiths, who was the master of metal, fire, and volcanoes in ancient Greece, should also be mentioned in this context. He is a powerful, albeit somewhat liminal divinity whose deformed feet are explained by different narratives linked to his falling from the Olympian abode where he was born. His cult is associated with the birth of comedy on a par with Dionysos. He is consistently found in relation to laughter in rituals and entertainments. He has been dubbed "the hobbling humorist," "the club-footed god" (Hall 2018). Interestingly, one of the ancient Greek adjectives used to characterize him is *kullos* [deformed, crippled], a word that might be the origin of the puzzling term "coulro-phobia," used to designate "the fear of clowns." The study of historical phonetics shows indeed that geminate consonants such as "ll" tend to dissimilate in various context. This would be all the more likely in this case since Hephaistos is traditionally qualified as being "*kullo-podiôn*" [with deformed feet]. Indeed, both "l" and "r" are liquid consonants and dissimilation can be triggered by the nature of the following consonant in compositions. In this case, "p" is a bilabial plosive and would prompt the production of a sound close to apical "r" as a natural transition from the liquid "l" to the plosive "p." We have to assume that "coulro" in the sense of "clown" found its way in modern English, most likely through a scholarly channel.

But there is more, Hephaistos is often represented in the iconography with feet pointing backwards. This evokes the frequent transformation of the feet of clowns through oversized shoes that cause their typical awkward gait. We can recall Aristotle's definition of the comic as representing the ridiculous arising from ugliness, oddity, mistake, or deformity not causing pain (Golden 1984). This used to apply to the mocking and bullying of lame or hunchback individuals in everyday life before contemporary standards of inclusiveness and civility repressed this tendency of the crowd to target physical or psychological abnormalities with laughter.

Religious celebrations and ritual performances have generated in most, if not all cultures in the world, secularized spectacles that still preserve features from their origins such as the formality (or prescribed informality) of the acting of special individuals in more or less radical disguises and the deep emotional involvement of the participating audience (Toffin 2018). It is not an insuperable stretch of the informed imagination to take a long view of the constant stream of enactments of the foundational narratives through which humans attempt to make sense of the mysteries of their existence through acting out the chaos from which a fragile order emerged. The universality of sacred clowns has been documented by Laura Makarius (1974).

Clowns and tricksters, under any other name, are characterized by their systematic flouting of the rules that define the cultures in which they enact their antics either in narratives or in live performances. There are, though, two ways of looking at their transgressions. Theoreticians have tended to posit cultural sets of injunctions and prohibitions as the background upon which the non-respect of these rules is assessed. Cultural norms are taken for granted and transgressors are defined by their actions with respect to these codes of behavior. As long as they are conceived relatively to pre-existing rules they break "for fun," their actions do not jeopardize the unquestioned power of the cultural norms. However, we cannot eschew the question of what kind of state of affairs preceded the instauration of cultural habits and laws. Looking upstream rather than downstream totally changes the vision of cultural evolution. Many traditions name this unthinkable state "chaos" or equivalent terms that convey a sense of unconceivable amorphous anomy and uncertainty. The transgressions that restore that previous state of disorder from which order arose, are of a very different nature. They embody a wildness that cannot be policed by laughter but overwhelms the participants who embrace this delirium during which the whole cultural edifice of the civil and religious order collapses. At times, tricksters subvert the law of the land through applying it to the letter. As Gilles Deleuze (1971: 77, quoted by Little 1993: 118) noted: "We all know ways of twisting the law by excess of zeal. By scrupulously applying the law we are able to demonstrate its absurdity and provoke the very disorder that it is intended to prevent or conjure."

The Vidûshaka does not so much break the rules as he acts outside of them. He is both before and beyond the norms that sustain the current social contract, and thus transcends the very notion and reality of cultural and religious order.

It is in this sense that we can consider his uncharted behavior as sacred. He straddles the unknown outside, the realm of unpredictability. He rides what Karl Friston (2010) calls "free energy," that feared solvent of boundaries and binds, that haunts the core of the law-and-order niche of civilized humans wherever they have settled on the earth and in which everything is relatively predictable.

Sunthar Visuvalingam (1989) points out that the Vidûshaka is regularly depicted profaning all the values of classical brahminhood so as to earn the mocking label of "brahmin par excellence." Yet constant allusions, sometimes in the form of teasing, are made to the formidable—actually magical—power of the apparently timid and gluttonous Vidûshaka who revels in making abrupt enigmatic remarks dismissed as puerile jokes and in breaking all language rules. Absolute power (*mana*) is released through the transgression he enacts with violence or indifference as if he were immune to guilt. He stands outside the canon of human physical proportions, fitness, and beauty as well as the standards of moral decency that were elaborated through eons of civilizing processes. He may evoke by many aspects, Loki, the supreme trickster of the Old Norse myths whose paradoxical nature and deeds are described in the Eddic tales. Loki is both friend and foe of the divinities, both blood brother and traitor of the radiant Odin, "He defies boundaries and his apparent and uncompromising liminality presents a continuous challenge to those who would try to understand and categorize his nature" (Krasskova 2010).

Students of the Vidûshaka (e.g., Bhat 1959; Kuiper 1979; Parikh 1953) characterize his persona as embodying deformity, often hunchbacked, gluttony, contrary speech, obscenity, impertinence, and holding a crooked stick. His way of speaking is compared to a "wicked monkey" or having "the voice of a donkey" (Bhat 1959: 51). He wears sloppy or outlandish clothes and his face is disfigured by stripes of dark colored makeup. A photograph of a modern Vidûshaka on the Kerala stage shows a broad lateral enlargement of his mouth and his eyes through dark makeup (Bhat 1959: 49). His transgressive behavior on many levels causes a liberating laughter mixed with disgust, shame, indignation, and fear. His role in the Sanskrit drama has been obviously codified so that his appearance and actions are framed and relatively contained within the mainstream cultural context. However, the origin of these classical performances has been traced back to new year festivals in archaic Rigvedic cosmogony that, like the Greek Dionysia, the Latin Bacchanalia and Saturnalia, and the Hindu Holi celebrations witnessed the irruption of a primal chaos. Similarly, the resilience of unruly carnivals in their modern forms that are mostly subdued heirs to the still more excessive Mediaeval feasts of fools (Chambers 1903), thrive on transgressing the socioreligious norms and reversing established hierarchies.

Significantly, the Vidûshaka is the only one who can address the hero of the drama, usually the king, on equal terms. So does the circus clown whose disrespect for authorities is one of the hallmarks of the role, such as in the classical exchange in a mocked military context in which the "officer" scolds the new recruit by calling him "idiot" and the clown-recruit retrospectively construes this interaction as a mutual introduction between peers and replies, formally stretching his hand toward the officer: "Pleased to meet you. My name is so-and so," thus reverting to a pre-cultural state of social relations in which institutional hierarchies had not emerged yet.

It is quite remarkable that the descriptions and the extant iconography of the Vidûshaka match quite closely the iconography of the early prototype of the circus clown, Joseph Grimaldi, whose fame in London during the Regency prompted artists to produce prints and portraits that make possible a precise assessment of the distance between his natural handsome face and the disfigurement of his makeup as it can be noticed in the series of prints and portraits published in his biography by McConnell Stott (2009).

Let us note that on the eastward end of the Indian cultural diaspora, on Sumatra, Java, and Bali, the clowning characters in the Wayang plays that perform episodes of the Ramayana and Mahabharata also wear disfiguring facial makeup, particularly Bagong, the most impertinent of the four comic characters, the Punakawans (Bouissac 2015: 188–95). Cultural patterns such as narratives, music, and theatrical performances migrate and adapt to new contexts through conquests, trades, or nomadism. Given the antiquity and resilience of Hindu civilization that relentlessly spread over three millennia through Southeast Asia and to a lesser extent westward, notably by the Gypsies, it is not surprising to identify the perpetuation across time and space of a symbolic figure whose fundamental cultural properties survive in its avatars.

However, it is important to note that these "semiotic disturbances" that reshuffle or undo the cultural norms take the form of rituals rather than riots. Festivals and rituals are contained in predetermined time and space slots, and correlate usually with relatively stable cultures. When sociopolitical forces appear to be in flux and threaten the degree of predictability that defines a culture by increasing the intrinsic uncertainty that is at the core of the human nature, transgressions are criminalized. Symptomatically, when in the 1950s the American capitalistic structure was under assault from communist ideology, the subversive humor of Charlie Chaplin became suspect and there was concern in the higher spheres of the government that his long-standing popular appeal through the cinematographic medium could overflow into the politics of real life. It is at that time that secret investigations of his British background took place and that Chaplin left the United States and settled in Switzerland.

A Modern Master: Charlie Chaplin

Don't forget that your great grandmother was a Gypsy. Keep that in mind.
Charlie Chaplin in **Chaplin: The Waterville Picture**, a documentary by his grandchild Arthur Gardin, 2012

The importance of Charlie Chaplin (1889–1977) as an inspiring source of modern clowning cannot be overstated. Like the historical Joseph Grimaldi, the mythical Loki, or the ritualistic Vidûshaka, he embodied in his productive artistic life a cultural icon whose haunting presence is still perceivable in the twenty-first century. It has come to light in recent years that Charlie Chaplin was born to a British Gypsy mother whose father once owned a small circus. He grew up in miserable conditions in East London in a dysfunctional family of entertainers. His mother was a singer and his father a traveling actor who died early. His own autobiography recounts his episodic stays in a workhouse, this Victorian institution in which authorities used to lock homeless and unruly children to provide them with rudimentary accommodation and exploitative employment. Charlie Chaplin entered the realm of entertainment at around ten as a child actor who was quickly noted for his unusual talent. His success as a member of a troupe that performed in the United States in 1910 and 1912 brought him to prominence, an opportunity he quickly seized to enter the Hollywood world of the emerging silent cinema with a knack for business typical of many Gypsies. His persona, the little tramp with his signature mustache, hat, gait and cane, fast became an endearing character whose power came from the fact that he was not so much transgressing the rules of good manners as he was creating an insolent world of his own, parallel to the stifling norms of the current mainstream society. Common people, as well as the cultural elite, could relate to the liberating energy of his genial slapstick comedy with an added touch of romance. The silent medium reached out to a universal audience beyond the linguistic borders. Charlie Chaplin introduced his fans to a world of regenerating primordial chaos. In 1928, one of his masterpieces, *The Circus*, was awarded the highest Hollywood distinction that, at the time, was not yet called an "Oscar." The Academy had received several nominations for the film and honored Chaplin with a special award for "versatility and genius in writing, acting, directing, and producing." He is considered one of the cultural icons who defined the twentieth century.

Charlie Chaplin's ethnicity came to light only recently, in large part thanks to his children who publicized a letter that was found in a secret drawer of his desk. Chaplin himself had contributed to the legend of his London birth. In a society that relentlessly stigmatizes Gypsies, the contrived invisibility of one's origins is an imperative, mainly for someone who aims to rise to economic, artistic or political prominence. The posthumously disclosed letter was addressed to Chaplin by an old Gypsy to let him know that the truth of his birth was that he was born in a Gypsy settlement near Birmingham, in the caravan of the Queen of the camp. As one of his sons noted, if Chaplin had not treasured this information he certainly would not have locked it in his desk. It is clear from the testimony of his children that Chaplin was aware and proud of his Gypsy lineage.

A bronze statue of Charlie Chaplin stands in a southern Irish town in the Cork region, where, in his later years, he used to take his summer vacations with his family. In *Chaplin: The Waterville Picture*, a forty-minute documentary narrated by his grandchild Arthur Gardin, we are told that "His great grandmother was a Gypsy from Cork. That Gypsy gene was something he was very proud of." Furthermore, an Irish chauffeur who used to drive Chaplin and his family around the region, recalls that once, as they were coming back from the beach, they happened to come across a group of Travellers on the side of the road. Chaplin asked to stop the car and he went to greet them. Upon returning from this brief meeting, Chaplin told his children: "Don't forget your great grandmother was a Gypsy. Keep that in mind!"

The profile and demeanor of Charlie Chaplin, who was popularly known as "Charlot" in some European countries, was so salient, both visually and psychologically, that circus artists all over the world imitated his signature costume and behavior. The "little tramp" was duplicated even in Asia in circuses, theaters, and on the screen. It was relatively easy for artists to model their makeup, gestures, and way of walking after having seen again and again the numerous silent movies Chaplin had produced.

The celebrated clown Charlie Rivel, for instance, was one of the several hundred clowns who first relied on this imitation to secure some success with their public. At the beginning of his career "Charlie" Rivel excelled to the point that after threatening him with a lawsuit, Charlie Chaplin joked that he was not sure any longer who was imitating whom. The mimetic reproduction of a characteristic appearance and acting, a phenomenon that is rampant in the clown culture, remains, though, a superficial move that creates a mere image of the original icon. During the twentieth century, many clowns cashed on their ability to visually evoke their model, but Charlie Chaplin articulated in his cinematic art a substantial discourse that was not easy to emulate. Charlie Rivel eventually cast this disguise away and invented his own persona. Charlie Cairoli, whose first stage name was "Carletto" (little Charlie in Italian), succeeded in adapting the Charlie Chaplin outfit and wit to the Post–Second Word War British public, and was able to provide his traditional slapstick comedy with deeply relevant contents to the point of creating an icon of his own. Nowadays, imitations of Charlie Chaplin have disappeared from the circus ring as only cinephiles and some fans still watch the silent movies that brought Charlie Chaplin to universal fame. As one of the last echoes of this influence, a young Ukrainian juggler, Vladimir Omelchenko, a decade ago, still performed his fledging act dressed as "Charlot," including the mustache, the hat, and the walking stick, but it is doubtful that anybody among the younger spectators could truly relate to the allusion. Omelchenko has now abandoned this outfit as he emerged as a supreme rola-bola acrobat. Cultural forms, such as patterns of performance, generate other forms through imitation, modification, and selection by the public. As we have noted again and again in this book, circus celebrities are fast erased from collective memory.

The original Charlie Chaplin, though, cannot be reduced to his signature outfit and demeanor. His acting has been characterized as a "visual Esperanto" that transcended linguistic and political borders. Albert Einstein expressed his admiration for Chaplin's universal appeal, stating that, without uttering a single word, he was understood by everybody. There is more in Chaplin's art than meets the eyes. His persona has been outwardly characterized as an outcast, a pariah, a downtrodden tramp, a disenfranchised citizen. But, on the contrary, he embodied the free energy that thrives outside the iron cage of society by acting against its constraints not from inside but from outside, from a creative utopian space. He does not oppose or transgress any particular rules; he ignores them and triumphs without apologies. He is the trickster, the true clown, beyond good and evil; he instigates the regenerating chaos from which novel meanings can always emerge.

The philosophers of the Frankfurt School, known for their fierce criticism of the modern communication order and the popular culture it promoted as a mere commodity, made a signaled exception about Charlie Chaplin. Theodor Adorno, who was an admirer of Chaplin, stated: "One can well imagine that Chaplin's cryptic dimension, or precisely that which makes this most perfect clown more than his genus, is connected with the fact that he as it were projects upon the environment his own violence and dominating instinct, and through this projection of his own culpability produces that innocence which endows him with more power than all power possesses. [...] in Chaplin, this is the utopia of an existence that would be free of the burden of being-one's-self" [Translated by John MacKay] (1996: 58–60). Horkheimer and Adorno, (quoted by Fuchs 2016: 78) identify the locus of this redeeming energy in no other place than the circus: "Traces of something better persist in those features of the culture industry by which it resembles the circus (2002:114)." But Adorno's insight goes further as he pertinently relates the clown with the animal in the circus context. After having defined Chaplin as the clown of clowns, a kind of "*ur-clown*" of his time, he states: "Psychoanalysis tries to relate the clown-figure to the reaction formations of earliest childhood, before any crystallization of a stable self [...] more information about the clown is to be found among children who, *as mysteriously as they do with animals*, communicate with his image and with the meaning of his activity, which in fact *negates meaning*" (1996: 59) [my emphasis].

Two Kinds of Laughter

To truly laugh, you must be able to take your pain, and play with it.

Charlie Chaplin

Laughter is commonly considered in the singular form. Since there is only one word in English that denotes this acoustic neuromuscular phenomenon which usually occurs in social contexts, its unproblematic ontology is taken for granted. However, even if one excludes the physical effect of tickling and pathological laughing caused by physiological disruptions of the central nervous system, several distinct kinds of laughter can be identified on psychological and situational grounds. Psychologists and sociologists have proposed categories such as affiliative and etiquette laughter that contributes to build spontaneous social cohesion to the point of taking the form, at times, of a contagious behavior. There can be contrived or genuine laughter, the latter emerging irrepressibly from unconscious brain events. Some students of laughter mention chuckling and snorting, or smiling as a silent version, at the lower end of a scale that leads to belly laughing, even howling to the point of choking. As a response to clown acts, there is no doubt that this reflex is mediated by cognitive processes that are not fully understood yet (Bouissac 2015).

Two markedly different kinds of laughter will be considered here in relation to the reception of clowning: repressive hilarity and elated laughter. The former could be called the Bergsonian laugh, the latter the Nietzschean one. This makes reference, respectively, to Henri Bergson's theory of laughter, according to which the social function of laughter is to repress deviance from the norm, and to Friedrich Nietzsche who celebrated the liberating laughter of the prophet who emancipates himself from the rule of the enslaved masses (Bergson 1911; Nietzsche 1995).

The Bergsonian laughter, echoing Aristotle, is a social behavior that is associated with mocking or even bullying those individuals who do not conform to the expected appearance or demeanor that is the current rule of social propriety. It may apply to the way one is dressed or the way one speaks such as making grammatical mistakes, having a foreign accent, or stuttering; the manners of walking or eating; abnormalities of the body such as hunchback or limping; and, naturally, the transgressing of expected social behavior with respect to hierarchy, gender norms, or logical reasoning applied to solving simple problems; the mindless mechanical reactions similar to those of an automat. We can recognize in that open-ended repertory of deviance many defining features of traditional circus clowns who deliberately contrive their ridiculous costuming, outlandish staging and slapstick performing so that they can play the justified role of scapegoat, not only suffering pranks and blows from their authoritarian partners but also triggering the "repressive" laughter of the audience. This laughter expresses the triumph of the crowd over the non-conformists that flout the rules. From this point of view, there is continuity on a scale going from the bullying of special kids in the schoolyard and the trolling on line of out-of-the-norm individuals to the loud laughter of a circus audience, although the latter is somewhat more codified and thus becomes the mark of professional success in the world of popular entertainment. The circus clown, though, is generally construed as a social outcast and a pathetic character in the literature that interprets and amplifies its symbolic status in society.

The Nietzschean laughter is of a different nature. It is akin to the divine madness of the Buddhist enlightenment when the cosmos reveals itself as an impenetrable joke. Nietzsche brings up the issue of laughter in the third part of his prophetic *Thus Spoke Zarathustra*. For him, the corrective laughter, in the Bergsonian sense, is the laughter of the herd, the oppression of conformism. The laughter he celebrates is the sign of the radical emancipation from the constraints of a doomed civilization that strives to maintain a mediocre average. The Nietzschean laughter signals the advent of a new, triumphant mankind. It is the sudden liberation of the free, Dionysian energy. It is not "laughing at" but "laughing with" that transcends borders and differences. It is quite noticeable that, when we watch Charlie Chaplin's silent movies, we do not laugh at him personally, whatever he happens to do, but we participate in a collective laughter with him in an integrative, rather than excluding mode. This is markedly different, to remain in the cinematic domain, from our laughing at the pathetic looser, Mister Bean, created by Rowan Atkinson. Let us remember the episode, in Chaplin's *The Circus* (1928), that shows the regular traditional clowns of the time going through their worn-out routine on a revolving platform at the center of the ring. A glance to the audience betrays the boredom of the front row spectators. Suddenly, "the little tramp" appears running away from a policeman who tries to catch him. In the blink of an eye, they both find themselves running around on the revolving wheel, instantly transforming the chase into an infinite loop. A new glimpse of the audience shows them laughing uproariously. In this sequence, Chaplin makes us laugh with him, not at him, not even at the policeman who tries to catch him. It reveals something absurd about society: the relentless, losing efforts to control free energy caught in the vertigo of an endless loop.

The Twilight of the Clown: Off-Limit Humor

All this removal of great comedy shows because they show black face or men dressing up as women is an absolute JOKE! It's pissing me off so I can only imagine it's going to make racism/sexism worse around the world as the grip goes tighter and tighter over people expressionisms of life! It's perfectly fine for the 'minorities' to joke about the 'majorities'! Right? I can't even watch the news now. It's a [expletive] *pisstake* (sic)! [expletive] *being a clown with all this crap going on, all you will be left with is dick and fart jokes ... Kill me now!!!*

Sacha Santus, British clown, **Facebook**, June 10, 2020
(Quoted with permission of the author with expletives removed)

The clown as a trickster, on the screen or in the ring, cannot pass muster with the guardians of the contemporary standards of inclusive civil harmony. Like the exploitative breeding and training of performing animals which, as non-human persons, are considered to have inalienable rights, the clowns' indifference to the current norms of propriety are unpalatable for many influencers of the current zeitgeist. How to be a successful clown while conforming to "political correctness"? This public discourse that opposes discriminatory behavior of any kind may be construed as a sign of progress toward an advanced stage of civilization that eliminates the scourge of racism and sexism but, by the same token, it impairs the human capacity for transcending the constraints of culture and exploring the nonsensical chaos that lurks under the surface—in the same way as the inclusion of animals among full-fledged social agents virtually brings them into the fold of civil laws but glosses over the wildness that, ultimately, must be controlled for the sake of human survival if this ideology were to reach its ultimate consequences. Such censorship, which often takes the form of self-censorship, misses the point of the clowns—whether sacred or not—that is to challenge all norms and to question their validity without jeopardizing their existence. The new sensitivity to their essentially ritualistic performances signals the pervasive cultural anxiety that characterizes contemporary societies. The creeping motions of the tectonic plates of the civil order—if we can use such a metaphor to describe the global semiotic changes that question the status quo—convey a sense of uncertainty. If cultures offer the security of stable semiotic constructions, the upsetting of norms, values, and categories toward unknown configurations create sheer panic in many if it spills out of the ritual frame. It is hard to focus on the beauty of a landscape from the midst of an earthquake when everybody has to run for their life. Even small motions of the ground on which we stand do alert us to greater upsets.

Let us take the example of an original gag that was successfully performed by Peter Shub, a contemporary-style solo clown, at Circus Roncalli. This act was observed on October 1, 1989, in Stuttgart. Peter Shub does not wear clown makeup. He does not try to be cheerful and charismatic, rather looking bored and slightly aggressive. His nondescript raincoat and hat would blend well in a busy street of any German town on a rainy day. He carries the equipment of a photographer, a large camera obscura and a tripod. This is a classic clown act paradigm since the invention of photography, that has inspired many routine gags such as pretending to take a group picture of the circus audience by asking them to gather in front of the camera, an obvious absurdity made worse by the fact that Peter Shub unexpectedly extracts a very small camera from the large vintage one he brought with him to the ring. He then turns his attention to the tripod, makes it advance step by step as if it were walking. He behaves toward this inanimate tool in a way that humanizes it and when the tripod collapses in the center of the ring, Peer Shub looks up between the legs, suggesting that he is peeking at its genitals and, thus, suggesting a female humanization of the tripod since it is obvious that nothing is hanging from the acute angles formed by the three legs. This brief gag triggers laughter. However, it could be claimed that this invasive glance trivializes a form of sexual aggression while objectifying, if not even mechanizing at the same time the female body. His indiscreet gesture is indeed evoking the traditional but now illegal "upskirting" of macho culture. This is, though, a brief instant. Peter Shub now uses his coat and hat to dress the tripod as if it were a double of himself, and engages a violent male-to-male argument with it, including the production of a gun, through a clever manipulation that creates the illusion that the tripod has also an arm.

As I observed this act, some three decades ago, I noticed the laughter that signaled the impact of the sex-themed gag, but I failed to discern whether the women in the audience were reacting in the same way as the men. It is not clear whether Peter Shub still performs that gag but there is no doubt that sexist and racist jokes—as it is lamented by Sascha Santus who is quoted above—have become off limit for many entertainers.

The Clown and Its Discontents

There is a climate today where many people are turned off by clowns.

This statement by Gerry Flanagan appeared on October 31, 2018, in "Clown Theory," a Facebook forum devoted to clowns. This is a platform for interaction among comedians and individuals interested in discussing clowning from a philosophical or cultural perspective. This group also includes some people who are making a living through teaching the techniques of clowning either as private instructors who have some professional experience or in the framework of a circus school. However, this Facebook forum does not seem to attract professional circus clowns. Typically, Gerry Flanagan defines himself as a "teacher/director/clown practitioner" who is the Artistic Director of *Shifting Sands Theatre*, a company he founded in 1998. "Clown Theory" is an interesting window on the selective cultural appropriation of the makeup, props, and skills of traditional circus clowns by comedians anxious to legitimize their claim to belong to the immemorial trade of clowning through becoming the mentors, in their own terms, of new generations of students who contemplate a clown career as a life project. Will their dream come to a sad end when the population they endeavor to entertain or enlighten "are turned off by clowns"? Why this is so is one of the main issues confronted in this part of the book.

Becoming a professional clown through academic or mock-academic teaching is a recent cultural phenomenon that emerged during the twentieth century. Traditionally, clowns were exclusively produced by circus families which exploited their own resources of talent and the knowledge of the tricks preserved in their collective memory. Some among them were creative individuals who innovated within this tradition and enriched this trove of recipes to make their audience laugh. Often, successful artists begot several generations of clowns who specialized in this genre by exploiting the technical knowledge preserved in the family or the caste. Some could reach temporary fame at times when the circus was popular and their tricks and props were copied by other artists to the extent that it became difficult after a period of time to identify the actual innovator who had devised a particularly successful gag. That lack of historical knowledge, though, was mostly irrelevant for the survival of a performing art that was essentially ephemeral. Clowning was indeed largely an oral tradition that depended on the memory of a limited number of individuals. Modern technologies from the nineteenth century on have recorded some aspects of clowning performances. Nowadays, some computer-savvy artists post videos of the highlights of their acts for promotional purposes. Researchers have also endeavored to preserve, usually in the reflexive mode, visual and written descriptions of the performances they have observed (e.g., Bouissac 2015; Carmeli 1989; Remy 2002). However, something important is paradoxically lost through such appropriation of an oral tradition by scholarly literacy. This objectification of clowning and its popularization through the printed and electronic media contributed to the democratization of a quasi-sacred character to the extent that anybody now feels that, with a proper training, they can become a clown. Such a commodification is fueled by an educational industry that churns out an oversupply of struggling talents who often turn to teaching clowning as a way of making a living, or at least supplement the unpredictable income of professional performers.

This is the context of the discussions going on in the "Clown Theory" forum. One of the issues hotly debated is whether the mask or the makeup is essential for the art of clowning. Stand-up comedians do not bother with the complex transformations that traditional circus clowns apply to their face. They simply rely on verbal jokes accompanied by a range of expressive mimics that elicit laughter in their audience. Many contemporary clowns follow suit. Some major circuses have relied on plain looking comedians coming from the cabaret culture for their comic part. Significantly, the famed Swiss circus Knie featured two such characters for its 100th anniversary program in 2019. As a token homage to the tradition, though, a white-face clown, Yann Rossi, appeared in the opening of the show, playing the saxophone, dressed in his impressive Vicaire costume, but did not act in the usual capacity of this role in the program.

The White-Face Clown: The Waxing and Waning of a Cultural Hero

Pipo's plan was to display signs of elegance, authority, and firmness that verged on an ostentatious and authoritarian personality. He was successful in his attempt to reveal strength and intelligence to the point of appearing heartless and mechanical. His idea was to fashion a clown who exhibited those qualities of cultural refinement and sophistication verging on narrow-mindedness and intolerance.

Kenneth Little, Simulation of tradition in circus clown performance, **Semiotica** 85 (3/4): 234

During the last decades of the twentieth century, the dynamics of clown productions moved away from the traditional duo that had reigned supreme from well over 100 years: the white-face clown and the auguste. Their dialogic performances were sustained by a repertory of short comedies that have been documented with historical and ethnographic precision (e.g., Bouissac 2015; Nguimfack 2015; Remy 2002 [1947]). These usually unwritten scenarios staged the opposition of a dominating, sophisticated character interacting with one, at times two partners who were breaking the rules of propriety and decency through their attire and behavior, and were made to pay for their provocative transgressions. These latter mischievous actions, though, were the substantial core of the narratives and the character of the white-face clown served as a dramatic contrast that enhanced the antics of his unruly acolyte(s). It was clear that, in spite of the dominating persona of the white-face clown, the true source of pleasure and laughter for the audience was the tramplike, outcast auguste. The current century has witnessed the eventual emancipation of the auguste from his subservience to a symbolic master, to the point that nowadays white-face clowns are rarely featured in circus programs or appear as a mere nostalgic sign of the past. It should be kept in mind, though, that the white-face clown was a relatively recent creation of the modern circus. Its coded makeup, shimmering costumes, eloquence and elegance emerged in circus performances when comic characters were allowed to speak and evolved from acrobatic parodists to dramatic antagonists.

Many among today's older circus fans—as well as professional entertainers who embodied the white-face role through their artistic career—lament the waning of this icon that had been, for generations, one of the hallmarks of the traditional circus, at least in continental Europe. The trajectory of this cultural form offers an interesting opportunity to examine a striking case of semiotic evolution and the very notion of tradition that is central to the canonization, conservation, and reproduction of stereotypical cultural behavior. In her luxurious book, *Le costume de clown blanc* [The Costume of the White-face Clown], ethnologist Sylvie Nguimfack-Perault (2015) retraces the history of this character and the cluster of signs that defines him. This process of successive transformations from the late eighteenth century in England to its heyday at the turn of the twentieth century in Paris opens a window on the evolution of cultural phenomena.

How does social behavior become a tradition? To understand this dynamic, we must avoid two pitfalls: first, the impression that the origin of traditions is lost in deep time and that we have neither access to it nor control of its development; secondly, the belief that traditions never change over time. In fact, these two assumptions are parts of the semiotic engineering through which a social habit is construed as a norm. Once social behavior has succeeded in taking root in a culture under the guise of a tradition, it can muster a great deal of energy in the service of its reproduction, maintenance, and conservation. As a symbol of the cultural law and order, the white-face clown is not an endearing persona. Actually, it could almost be viewed as a "cultural monster," an exaggerated representation of ruthless and pitiless authoritarian power. Its face is designed to inspire fear rather than love. It has been uniformly whitened so that it cannot display any human feeling through the range of natural hues caused by the flux of blood under the skin, or through the meaningful contractions of the numerous facial muscles that constantly convey various attitudes and emotions. White is the color of death, marble, vampires, or zombies. The black marks above the eyebrows and the violent red around the lips and ears are not reassuring signs. To distinguish themselves from one another, white-face clowns had only the shape of the artificially painted eyebrow to play with, hence the emergence of the notion of "signature" in the context of the artistic competition that soon arose from the popularity of clown acts in circus programs. The appearance of the white-face clown is more akin to a mask than a makeup that would enhance the attractiveness and expressive potential of the human face. Taken out of context, it is truly frightening. Significantly, in the little comedies that are performed in the ring, the white-face clown impersonates policemen, military commanders, conductors, umpires, and enforcers of all kinds as the theme of the interactions among the performers requests. These avatars are indicated by the adjunction of a hat or a prop typical of these respective functions. In the standard versions of these "improvised" plays, the white-face clown leads the team through the dramatic action and presides over the resolution of the conflicts when, at the end, the whole cast leaves the ring, often playing music, in a well-ordered march.

Another important feature of traditions is that, as they emerge from free variations, they are not deliberately designed as coherent wholes. They often crystallize as bricolages endowed with striking patterns that impose themselves as visually compelling prototypes. Sylvie Nguimfack-Perault (2015) documents the emergence of the glittering costume that became, at the turn of the twentieth century, an archetypical attribute of the white-face clown. Historical iconography suggests some continuity with an outfit noticeable in the *Commedia dell'arte* and its conservation with variations in the British pantomime in which Joseph Grimaldi rose to fame and set the standards for the modern clown before unclear circumstances created the dramatic tandem of the white-face and the auguste. Soon, the former became associated with a shapely apparel made of colorful fabric incrusted with minute shimmering elements, such as pearls and rhinestones. The demand and the competition among clowns created a specialty within the theater and circus costumes industry. In Paris, the workshop of the Vicaire family gained prominence in this trade. Although there were other smaller companies that catered to the needs of artists and music halls producers, Vicaire was a must for those who could afford the cost. Charles Vicaire invented around 1920 a new machine, based on the adaptation of contemporary sewing technology, that made it possible to automatically add rhinestones to fabrics. Nguimfack-Perault has detailed, in her ethnographic study, the role of Charles's son, Gérard Vicaire, upon the innovative creation and standardization of the white-face costume during the twentieth century. We can follow through her account based on interviews with Vicaire who had specialized with passion in this branch of the family company, the emergence of a cultural form that progressively became a "tradition." As a designer, he offered different patterns of costumes adapted to the body type of the clowns who sought his services. Fads and fashions played a part as artists were prone both to imitate and outdo their successful colleagues. Vicaire was also a productive painter of colorful motifs to be embroidered on these costumes. These figurative or abstract representations, abundantly reproduced in Nguimfack-Perault book, were not inspired by a preexisting tradition but sprung from the creative imagination of an individual costume maker who brought brilliance and luxury to a circus character who had become, perhaps in part because of his re-invented costume, the focus of attention among the comedians of the ring.

The dramatic reign of the white-face clown, though, was relatively short. His authoritarian character was ambiguous and variously received by the audience. He was redeemed by his musical talents and, nowadays, appears in some spectacles in this capacity, as a kind of nostalgic and poetic quote from the past, oblivious of the famous cruelty of some of them who were wont to abuse their auguste partner both verbally and physically in order to provoke laughter. Economic reasons have been suggested for this demise: on the one hand, the sets of "traditional" costumes were difficult to transport and maintain in prime shape; on the other hand, popular augustes would easily do away with the expenses of hiring a white-face partner when they were confident that the ring master could minimally fulfill the part in their dialogued sketches. However, the destiny of the white-face clown was probably more surely doomed under the pressure of sociopolitical evolution that undermined the legitimacy of a dominant figure that had no qualm triggering laughter by harassing and hitting downtrodden representatives of those who were perceived as members of the lower class such as peasants or tramps in the context of urban elitism, and Africans at the time of triumphant colonialism.

There were advanced symptoms of the semantic change at work during the later decades of the twentieth century. For instance, after having served as the victimized auguste of his father, Jean-Marie Cairoli, a prominent white-face clown known for his rough comedy style, Charlie Cairoli inherited the mantel and soon developed a new style of performance in which the auguste was the focus of action and attention. Significantly, the white-face clowns he hired as partners for a while at the Blackpool Tower Circus in England were not dominant but truly served his gags. In fact, there were narratives in which the white-face was construed as the bad guy to the point of being spontaneously booed by the audience, a reaction that the star auguste exploited to his advantage. In the 1970s, though, Charlie Cairoli stopped using a white-faced partner and had the antagonistic part of the comedy perfunctorily performed by the ringmaster.

The tendency to dump the white-face clown role is recorded by circus chroniclers about two decades earlier when the celebrated auguste Rhum (Enrico Sprocani) decided that he did not need to cope with the demands of such an expensive colleague and created original versions of comic sketches with a partner formally dressed as a straight man. Circus historian Tristan Remy (1986), a friend of Rhum who documented his biography in a privately published booklet, details the tensions that undermined the relationship between the auguste and the whiteface clown over the mid-twentieth century, a process that involved both personal factors and more general cultural changes.

Figure 29 A typical costume of white-face clown: Yann Rossi (from the duo the Rossyans) wears a creation of Gérard Vicaire made of luxurious fabric and elaborately decorated. Photo credit: Serge Fleury.

An anecdotal evidence of this evolution was observed in 1995 at German Circus Krone where that year's program featured the Toni Alexis Trio a Spanish troupe including a white-face and two augustes. For the first time, in my long experience of the circus, I witnessed a white-face clown receiving blows from the auguste. "Traditional" routine had the former initiating mock violence of various degrees of intensity against the latter, but these blows were never returned or, if there were attempts to reciprocate on the part of the auguste, the white-face always managed to avoid being hit and the auguste perpetually

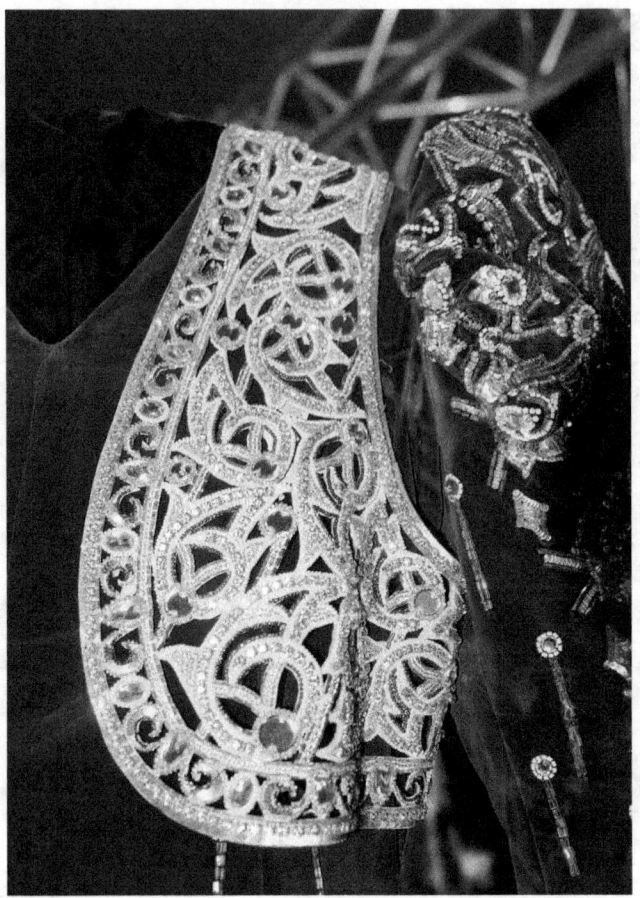

Figure 30 Detail of the embroidery on a white-face's costume. Photo credit: Serge Fleury.

remained at the receiving end of the cycle of kicks and slaps. It was noticeable that, in the Toni Alexis Trio act, the breaking of this convention triggered a strong response from the audience that burst into laughter when the white-face's arrogance and aggressiveness was suddenly put down by a slap on the face. This ultimate transgression on the part of the auguste was a sure symptom that the "traditional" white-face was on the wane. This circus icon, though, did not totally vanish but it does not appear to be a productive paradigm any longer in the meaning-making circus matrix, increasingly fulfilling a role of nostalgic allusion or even a mere simulation as anthropologist Kenneth Little suggested three decades ago in his discussion of this tradition (Little 1991).

Black Face Matters

Chocolat's auguste was a would-be man of the world, a fool attempting to appear dignified but rarely getting away with it. It was reasoned that if the auguste were meant to be on the receiving end of all the slaps and kicks, then these blows would be more amusing if the auguste were an impeccable gentleman.

John Towsen, Clowns 1976: 219

The redundant whiteness of the face of the clown who embodies cultural domination has always been taken for granted by the European public over the last two centuries. Cultural codes are unproblematic within the population which foster them. They are tacit norms that define reality itself. Caucasian audiences may discuss the origin and meaning of the white-face clown's makeup but the whiteness itself is not an issue. Contemporary reflection on clown faces in a wider sociopolitical context reveals deeper implications pertaining to exclusion and racism. In a post published in the Facebook Public Group "Clown Theory," Jon Davison calls attention to a Dainty Funk's black perspective on reclaiming some of the racist roots of clowning: "The Racial History of Clown Face" [youtube.com: CLOWNS ARE RACIST]. This passionate, illustrated lecture offers invaluable insights on the history and meaning of clown makeup, mostly from North American point of view. It also pertains, among other aspects, to the minstrel tradition of the blackening of the face and its racist roots. In a subsequent comment, Christine Lesiak points out that clown makeup presupposes white skin and other cultural assumptions as a base and she invites BIPOC [that is, black, indigenous, and people of color] to share their thoughts and experience concerning the issue of makeup. Others have addressed the meaning of white makeup in a various historical and cultural context, for instance social anthropologist Magnus Course documents and discusses the trauma of becoming white with respect to the antics of the Mapuche ritual clowns in southern Chile (Course 2013).

It should be clear that there is more at stake than mere innocent play in the various chromatic modifications of the face in clowns makeup. In the repertory of traditional clown comedies, making visible minorities—or by the same token disabled persons such as being lame, hunch back, deaf, or stutterer—the targets of jokes and pranks was considered good sport. The American Indian theme is still nowadays perpetuated without any hint of discriminatory guilt by some clowns in acts in which the white face represents a cowboy, an officer, or a bar manager and the auguste wears an American Indian feather headgear. Expectedly, the latter is the butt of the gags that ridicules him, thus re-enacting symbolically the conquest of the west and the extermination of the indigenous population. The implied social violence that is represented in these comic performances is fundamentally dissymmetrical, aimed at tramps, derelicts, blacks, and women who are systematically parodied through grotesque attire and misogynistic jokes.

The history of clowning in France, particularly in the several permanent circuses that existed in Paris in the heyday of the dialogic genre at the turn of the twentieth century, features a legendary team formed by a British clown-acrobat, Footit, and his black partner, Chocolat. Dubbing a black man who was a former slave from Cuba "Chocolat" [chocolate] was meant to be humoristic by virtue of foregrounding the color of his skin in the colonialist context of the time. Moreover, food names are demeaning when they are applied to persons. The German auguste Hans Wurst [sausage] is a telling example of this paradigm.

Starting their performing partnership in the late nineteenth century, Footit and Chocolat rose to stardom in the circus world. The latter's role was to be the one who get slapped and Footit was famous for his cruelty. Beating up a downtrodden character was then a recipe to elicit laughter. His very ethnicity qualified Chocolat for the auguste's role. Indeed, Chocolat did not wear the traditional makeup of the auguste and was dressed with a tuxedo, white shirt and gloves, and shiny black shoes. According to the prejudices of the time, the formal attire of a gentleman associated with a black man was considered sufficiently hilarious. In one of their acts, it was Chocolat who was kicking Footit to make him stop singing a stupid song. However, significantly, Chocolat's violence was defeated by the unflappable resilience of his partner to the point that, at the end, the repeated kicking exhausted the kicker who collapsed while stolid Footit kept singing while being carried out of the ring by circus hands. In no way could this black auguste win. Chroniclers reported the following dialogue in which Chocolat was declaring that he was thirsty. "Do you have money to pay for a drink?" Footit replied. The answer was "No!"—"You have no money? Then, you are not thirsty" was Footit's imperious answer (Rémy 1945: 116).

Nevertheless, Chocolat was celebrated for his excellence in this subservient role that fitted his tumbling virtuosity. His fame culminated in 1890 when a nautical pantomime titled "Chocolat's wedding" was staged at the popular Nouveau Cirque. Once again, the comic thrust of the narrative was the physical and psychological battering of the black man. The arena of that circus could be lowered and filled with water. Chocolat, in a mock formal suit, was the groom and the bride was a lovely blonde. The wedding party entered the ring on boats but soon the apparent good order collapsed: the boats sank and the bride eloped with drunken students. Chocolat was desperately running to catch his bride to be. The pantomime mostly consisted of well-choreographed hectic tumbling and jumping in which Chocolat was the ridiculed hero. The resulting chaos was the expected outcome of a mixed-race wedding in the sociopolitical context of a time when France was engaged in the "civilizing" of its African colonies and the "black man" was the iconic representation of the incompetence and awkwardness that characterized the auguste in the circus ring.

This paradigmatic example shows the extent to which the transgressive dynamics of clowning relates to the deeper semiotic structures that historically define a culture. The systemic racism implied in the colonialists' sense of superiority regarding the low status of "uncivilized" natives of exotic lands accounts for the guilt-free representation of dissymmetrical physical and verbal violence. A successful exchange that was noted by chroniclers of the time consisted in Footit repeating a dozen times in various forms and positions "You are an idiot!" and being told at the end by Chocolat: "I had understood the first time!" (Rémy 1945: 115). To make things worse with respect to current standards, Chocolat did not have to blacken his face to perform his role but other artists would do so frequently as the minstrels' tradition shows. It is extremely unlikely that the plots and antics that supported the success of Footit and Chocolat, as well as other performances based on the same model, could survive in today's Western cultures in which ethnic relations are in conflictual flux and generate tension and uncertainty. This suggests that transgressive representations correlate with robust systems of semantic oppositions that account for the stability of a worldview, irrespective of its moral and legal legitimacy. Clowns straddle the fine line between order and chaos. Performances can reach a critical threshold that switch their mode from ritual to riot.

The Crucifixion of the Clown

Can comedy survive in an age of outrage? Comedy is such a simple thing. One person tells a joke. Another person laughs. The end. Simple. Except, as every comedian knows, simple does not mean easy. Not only do you have to make someone laugh (which is hard) if you are a comedian, you have to make them laugh in the right way. At the right thing. For the right reason ....Who is going to take offence?

Miranda Sawyer, ***The Guardian***, July 28, 2019

Clowns are not vanishing as fast as the wild animals from circus programs but, as lions and zebras are replaced with horses, cows, and dogs; their humor tends to be domesticated, so to speak. We can observe a softening, if not an infantilizing of their gags and jokes that must be within the boundaries of political correctness lest their career be jeopardized. To make things worse for the acceptability of their traditional art, some high-profile clowns in recent years have been prosecuted for sexual harassment in the context of the "me too" movement, and instantly disappeared from the ring and the stage.

Solo clowns have now mostly become the rule. Deprived of the partner who served them as an enhancing contrast who also had the function of leading the game, the augustes are on their own and have largely abandoned the heavy traditional makeup and outlandish costumes in order to defuse the fear and hostility that these facial and bodily transformations may cause once they address directly the audience rather than their white-face antagonist. However, as a consequence, they lose the relative anonymity that a mask or makeup provides to protect their responsibility when they engage in transgressive performances. A minimal makeup does not guarantee immunity. These clowns' civil identity is not fully split from their performing behavior.

Furthermore, the dialogic nature of the sketches has turned into a speechless "monologue" as the Peter Shub's gag that was described above shows. This is quite different from the situation of standup comedians who usually benefit from the pulpit position on an elevated stage. The circus solo clown is encircled by the unforgiving gaze of the audience. An escape from that trap consists of making some members of the public—or occasionally some stooges—the focus of the audience's attention by driving them through actions that make them seem ridiculous and transform them into augustes by proxy. The magnitude of the transgressive gags that are permissible in such situations is considerably reduced through self-censorship in view of current standards of civility.

In interviews with instructors and students in a London "clown school," Mark Wilding (2019) reports that, when asked what is their connection with the "face-painted and floppy-shoed clowns of the public's imagination," a student replies, referring to the kind of clowning they are learning: "It's an art form. It's just a completely different thing." She claims that this new type of clowning offers innocence, freedom, vulnerability, something deeper than other forms of comedy. How are these clowns different then from standup comedians? "Standup is about your ideas and how clever you are, and this is about who you are as a human being." Indeed, standup comedians are pitiless. They make their audience laugh at various categories of people they stigmatize for reportedly making or saying stupid things, rarely do they aim their aggressive wit toward themselves. By contrast, the new solo clowns tend to elicit laughter in their audience by acting silly or failing in their ill-conceived attempts to achieve their goals. Self-deprecation is an introverted behavior, a kind of suicidal performance that may denounce the absurdity of cultural norms or even life itself, but cannot upset the world order and cause a riot.

There is a productive clowning paradigm that re-orients the transgressive process from the outward cultural norms toward the tacit rules of performance themselves through staging failures in a systematic way. George Carl (1916–2000) exploited that comic vein with utmost efficiency as he was flouting all the felicitous conditions that are the foundations of a successful performance (Bouissac 2010: 127–36). George Carl's act was performed with great success both in circuses and varieties. It has been recorded many times and remains available on line in video form that other artists can watch and emulate. Clown Sascha Koychev, for instance, posted in Facebook an impressive imitation of this act by his thirteen-year-old son Alex. Among contemporary clowns, Cesar Diaz, inspired by Carl's example, illustrates this method that displays the corrosive effects of self-deconstruction (Bouissac 2015: 99–102). The laughter these clowns elicit in their audience tends to target the human condition itself of which their own predicaments is but an example, rather than assaulting stigmatized minorities and deviant behavior or raising the specter of primal chaos. In that paradigm, the clown creates group unanimity against himself, turning his transgressive persona into a sacrificial scapegoat.

The semiotic saga of a visual logo that had reached global currency in the late twentieth century is symptomatic of the social demise of the clown. The fast-food restaurant chain McDonald's started in the early 1960s to use a clown as promotional tool to attract children. The stereotypical image of a clown with red hair, white face, red nose, enlarged red lips, and bright yellow attire, became the striking mascot of this corporation and was stylized as a visual logo that adorned the restaurant outlets globally under the moniker of "Ronald McDonald the clown." However, as the perception of clowns shifted from childish innocence toward the sinister aura of creepy characters, the McDonald company decided to retire their mascot in 2016 as it had become a liability rather than a commercial asset.

Finnish visual artist Jani Leinonen, a critic of the corporate culture and its imagery, took notice of this tragic end and dramatized this turn of event by creating a sculpture representing the McDonald clown crucified on a large wooden cross in a position replicating the traditional Christian representation

Figure 31 "McJesus" 2015. Acrylic on resin. 218 × 146 × 50 cm. By Jani Leinonen. Photo credit: Vilhelm Sjöström. Published with the kind permission of the artist and the Zetterberg Gallery, Helsinki.

of the crucifixion. As he had titled his work "McJesus," its exhibition, in January 2019, in a Israeli museum in Haifa caused a stir among the local Christian communities and was eventually removed following protests (Dwyer 2019). There is more than anecdotal value in this provocative merging of activism, commercialism, clowning, and the sacred. It brings forth the plight of the clown through the symbolic immolation of a circus icon.

Free Speech and the Clowns: Is Jordan Peterson a Trickster?

In recent years, I have had to seriously edit my routines with my wife for the majority of audiences. The verbal banter we did in the clown act has had to be seriously curtailed as the audiences in Germany, France, and the UK deem it too sexist, which of course is not the intention; she is the 'White Face clown', the figure of authority, and I am the Auguste; so the conflict is what makes the comedy. We have had to change a lot.
 British clown David Konyot, August 2, 2020 (personal communication)

We encountered Jordan Peterson at the end of the previous part of this book when we noted that his ideas are found attractive by some animal trainers who feel they are the victims of the contemporary ideology that Peterson attacks.

Let us recall that the clinical psychologist from the University of Toronto gained a late celebrity in his academic career through his provocative fight against the sociopolitical inclusive norms that now tend to prevail in the twenty-first century, at least in democratic countries.

He first caused a stir in his home university when he refused to abide by new instructions concerning the acceptance of pronominal changes that were aimed at restoring the grammatical gender balance that had been tipped for ages in favor of the masculine forms and accommodating trans identities. For him, the traditional system of personal pronouns in English enshrined the legitimate masculine order and doing away with it could only invite chaos. But his fame among conservative constituencies reached a peak when he attacked Bill C-16, a Government Act voted by the Canadian Parliament to amend the Human Rights Act and the Criminal Code by adding gender identity and gender expression to the list of prohibited grounds for discrimination. He thus caught the tide of mounting anger and frustration of mainly white males in the western world and became a kind of prophet of the traditional patriarchy that had defined for centuries not only academia but the whole spectrum of political and cultural institutions. He endeavored to lead a crusade against modern liberal culture.

Jordan Peterson's aggressive, divisive rhetoric became, during the second decade of the twenty-first century, the focus of attention of the media outlets that cultivate controversial debates that attract wide popular audiences. There was no nuances in his brutal approach to the tenets of the new inclusive norms. Claiming, among other accusations, that the academia had become a hotbed for Neo-Marxist indoctrination, he denounced the pernicious effects of the fountain heads of Postmodernism and Feminism aiming to undermine the foundation of the Patriarchal civilization with which he identified. One of his favorite targets was the censorship of free speech that victimized those who tried to express dissent, causing some professionals to lose their position or be ostracized by the majority. He promoted his ideas through lucrative lecture tours and an insisting presence in social media such as Twitter, Facebook, and Patreon, eventually creating his own platform called Thinkspot destined to be immune to any form of censorship. His 2018 book, *12 Rules for Life: An Antidote to Chaos*, through which he promoted a kind of Victorian-era ethics, with trivial self-help advice, often expressed in contemporary urban slang, was an instant international bestseller. Morphing himself into a cultural warrior confronting the modern liberal culture, he has been the occasional victim of the oppression he denounced when his lectures were cancelled under the pressure of local objections to his ideas.

However, Jordan Peterson is neither a political theorist nor a revolutionary leader. He is rather an efficient entertainer who engages his audiences, shocks or delights them, and occasionally makes them laugh at the strawmen or women he accuses of destroying the values of the good old times of male dominance he cherishes. His rhetorical excesses liken him more to a trickster than a prophet. He excels at unwittingly parodying himself. His performances are rituals rather than riots. For instance, watching on YouTube the lecture on "political indoctrination on campus" he delivered on November 16, 2017, at the University of Wisconsin—Madison, provides evidence that he runs some kind of academic campus rampage similar to the Krampus celebrating the Germanic winter solstice. In a truly trickster mode, he "deconstructs" his *bêtes noires*, Michel Foucault and Jacques Derrida, using the very postmodern methods they promoted. Like all tricksters, he profanes and mocks the foundation of a cultural order, either past, present, or future, thus unveiling their transitory existence and their fragile consistency. In truly trickster mode, though, the fortune he made with these antics allows him to have the last laugh.

This is precisely what traditional circus clowns do, hence the affinity that some can feel with Peterson's fight for free speech. As we have shown in this second movement, clowns are increasingly constrained by the standards of the new liberal culture. I asked British clown David Konyot to provide some examples to include in this book. David performs with his wife who plays the role of the white face clown but does not wear the traditional makeup and attire. She embodies authority as a woman. He is the auguste of the pair with the red nose, shaggy hair, and baggy pants. "As my wife is taller than me we accentuated this so that I was the more sympathetic figure against her stature and the conflict we set up is that I want to play music and she has announced a magic trick that she wants to do, and I am just an annoying interference. Because we are both multilingual we can do a lot of 'patter gags' which is where the present PC [political correctness] and 'woke' agendas come into play. Examples from our English and German routines: During the part where she keeps taking my instruments away, I say: "Where is your sister and what have you done with Cinderella?" [implying that she is nasty and ugly like the two sisters of beautiful Cinderella]. Since my wife is herself extremely beautiful, this actually works against me but I still get a laugh. A little later I play the musical theme from the film *The Good, The Bad, and the Ugly* and, looking at the audience I say 'the good' pointing to myself and 'the bad' pointing to my wife ... and just say nothing more, again because of her good looks. It is really an inverted gag but I always got a laugh. Now, last year in Germany, both these gags got a different reaction that is difficult to describe: the children still laughed but many of the adults didn't. Many looked around to see who was laughing. We changed our routine for a more traditional approach, less verbal comedy and more old-fashioned routines which I don't like to do as they limit our possibilities of finding new 'bits' to do. This year we are in Hungary, the verbal gags are working as they should. The act is going extremely well and we are back to our 'ad-lib' style of comedy."

These remarks show how sensitive clowns are to the reactions of their audience. They perceive subtle feedback as their actions unfold, and modify their performance according to the effects their gags produce. This allows them to fine-tune their comedy in response to the perception and reception of their gags. The examples provided by David Konyot brings fodder to Jordan Peterson's argument as it demonstrates the impact of the liberal culture on freedom of speech in a popular performing art like the circus that responds by self-censorship lest it become the target of boycott or prosecution.

Figure 32 British clown David Konyot writes: "My family, like many others, have plied the circus trade for centuries. From my mother side, I descend from the Blumenfelds whose ancestry can be traced back to the mid-17th century when an Emmanuel Blumenfeld, 'Gaulker and Seiltanzer' [traveling entertainer and rope walker] brought three elephants in the town of Wuppertal. On my father side, are two British circus dynasties, the Fossetts and the Yeldings. I have over 60 years of circus experience as ringmaster, producer, and clown" (2020). Photo credit: Gályász Ferenc.

David Konyot's next example is still more telling as it connects this dynamic with animal acts:

> We do a short 'reprise' [brief interlude] with me dressed as a sea lion, all in black with flippers and a balaclava. It is a very funny gag which ends with me playing

The Blue Danube on bicycle horns. The gag is not the problem, but when the Ringmaster announces: 'Ladies and Gentlemen we now present Cedric the sea lion', there is an audible reaction in the UK, Germany, and other countries with active anti-circus animal campaigns, until they realize that it is a parody when I waddle in the ring. Then, they laugh but the original reaction is interesting. I also 'hypnotize' a giraffe that is a blow up toy, a gag from over twenty five years ago, but I get now a different reaction as well (personal communication).

These last examples are very representative of the toxic atmosphere in which traditional clowns now perform. The pressure to conform to the new standards of civil inclusivity condemns them to restrict the range of jokes and gags that had been their bread and butter for ages. We may wonder now what is the limit of permissible humor and, even, whether comedy is simply becoming impossible since it is precisely the capacity to break taboos and mock the cultural norms that is the ritualistic foundation of clowning. If clowns are expected to submit to the common decency of the day as if they were regular members of the society in which they perform, and avoid to transgress the rules, whatever they might be, they are not clowns any more. In myths, narratives, rituals, and performances, the tricksters are never politically correct because it is their sacred role not to be so. Turning away from this challenge is driving circus clowns to irrelevance and, ultimately, self-inflicted erasure from the cultural landscape, leaving space for tragic jokers like Jordan Peterson or Charlie Chaplinesque dictators to wreak havoc in our lives rather than in a circus ring.

5

Fourth Movement

Maestoso Appassionato

Bodies

Koan: *"Bodies never stop falling."*

What Is a Body?

There are several ways to look at and understand a human body. Like any other mammal, it has a visible outside and an inside that cannot be directly perceived by an observer in normal conditions. The inside is primarily a flexible tube that ingests food, digests it, and excretes the waste. Early organisms are such types of tubular slugs. In more complex animals, the tube has specialized into functional parts and has evolved auxiliary organs and appendages. It is always possible, though, to take apart this inner tunnel around which the rest of the body is organized.

However, a still more essential component of the invisible inside is the nervous system which processes information from the environment and the inner organism itself to produce appropriate responses to constant inputs. It forms the deepest aspect of the body since even the primeval tube would not be alive without a rudimentary nervous system. Contemporary technologies of imaging make it possible to visualize the whole nervous system of humans, which, from the brain to the toes, runs inside the live body. When this complex network that maps the body from the inside is represented, we are confronted with the unsettling, alien-looking organic pattern that inhabits all the other live bodies with which we interact. There may be subtle differences from body to body but this inner dynamic structure is fundamentally common to all primates, including humans, and beyond.

Figure 33 The artist's body unfolds with total grace and insistence in the revealing glare of the circus ring. Here, Romina Micheletty, heir to a long family tradition of circus acrobatics, displays her contortionist and hula hoop skill in a brief pose offered to our contemplation. Photo credit: Christian Hamel.

Figure 34 Magician Christopher Eötvös Dobritch, the scion of a famous Hungarian circus family, introduces his partner (Elizabeth Axt) whose shapely body will soon be folded and locked into a small container. Photo credit: Gályász Ferenc.

Still deeper, in the invisible inside, lurks the infinitesimal genetic code made of DNA and other nucleic acid molecules, which controls the development of both the inner and outer body as well as its biology and the hard-wired parts of its behavior. This ultimate dimension of the body only very recently came to the awareness of humans through insightful theorizing and the invention of extremely powerful microscopic imaging technology. This knowledge has opened the way to genetic engineering that makes it possible to modify some selected aspects of the body through interfering at the very source of the development

Figure 35 With charm, elegance, and cruelty, Christopher will thrust through the container four sharp swords … Photo credit: Gályász Ferenc.

Figure 36 … and will forcefully dislocate the pierced body that rests inside, before, like in the notorious Indian rope trick … Photo credit: Gályász Ferenc.

Figure 37 ... he gracefully restores the body of his victim to her full, resplendent integrity. Photo credit: Gályász Ferenc.

processes thanks to CRISPR technology that makes it possible to edit genes (Vidyasagar 2018). At the same time, it has brought to light the information script that all bodies have in common like a musical score upon which life plays its rich variations within the constraints of its diverse environments.

When we refer to the body, though, we usually mean the outer body through which we interact with each other, the live bounded surface that biologists call the phenotype, the source of beauty and the beacon of desire. We apprehend human bodies, including our own, with all our senses. It is this visible body that the circus displays, groomed to perfection in the glaring light of the ring, moving through all the possible configurations of its parts, bouncing from the ground, lifting itself and ascending ropes and straps, hanging high by a grip of the hand or a hook of the foot, letting go at times for a brief challenge to universal gravity before grasping life again at the anchor of a bar or the wrists of a partner. We must not forget, though, that behind these moving images the will and skill of the artists have relentlessly trained, rewound, and schooled the complex mechanisms that have evolved, hidden by the skin, over the deepest abyss of time.

Modes of Survival

October 1992, Nagarahole National Park, India. My friend Kikeri Narayan, an anthropologist at the Central Institute of Indian Languages in Mysuru, is taking me and my Indonesian assistant Jajang Gunawijaya to a wildlife sanctuary that straddles the states of Karnataka and Tamil Nadu in southern India. The jeep proceeds carefully through dirt roads and forest tracks. Kikeri briefs us on the forest tribes he has spent a decade studying in order to record their language and create an appropriate script to contribute to the survival of these strictly oral cultures. On the way, he mentions that these nomadic populations have to cope with the danger of wild elephants, particularly unpredictable rogue males, with which they share their territory. "Their children learn to climb trees before they can run!" I ask if he was himself in such risky situations during his stays with them. "Yes, once, I was chased by an elephant. I knew that I had to run in circle, not straight ahead because this slows down the animal. I could not climb trees as fast as the Jenu Korubas did. The elephant was persistent. Suddenly, they realized that I was in real danger to be killed. All the men came down, rushed toward the elephant and instantly built a human pyramid that was much higher than the animal and shouted as loud as they could. The elephant turned away. Size matters. They told me that it usually works but, of course, elephants are unpredictable. I am grateful to them for my life."

Humans, like most primates, are an intensely social species whose members share knowledge and cooperate to meet the challenges of survival. Coordination and combination of muscular resources enable humans to multiply the capability of single bodies to temporarily build a super organism, so to speak, to achieve a goal such as reaching something high above the ground. This technique of compounding the potential of individual bodies over several levels of altitude requires training and practice. Acrobats can astonish their audience by constructing complex human scaffoldings made of two or more bodies that rely on strength and balance to reach a state of vertical stability. Grasping hands, lifting bodies, in cooperative and synchronized collective tasks are examples of adaptive behavior developed by cultural nurturing. However, ultimately, survival is an individual affair. Before benefitting from the social comfort and security provided by the group in challenging situations, every human being has to be able to fend by themselves. We all are born and die alone.

Life on the Brink of Death

In the traditional circus, a solo trapeze artist is not someone who has merely mastered the skill of keeping their balance on a swinging bar hanging above the ground. It is someone who achieves this feat at a height that makes failures harmful, or even lethal. One of the most daring skill is definitely the specialty known as the "trapeze Washington" whose invention is credited to Keyes Washington (1830–82). It consists of an apparatus similar to static or swinging trapeze but with a heavier bar that includes in the center a small circular support on which the artist can perform a headstand in addition to other feats of balance. It is a demanding discipline in which both men and women have excelled.

In the second part of the twentieth century, the most celebrated figure in this balancing skill was Pinito Del Oro, a glamorous Spanish woman from a circus family who performed these risky tricks with charm and elegance. She fell down from the trapeze three times in her artistic career but recovered from the bone and skull fractures she suffered and, each time, returned to the ring after her convalescence.

In the later part of the century, French aerialist Gérard Edon gained international fame in the same discipline. His hands-free frontal balancing on the swinging trapeze was all the more impressive since the bar of the trapeze was six meters above the ground and close to two meters higher when the trapeze was in full swing. When he performed for a season in the then prestigious Blackpool

Tower Circus, his condition of employment implied that he should not use a safety net since, in the "special schedule" appended to his formal contract, the mention "the Management require that the act shall bring over and use a safety net" was crossed out. During his thirty-year career in this high-risk specialty, "no lunge or net" was explicitly spelled out in the formal hiring documents. Gérard Edon's remarkable career has been documented by Andrea Negrelli in an interview illustrated by video excerpts of his Washington-trapeze act. https://www.facebook.com/100008400363590/posts/2408439902779332/

As a boy, Gérard loved the circus. He was born in Paris at a time when there were, close to his home, two permanent circuses that performed most of the year. He soon decided that he would be an aerialist but his father objected and sent him instead to a professional school to become an electrician. He complied but would not so easily give up his dream. At seventeen, while working in his trade, he joined a gymnasium where some circus artists used to train and practice. He was welcome and received advice from seasoned aerialists who encouraged him to choose the trapeze Washington as a specialty that would provide him with more independence and stability than if he were to work as part of a flying trapeze team. He bought the equipment and, while being fully employed as an electrician, spent two hours a day at the gym. Three years later, in October 1960, he was offered his first contract at *Cirque Medrano* in Paris. This was the beginning of a successful international career that lasted thirty years in all the most prestigious venues. Extreme aerialists, at one point, understand that they have reached a limit. The body cannot be pushed further any longer without increasing the risk of fatal failure. At forty-eight, Gérard Edon felt he had to stop and he pursued a professional life in the circus first as ring manager, then as a professor of acrobatics at the *Centre National des Arts du Cirque* [National Center for Circus Arts], a French institution designed to train young men and women who want to embrace one of the circus disciplines.

Let it be Pinito del Oro, Gérard Edon, or other high risk acts, their daily unprotected performances secured for them a star treatment in the program, if not necessarily commensurate weekly fees. Nevertheless, the amount of money that circus producers were prepared to pay such artists was proportionate to the degree of lethal risk they were taking. This implies that putting one's own body at stake in a extreme constructed situation commanded then, as it still commands now, an economy of death underlying this kind of acrobatic performances. There is a demand for high-risk acts that are, at the same time, reliably performed but cannot entirely be foolproof if they are genuine. Even if we factor the dramatic staging of these acts that may make them appear to the audience still more dangerous than they actually are, and even if we keep in mind that these men and women are not suicidal but have acquired their remarkable skills through arduous training and regular practice, the possibility of a fall is always present to their audience as well as to their own mind. The semantic register of death is redundantly indicated by the ominous music used, the special announcements uttered with a tragic intonation often underlining the absence of a safety device, and through the very names given to these acts such as, for instance, "death defying trapeze act", "wheel of destiny", "ladder of death", or *"salto mortale"* [mortal leap]. Whether they come from a circus family like Pinito del Oro, or from mainstream society like Gérard Edon, these individuals negotiate their body in a kind of high-stake gamble while making sure that they do all that is in their power to secure a winning outcome.

In his candid interview, mentioned above, Gérard Edon recalls that he always intensely focused for five minutes, in silence, before entering the ring and that each stage in the act had been thoroughly rehearsed. There was no place for improvisation, only a move at a time, following a rigorous score. He was never oblivious of the danger that was constantly present. He needed to visually control the whole inner configuration of the tent or the premises: the context below, around, and above him, from which he was getting his cues for maintaining his perilous balance on the stable or swinging trapeze bar. This is why the performing space had to be constantly visible, even if flooded only with a dim light. As he matured technically and artistically, he felt increasingly comfortable implementing his routine, although he never took anything for granted. Standing on a bar, high above the ground, hands-free, he was always conscious that he was on the brink, on the thin edge of a cliff. No misstep was allowed.

These acts are all the more successful as the artists are young and charismatic. It seems that their charm and beauty enhance the anxiety of the audience and give rise to an indescribable awe that is probably akin to the feeling of transcendence experienced by the faithful who attended human sacrifices in ancient—and sometimes more recent—religious rituals. The skimpy outfit of Pinita Del Oro enhanced her vulnerability. The elegant, light-colored costumes of Gérard Edon conveyed an impression of defenseless innocence. These high-risk aerial acts may appeal to a deep human drive to treat death as a predator and to temporarily protect the community through sacrificing desirable prey to the grim reaper's insatiable hunger. For many spectators, the sight of beautiful young men and women straddling the fine line between life and death is unbearable and it is quite common to see some members of an audience who close their eyes or obstruct their view with their hands to avoid watching the most dangerous tricks.

Figure 38 Commenting this photo that he selected for this book, Gérard Edon mentioned that it revives for him a moment he really feels from inside. Photo credit: Serge Fleury.

Figure 39 Frontal balance on the swinging trapeze. Gérard Edon's contract with the Blackpool Tower Circus specified that no safety lunge or net were to be used in this act.

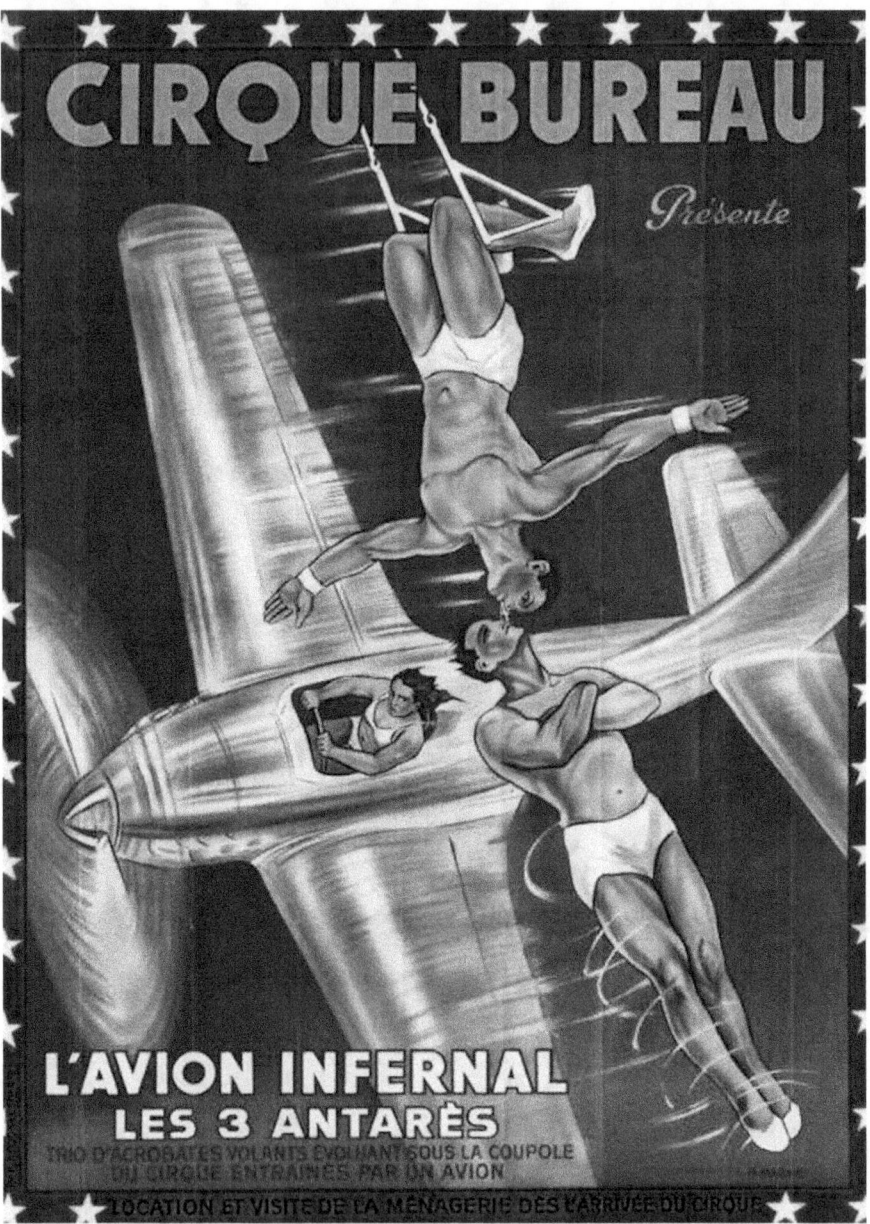

Figure 40 The Antarès. This poster of Circus Bureau from the 1940s represents the dramatic finale of an impressive aerial act. There have been two generations of this act as the children took over when the parents retired. Unfortunately, it had a tragic end when the man hanging from his teeth fell to his death in 2006 when the leather contraption he was holding in his mouth ruptured.

Epiphanies

An epiphany is a term of literary criticism for a sudden realization, a flash of recognition, in which someone or something is seen in new light.
Richard Nordquist, Humanities > English, thoughtco.com

While the possibility of death is always underlying high-risk acrobatic performances, bodies manifest themselves in the circus ring as immune to the slow decay of age, thus dramatically emphasizing the magnitude of an eventual tragic outcome. Swiss writer Charles-Ferdinand Ramuz (1878–1947) poignantly orchestrated this theme in his short essay *Le Cirque* [The Circus] of which several versions appeared between 1931 and 1936. In the latter, he describes the evening in a small town in Switzerland when the inhabitants are taking a walk after dinner before going to sleep. It is a routine activity that does not arouse much interest for the surroundings of their everyday lives. Ramuz reflects that the repetition of this ordinary ritual cannot make us forget that death will eventually happen because everybody is continuously and irreversibly aging whether they realize it or not. Suddenly, the crowd comes across a circus with blaring music, enchanting colors, and exotic banners showing wild animals in African, Asian, and Arctic landscapes. There is also a sign that stands out with a mysterious promise, in large, red luminous letters, above the entrance of the circus: MISS ANABELLA. This overload of information deeply transforms each of the individuals in the crowd and, once inside the tent, their separate identities will fuse into an unanimous, forgetful enthusiasm.

However, before taking that step into the dream, Ramuz wanders behind the circus and catches a glimpse of a woman in her small living quarters, standing in front of a mirror. She strips out of her ordinary clothes, rather automatically. Now, almost naked, she looks at her own body showing the marks of aging, with some skin stains and a somewhat flabby belly. Then, methodically, she spread a lightening makeup on her face and arms; she tightens her waist with a belt that she strained to buckle as tightly as possible; she slips into a shiny leotard; she reaches for a lipstick that she applies to her lips; she flashes a smile through the brilliant red of her mouth. The metamorphosis is complete. The spectacle can start.

Back inside the circus, Ramuz shows her glorious entry in the ring and her sublime ascension along an inclined wire under the spotlights. Once at the top, she dances as she were floating in the air, immune to gravity, smiling with a mixture of insouciance and seduction, lightly bouncing on the cable that has become almost invisible, seemingly carried by the music. Out of time, out of age, her body is youth and life itself. Below, they don't know any longer who they are, where they are. They had come in as separate bodies. Now, they feel as if they were a single, multiple being, shaken by the same fear, the same joy, at the same time. The writer himself is deeply affected by his evocation: " … and I am myself, seated at my desk, overwhelmed by a broad light that pours on me and my paper as I am writing." [… *et je suis moi-même tout envahi à ma table par une grande lumière qui vient sur moi et sur mon papier, pendant que j'écris.*]

The Body Brought into Play

Life is being on the wire. Everything else is just waiting.
Karl Wallenda, high-wire artist (1905–78).

Epiphanies come at a cost. It involves gambling one's own body. Acrobats work hard, though, to put chance on their side in this game but they know that unexpected failures of their stamina or their equipment can bring disaster at any moment. Their demeanor strives to deny their vulnerability. They paradoxically represent the very opposite of death. In his fictional account of a female high-wire dancer, Ramuz rightly points out the distance that exists between the appearance and reality of the radiant circus bodies, and exploits this perceptive intuition to reflect on the delusional enchantment of the audience. What is left out, though, is the fact that between the slowly decaying body of the acrobat—that is universally shared by all humans—and the brilliant performance on the wire, there is a full life of hard work that has molded this body into the esthetic live object he admires. Circus artists pay a heavy price for their ephemeral glory. Let us listen to my late friend, Madeleine Rousseau (1925?– 2011), who had created with her husband René, a double-trapeze act that was considered the best in this daring discipline at the time.

In the circus world of the 1950s, an act was often mentioned with awe: **The Geraldos**. *I was introduced to them by Antony Hippisley-Coxe, the author of a landmark book,* **A Seat at the Circus** *(1951), who provided me with their address in Florida at a time when I was doing research for my doctoral dissertation that required technical information about acrobatics. Born in France, René and Madeleine Rousseau had developed a stunning double trapeze act that had performed in most major European circuses under the stage name "The Geraldos"* *until they were hired by John Ringling to be featured as the stars of the aerial display in the center ring of Ringling Bros. and Barnum & Bailey Circus from 1949 until the circus ceased its traditional touring in 1953. Between 1968 and the mid-1970s I regularly corresponded with Madeleine, and I met her and René in person on several occasions in Florida as well as in Toronto whenever they happened to be part of a visiting circus show.* [This correspondence has been deposited in the archives of my circus fieldwork at the Pratt Library of Victoria University in Toronto.]

In acts in which two acrobats perform tricks high above the ground, usually one of them is the flyer and the other one the catcher. There are several figures that have in common that the flyers release the grip they hold on the bar and are caught in mid-air by their partner. In the Geraldos' act, each one was in turn catcher and flyer during 8 minutes of breathtaking various leaps from the trapeze to the other's grasp with increasing degrees of obvious risk. They were performing without being tethered and without safety net. They fell twice but, after a lengthy recovering from broken bones and shattered organs, and a full year of retraining, they returned to the ring to perform their signature act. When I met them, they had moved to still daring but less intrinsically dangerous performances. The following is an extract from a four-page text written in French by Madeleine to explain to me the details of their act. It includes some reflections about the state of mind of the artists themselves and the constraints that their art imposes on their everyday life.

"The Geraldo Act 1943–1960. Duration 8 minutes. Music: the music is sacred, mainly the waltz, as nobody ever used this music that had been composed for our act by a circus music conductor. It perfectly accompanied our movements to the point that it can be said that we were dancing while working. I studied ballet for several years before starting acrobatics, and René also had some dance training. The act includes a succession of flying tricks without any posing between them. [This means that the rhythm was intense since they were not stopping from time to time to strike a pose in order to take their breath]. *This demanded extreme concentration, well-developed reflexes, great strength and flexibility in the muscles of the abdomen and the back, resistance, and versatility of the shoulders. Note that the only fixed point was the hocks of the knees of the catcher hanging from the trapeze bar.*" [Madeleine, then, describes technically some of their tricks. All have in common that one of them releases his or her grip either from one of the two trapezes or from the hands or legs of their partner. In free fall for a fraction of second the muscular impulsion that initiates an upward movement offers an extremely brief window of opportunity for the catcher's hands to grab the flyer's wrists or insteps and prevent a crash to the ground. Figure 42 gives a more vivid impression of the actual situation as it shows Madeleine holding René's wrists just before he will release his grip and be caught by his ankles.]

"We had two terrible accidents. The first one was the worse: we were in hospital for a full year followed by a year of reeducation. Then it took us about a year to re-train for the act. We made it, though. However, after the second accident, we stopped the act and developed less risky aerial performances such as flying trapeze, exercises hanging from a revolving plane fitted with a trapeze, and, now, the wheel of death. [Madeleine pursues by listing the qualities that artists engaged in such acts must have]. 'Not to be afraid of hard work; nor of long hours of training; not to be afraid of being afraid; nor of pain; nor to be hurt again and again; nor to be a tyrant for oneself; nor to end up with nothing.' [...] This demands self-discipline: no alcohol; no smoking; no tea; no excess of any kind; control of the diet to optimize one's weight, reflexes, and strength; avoiding chatting too much, political or other discussions that distract from the necessary concentration and scatter one's energy."

[The text also includes some notes on the counterpart of the artists: the spectators]. "After this endless struggle with oneself and moments of despair when things seem hopelessly impossible, suddenly it works! Then, [the challenge is] to get the public, to hold the public, to capture its emotions, its attention. This is as exhausting as developing a new trick. While we work, we feel the audience. If we fail to arouse their interest, to bring them pleasure, to cause fear and anxiety in them, our motivation slackens and abandons us. We lose the ground upon which rests our existence as artists. Sometimes, we find it difficult to communicate with the audience because it happens that we are tired or depressed, or not up to our best."

Indeed, both psychologically and economically, performers cannot be conceived independently from their spectators. These are the two faces of a single and same phenomenon, like the recto and verso of a piece of paper and, in the traditional circus, this relationship is deeper than meets the eyes. First, it involves physiological echoing, so to speak, in as much as the mirror neurons of the spectators play out in response to the movements of the acrobats in the context of the unstable situation they have created; then, imaginary anticipation of the possible outcome that entails unbearable uncertainty; and, finally, a deep empathy mixed with an underlying feeling of guilt since the performance is, in some manner, commissioned by the public for their own pleasure and excitement. The best demonstration of this unique experience that recurs at irregular intervals in the annual cycles of the visits of traditional circuses is to compare it with the acrobatic performances produced by the contemporary circus that mostly eschews high-risk disciplines and features instead the athletic prowess of the performers by using lower trapezes and other apparatuses, or ensuring the safety of their artists with lunges and inflatable ground mattresses. The skills and esthetic value of the performers are foregrounded but there is a marked difference with the emotional involvement that characterizes the participation in a ritual during which humans put their own life on the line. Note that I am not arguing here whether this is ethical or legal for individuals to engage in such potentially self-harming behavior, nor for producers to feature and advertise this kind of death-defying acts. It is a fact that first must be recorded since it is a constant element of the traditional circuses to promote their spectacles through emphasizing the extreme danger to which some of their performers expose themselves. Fundamentally, aerialists, like any other circus artists, are performing to earn a living, not to stage a public suicide. Nevertheless, reality is more ambiguous as dangerous acts betray, to the least, a fascination with death on the part of both the artists and the public that consistently yields to this attraction and sustains its economics. This issue came to the fore in March 2018 when a French acrobat, Yann Arnaud, who had been hired by *Cirque du Soleil*, lost his grip and fell to his death during a performance in Tampa, Florida. *The Guardian* (March 26, 2018) quoted a comment that Arnaud had added to a photo of himself gripping the strap he had posted on Instagram: "After so much work and training and staging, our strap duo is finally in the show tonight. It is time to go for it." The reporter, Simon Usborne, expectedly discusses the ethical issue that nobody can fail to raise when confronted by such a tragedy. From an interview with the founder of the British Zippo Circus, Martin Burton, Usborne extracts the following: "Circus is a funny old beast, because people want to be excited and thrilled, but they definitely don't want to see an accident, but people also want to feel that they might see an accident, so we have to walk a fairly fine line between, well, acting and perceived danger." The report concludes with quoting the website through which a Brazilian aerialist advertises his act: "Swings and walks upside down 30 feet above the audience with no safety nets or wires."

Greatness and Misery of Acrobats' Bodies

Nowadays, when I happen to mention "The Geraldos" among circus fans, I draw a blank. Only some rare survivors who were their contemporaries remember their fame. Nobody, though, can describe in any technical detail the tricks that established their stardom. They worked before the era of the intense

Figure 41 René et Madeleine Rousseau, "The Geraldos," ca. 1950. Author's collection. Photo credit: H. D. Coghlan.

technological visual culture that spun a flood of videos. Filming existed but was not yet democratized to the extent it is today. Only exceptional circumstances such as the needs for a documentary, could have justified the complex challenge of bringing up a movie camera to their level above the ground and catching their movements at the right angles without interfering with their performance. However, there are some photographs and some line drawings such as the one that they had printed on the right lower corner of the paper they used for their correspondence that bear witness to their past achievements. Since then, other acrobats have produced stunning acts that, in turn, have been forgotten. Circus glories are fast erased from the collective memory. Their ephemeral beauty and

Figure 42 The Geraldos: High above the ground, without a safety net, catching insteps to insteps to stop the fall. Photo credit: Carl H. "POP" Haussman.

triumph are blown away by new wonders and the natural decay of oblivion. They are sacrificed to the ruinous power of time. Why, then, do some people choose this way of life?

For many acrobats, this is not really a choice. Children born in circus families are trained very early in the basics of acrobatics. Some of my Facebook friends who own family circuses readily post videos showing the first attempts at developing in their young children a good sense of balance or their first steps in juggling skills. Their spectacles are as much as possible based on the artistic resources of the family or, at times, the extended family. Their livelihood is sustained by a subsistence economy as used to be the case

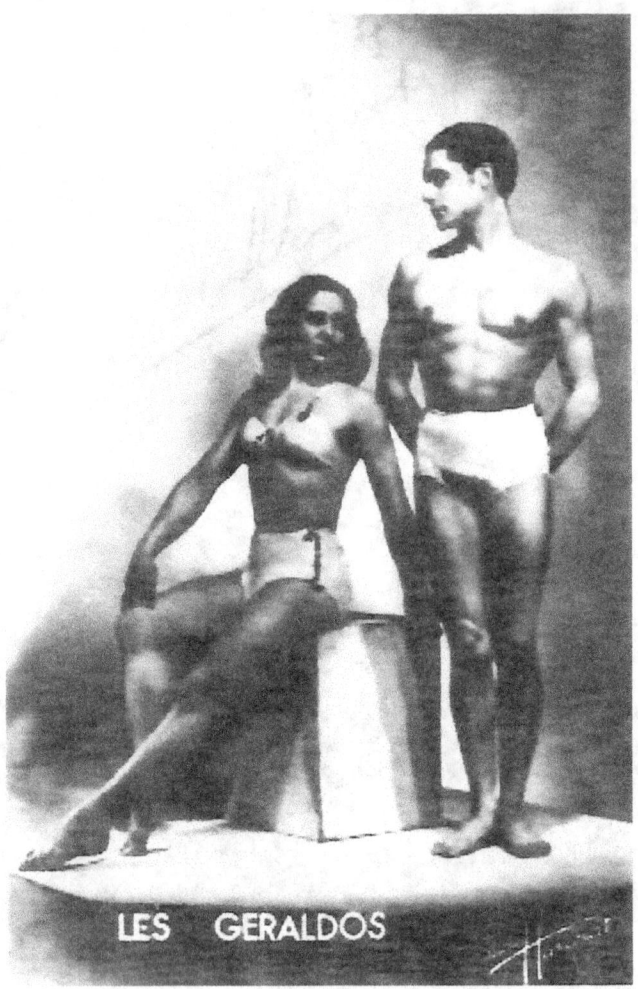

Figure 43 *Les Geraldos*, early promotional flyer. Author's archives.

for small, traditional farmers who could produce all that was needed from wheat to meat, to survive through the whole year when there was no dramatic drought or flooding. Most had to pay their share to the owners of the land if they did not themselves possess the fields they were toiling. Similarly, small circuses must be able to produce shows that justify the admission price by relying on the skills of the family. They often also pay a percentage of their income for the right to use a trade name more famous that their own, that ensures some degree of visibility and profitability to their presence. They borrow value from a symbolic capital owned by the descendants of families that have been very successful in the circus trade and could retire comfortably. The programs these families offer must be diverse and substantial through a mixture of acrobatics, clowning, and animal training. The latter is essential to their business because animals provide both exotic attraction and performance time even if they are in limited number and display only rudimentary tricks. The bulk of the show, though, comes from the family talents. It is not unusual that an athletic young man, like for instance the Czech Hynek Navratil Jr. from *Circus Humberto*, who is one of the sons of the owner, presents a lion act, assists his father in a bear act, displays his strength in hand balancing, and adds to the program his juggling and antipodist skills. Some circus-born artists further develop their exceptional talents in a particular discipline to become international stars through intensive and constant training, as was the case for Pinita del Oro who was mentioned above. However, the majority of them fulfill a succession of roles along the curve of their life, from demanding acrobatics in their youth to horse and other animal training, and clowning as age takes its toll on their joints, muscles, and reflexes. Circus is indeed hard work and a day-to-day struggle with economic, social, and psychological challenges rife with uncertainties, but the pain is usually mitigated by the mutual support that characterizes family units and the wider network of other families to which they are related. There is indeed a strong tendency to endogamy in the traditional circus population, resulting in reliable social bonds among several generations of first and second cousins, and beyond. There are, of course, like everywhere else, occasional family feuds and lasting enmity between groups, but as an ethnic minority constantly challenged by mainstream society, circus folks are usually comforted by a remarkable degree of solidarity. The crowd that weddings and funerals famously attract bears witness to this far-reaching family-based social web.

Negotiating One's Own Body: Benefit-to-Cost Ratio

No doubt there are risks that we would rather not run but that we undertake in order to gain other benefits.
Mary Douglas and Paul Wildavsky, Risk and Culture, 1982: 18

This kind of life, though, attracts outsiders who are prepared to submit their body to the lengthy and strenuous discipline that will allow them to become circus acrobats. While it is easy to understand this process in the case of those who are born in the circus, the choice deliberately made by individuals to engage in this way of life raises several questions. Gypsy and other Traveller children have no choice but to contribute to the family's survival through acquiring early appropriate skills and developing them according to their particular talents. Traditionally, and still in some cases nowadays, their lack of formal education deprives them from other opportunities. By contrast, the young people who decide to join the circus as performers in spite of having received a regular education are willing to trade a more or less secure existence for a life of uncertainty. Not only will they relentlessly put their body in jeopardy but they also will confront economic challenges. It is one thing to produce a decent acrobatic performance; it is another thing to secure a continuing stream of contracts with circuses and other spectacles that will provide a sufficient income.

A way to theorize this phenomenon is to consider that the fit body and mind of a young worker is, from an economic point of view, their only asset. Most members of the working class, both blue- and white-collar employees, alienate this asset by submitting it to the demands of the market economy in exchange for a more or less predictable life while abandoning to the capitalist the added value they create through their work. By contrast, an acrobatic career may be perceived as a way to escape this social condition by exploiting one's own body as a private capital and making it produce an extra value that will meet the demands of the entertainment industry but will command a better income. This is, though, a very competitive world and the incentive to push the acrobatic performance to an extreme is overwhelming. It amounts to a heroic re-appropriation of one's own body that is ostensibly displayed for social recognition, something that is denied to workers because all the credit for their production goes to the capitalist and its trade marks. In the circus, even if the financial profit mostly goes to the owner, at least the artists can enjoy the public expression of a deep appreciation. This feedback eventually increases the market value of the act and can command fees that are commensurate with the degree of spectacular risks taken by the artists. In addition, the time frame is an important factor. An acrobatic act is relatively shortlived because the body cannot be exploited indefinitely and accidents may always bring the act to temporary or permanent closure. Many outstanding acrobats, whether circus-born or outsiders, enjoy comfortable retirement in properties acquired thanks to their courage and talents.

Bodies Unbound

January 18, 2020, Monte Carlo, 44th International Circus Festival. As I snake my way through the crowd around the circus lot during an intermission, I bump into Alexander Lichner. We have been friends on Facebook for a while but I never had an opportunity to meet him in person. His trapeze act is remarkable from both the acrobatic and esthetic points of view. His charismatic personality shines through his energetic performance from the moment he starts climbing the rope that connects the ground level to his high-hanging trapeze. He punctuates his vigorous ascension with successive brief pauses marked by a gesture and glance toward the audience until he reaches the bar. Even if he uses a safety lunge for one of his most dangerous tricks—Alex has a lovely family and is not suicidal— his routine is daringly stunning, notably when he hangs by his heels, without the lunge, from the trapeze in full swing. As I freeze in front of him, he recognizes someone who always "likes" his posts. Our brief conversation is hurried and intense. We talk about his recent, unusual brief tenure as co-director of the Swiss Circus Royal—"That was a flop! I lost big in that short venture!" I am curious to know whether he comes from a circus family. "Yes, but they have lost interest in the business." The tone is almost resentful. "But my wife is a Quiros!"—the intonation is now proud. "They have a circus in Spain. I love the circus! There is nothing like that!" He radiates energy and passion. I hesitate to ask for a selfie with him. His phone rings. Too late. Alex moves away to answer the call. In the past, I have often admired the high-wire act of the Quiros who have performed in many shows all over the world.

*May 2, 2020. A new post by Alex on Facebook: a splendid photo of himself hanging by his heels from the swinging trapeze. His comment: "Live on the limit and enjoy your life because not everyone is lucky enough **to be circus**. Live on the limit and enjoy your life because not everybody is so lucky like circus people"* [my emphasis].

I have witnessed this enthusiasm in many young men and women, now in their twenties, who have been born in circus families and are driven by the same passion as well as a deep sense of being the proud heirs to a long tradition that has been running in their families for countless generations. Facebook provides an abundance of visual evidence of the continuity of body techniques that are taught by parents to their children as soon as it is safe to start training. The genetic filiation provides a lining, so to speak, to the cultural lineage that creates the reproduction of a distinct *habitus* that is added to the biological functions of the body and becomes existential rather than being a simple competence. The most appropriate comparison to understand this phenomenon of "being circus" as Alexander Lichner says, is the Japanese tradition of Kabuki actors.

This formal tradition is much more recent than the millennia-long uninterrupted transmission from generation to generation of the acrobatic skills that are the basis of the circus art and trade. The Japanese guild of actors, called *Naritaya*, was founded in the seventeenth century by Ichikawa Danjuro [http://www.naritaya.jp/English] The current, high-profile star of the Kabuki theater is Ichikawa Ebizo XI [http://www.kabuki21.com/ebizo11.php]. This is a stage name that perpetuates the dynastic formality of these popular actors whose performances embody ritualistic elements. Like jugglers or wire walkers, they accomplish their feats along recurring traditional patterns with the added value of their own style and personality. They feel existentially committed to "being" the incarnation of their roles that must be acquired through a demanding training both vocal, as they must produce the typical vocalizations of the Kabuki genre, and physical, since they must follow the rigorous codified demeanor required by their acting that includes quasi-acrobatic poses and movement akin to martial art as well as the credible impersonations of female characters. In April 2020, a documentary presented an interview with Ichikawa Ebizo during which the actor introduced his own young son, already costumed as a Kabuki actor and eagerly performing an appropriate role, as the one destined to succeed him.

Unexpected circumstances made Kabuki and circus acrobatics intriguingly overlap at the 44th International Circus Festival of Monte Carlo in the staging of a stunning Icarian act by the Martinez Brothers. The two young acrobats introduced their performance dressed as Samurais and manipulated Japanese swords for a brief moment until they emerged from their heavy traditional costumes of the type worn by Kabuki actors to appear in their functional, colorful leotards and start their Icarian tricks on the trinka. This brilliant act earned a well-deserved Golden Clown prize. One may wonder, though, how the Kabuki theme happened to merge seamlessly with the circus in this unique circumstance. The two acrobats are half-brothers, sons of a Hispanic–Japanese couple. Their actual names are Alan David Martinez and Arashi Kofukada. Obviously, the staging of their act surprisingly reveals an underlying compatibility between two distant cultural institutions on the deep level of the existential engagement of their performers. It also shows that the circus is more ruled by ritual codes than we usually think because we take for granted the formality of its performances and the genealogies that sustain this art.

But there is more. In the circus culture, like in the Kabuki tradition, there is a similar use of stage names that are carried from generation to generation—these names may be actual patronyms but have often been coined in view of various considerations. This behavior implies a dedication to their performing identity along a lineage that transcends their individuality. For example, the clown Pipo (Gustave Joseph Sosman 1901–70) had been trained by his uncle, Tony Sosman, and became an iconic embodiment of the traditional European white-face clown. A photograph of the early 1950s shows him in the company of his two-year-old son, Philippe (born in 1949), with a makeup and costume identical to the one worn by his father. Later, after the latter's death, Philippe became a new Pipo who performed like his father did with remarkable devotion to "being circus"—a stance also taken years later by Alex Lichner as we saw above—as Pipo insists in an interview with anthropologists Kenneth Little (1991). In the same vein, the appearance and demeanor of the celebrated Charlie Cairoli (1917–79) was perpetuated by his son who performed under the same name after his father's death.

A similar kind of filiation is found in some juggling and acrobatics dynasties. For instance, Bela Kremo (1911–79), a Swiss artist, presented his iconic hat and cigar boxes juggling act with his son Kris Kremo, born in 1951. The latter is now performing the same double act with his own son, Harrison, born in 1999. Another example, among many others, is found with the "Ferreri" dynasty, a stage name that hails back at least three generations of Spanish artists on the father's side and a much longer legacy of German circus folks, the Bueglers, on the mother's side. Miguel Ferreri enjoyed a successful international career as a low-wire acrobat, performing the whole traditional repertory on a tight cable: sword dancing, jumping, rope skipping, clearing obstacles, flic flac, and backward and frontward somersaults in the Hispanic style. His son Steven earned a Bronze prize in the same specialty as his father at the New Generation Monte Carlo Circus Festival in 2020.

I have been friend on Facebook with Steven and his elder brother Michael, a brilliant fast juggler who has won many distinguished prizes in various competitions during the last decade, including a "silver clown" in the Monte Carlo Festival. Both Michael and Steven are active Facebook fans and regularly post snapshots and videos of their training sessions and performances. For several years, I have been able to follow step by step the progress of Steven on the wire when the family was traveling with an American circus in California. For long, Steven exercised under the close watch of his father who was holding the lunge that would prevent dangerous falls. There are countless failures during that stage. A year later Steven was a part of the program at Circus Vargas, performing the basic tricks he had mastered, with his father standing nearby, ready to break a loss of balance and giving him discreet encouragements and advices. Week after week, it was like witnessing the slow blooming of a flower. Steven gained in assurance and poise. There were fewer and fewer missteps. His Monte Carlo performance was technically flawless, albeit a bit strained. Now, in the midst of the Covid-19 crisis, all plans for the season have been cancelled. The family is sheltering in their property in Seville. Regular videos keep appearing on Facebook: Michael pushes to new limits the number of balls he juggles and the fastness with which he throws and catches them. Steven intensely practices more difficult leaps and jumps on a wire that has been lowered closer to the ground for practicing. His father is often around, though, providing counseling. His Facebook friends, mostly other circus young men and women, or aunts and uncles, cousins, and colleagues sometimes jokingly comment with emojis or sarcasms when an awkward failure occurs, but also, frequently, with congratulations and heartfelt encouragements. The international act that will emerge eventually from this relentless training will have been midwifed not only through his own persistence and dedication but also by the knowledgeable and caring attention of his, and the circus's extended family. I remember with

Figure 44 Alexander Lichner slowly ascends the rope to reach his trapeze with strength, poise, and elegance. Photo credit: Nuria Torralvo Quiros.

Figure 45 Dramatic moment: the audience cannot fail to empathize with this precarious challenge to gravity. Photo credit: Nuria Torralvo Quiros.

emotion the photo that Michael Ferreri posted, a few years ago, on his way to Germany to compete in a young artists' festival: he was proudly traveling there with his grandmother Buegler. This is the kind of temporal depth and moral support that the outsiders who learn an acrobatic skill in the so-called circus schools and colleges will always lack.

The Visceral Circus: Bodies of Fear and Desire

Acrobats, with various degrees of innocence or contrivance, cater to the erotic pleasure of the eyes. There are relatively rare cases in which female or male

Figure 46 "Like an angel taking his flight," Alexander Lichner remains secured to the bar of the swinging trapeze by the sheer muscular contraction of his insteps. Photo credit: Nuria Torralvo Quiros.

artists stage their act with a deliberate intention to provoke sexual desire in their audience, but, in general, such behavior is not foregrounded in acrobatic performances unless they play for a cabaret audience. However, the inherently seducing behavior of circus acrobats is an implied part of their *habitus,* that is, the way in which they have grown up in a culture that aims at displaying their supremely fit bodies as the currency of their trade. It is most often a passive seduction in the sense that they abstain from excessive erotic provocations. However, they definitely work into their physical feats of balance, strength, and contortion appeals to the natural interest of humans for arousing visual experience. It suffices to compare the strictly functional practices in particular acrobatic skills that are very similar to any athletic training, with the staged versions of these specialties to perceive the added value in the latter, produced by the makeup and the usually minimal covering of the body with tight garments that reveal much skin and enhance curvatures and bulges. Smiles, glances, eye contacts, and gestures that are indiscriminately broadcast toward the public during the performance and while artists briefly pause to acknowledge applause and catch their breath, can at times be interpreted by individual spectators as aimed at them personally—and occasionally they are—thus arousing a deeper erotic or romantic interest. Circus posters tend to display scantily dressed iconic

Figure 47 A moment of triumph: Alexander Lichner takes a deserved heroic pose for the posterity. Photo credit: Nuria Torralvo Quiros.

female bodies in enticing postures and superbly fit males, some portrayed as movie heartthrobs, that may bias the actual perception of the real performers and color the memories of them we treasure. They are, though, more often than not in real life young men and women radiating unbridled seduction.

From the point of view of the audience, there are two parallel streams of attention in front of the unfolding of an acrobatic act: on the one hand, the physical and artistic skill that succeed in meeting a daunting challenge; and, on the other hand, the appreciation of the shapely bodies and individual personalities that evoke sensuality in the glare of the spotlight and the entrainment of the music.

Acrobatics bend, fold, stretch, and almost torture bodies in a way that reveals all facets of the skin that tightly envelops complex biological designs that call for

Figure 48 Back on earth, between the shows, Alexander teaches his daughter Denise how to master handstand balancing, a staple of the acrobatic art, under the loving gaze of his wife, Nuria Torralvo Quiros, the photographer. Photo credit: Nuria Torralvo Quiros.

a kind of festive, uncensored visual consumption. It amounts to a willful self-immolation of the artists to the secret intimate fantasies of their audience.

There is a primal subtext under the formality of acrobatic performances, akin to the threatening presence of the unsparing wilderness in trained predators, and the cosmic chaos lurking in the clowns' irrational demeanors. These are the three fundamental dimensions of the multisensory experience that unfolds in the very midst of the audience with the rigor and solemnity of a religious ritual that constantly alludes to the chance accomplishment of a human sacrifice.

A powerful circus icon that evokes the ultimate vulnerability of the human body is often staged in wild animal acts in which a scantily dressed male or female trainer confronts predators in the steel arena. A trick that only a few individuals can achieve consists of lying down in the sawdust at the center of the ring and prompting some lions to approach and crouch over them until a signal sends them back to their pedestals. In a previous book, I have described in detail the dramatic performance of the charismatic Henri Dantès (Bouissac 2012: 132) who completed his lion act at the fast pace of seven minutes, rather than the mistaken seventeen minutes that are indicated in that book. The highlight of the act was the lying down episode involving five male lions that were taking position in the roaring fighting mode while the young man was helplessly nailed to the ground by the sheer weight of the first two animals that lay upon his abdomen and chest. In this position, he was provoking the next ones with cracks of his whip to advance toward his body. As an assistant to Dantès for several months I can bear witness to the visceral impact that this feat had on the audience. During the intermission, he was regularly mobbed by female admirers, but his act had a wider appeal and still nowadays belongs to the circus's golden legend. Nobody has ever repeated it with the same bravado and esthetic perfection. Blood was often spilled during this act as Dantès was famous for taking risks and, defiantly, working too close to the lions.

However, even when staging routines are not deliberately geared toward the apparent threshold of death, wild animal trainers are as exposed to accidents as bold aerialists. In 1990, Catherine Blankard, a young woman who was performing in a skimpy outfit with lions at the Bouglione circus, found herself in a dangerous situation during the filming of an episode for an American television chain that featured her act. The six lions she was driving through their paces suddenly started a brawl and ended up fighting in earnest for dominance. This is a dreaded unpredictable situation. The Bouglione brothers were present outside the cage and immediately instructed her not to panic and to calmly walk backward toward the exit while they were distracting the animals with the water cannons that are always in standby close to the ring. Nowhere is the vulnerability of the human body more palpable than in the close proximity of predators endowed with powerful killing tools when they get out of control and switch to the wildest side of their nature. The body of the predators' trainer is all the more fascinating as it straddles the raw side of nature and the mastery of culture. It has to be part beast and part human. A powerful erotic dimension emerges from this infinitesimal cleft. It often calls for passionate, total surrender.

Circus folks are keenly aware of their appeal and often, during their act, scan the audience in search of promising eye contacts. This, of course, presupposes that the dimensions of the premises or the tent enable a sufficient degree of relative visual proximity with the spectators seated in the first rows. It is not the case, though, when performances take place in large-capacity big tops or in huge sports arenas. In industrial circuses such as the famed *Cirque du Soleil*, the distance of even the most expensive seats from the artists precludes the possibility of casting or catching a glance.

This was not the case in the small traditional circus that David Conway visited with a friend on a Sunday evening, some sixty years ago, in a suburb of Rennes in Brittany. He was then a university student from Wales who had been sent to France for both teaching English in a local boys' school and practicing at the same time the French language he was learning. Another student from the UK, a girl named Joan, had been assigned to another, nearby institution. In his candid autobiography (Conway 2020), David recounts that as they both were exploring the regional countryside during a weekend, they came across some circus posters. Since as long as he can remember, David was in love with the circus, the opportunity that presented itself could not be missed and he bought two first-row seats. The circus was a bit shabby but it was real, with horse smells, lions' roaring coming from the backstage, and a small live band. The first item in the program, after the pompous welcoming of the ring master, was the cage act, featuring "forest-bred lions". David, then, realized that he and his friend were the only people in the most expensive places, so close to the ringside that they almost could touch it. The lions were let in, followed by their "indomitable trainer, black-haired and handsome, bare chested and studiously morose." While the tricks of the lions and lionesses went on, David noticed the man "squeezed into red tights, with black leather belt and golden boots." At the end, there was applause and fanfare, but Joan leaned and whispered to her friend: "Was he staring at you or at me?"

David had not noticed as he had been focusing "on the forest-bred lions […] and on the crimson tights". At the intermission, he rushed to visit the zoo and came across Luca, the trainer, who welcomed him with a broad, engaging smile. After the show, as soon as the taxi had dropped Joan back to her lodging in the city, David prompted the driver to take him back to the circus. Thus started David's first love affair. For the next six months, until academic duties called him back to England, he shared his life between the school and the circus that kept touring the region.

Technological Evolution and the Perception of Risk

Keeping one's balance while dancing and somersaulting on a rope or on a thin braided cable anchored to two fixed posts and strained by a crank to the optimal degree above the ground is a challenge that no untrained person could do without promptly falling. Spectators watching an acrobat performing such a feat can be observed tightening their muscles in synchrony with the artist, mainly when the chances of a fall are apparently higher, and, once again, let us keep in mind that the younger the acrobats are, the more intense the degree of empathy. The spectators' anxiety is often increased by skillfully staged failures that seem to be genuine. The rhetoric of lethal danger is a part of the performance. In Catholic and Orthodox cultures, artists sometimes make the sign of the cross before "attempting" the most perilous tricks. Some in the audience hold their breath until the acrobat safely lands on the wire after a daring somersault. Some others, as it is frequently observed, cannot stand the stress of watching and close their eyes or raise their hand to block the view. We all have an intimate knowledge of the risks of losing our balance. Walking upright is something we had to learn early in our life and negotiating gravity is a constant imperative that does not allow errors. When our neuromuscular system ages, we often need to use a cane to provide us with an expanded basis of support.

The body-to-body empathy we experience while watching a risky acrobatic act has been explained in recent decades by some neuroscientists who demonstrated that primates have specific neurons in the frontal cortex of their brains that fire both when they perform an intended movement and when they perceive this same movement executed by someone else (Marsh 2012). Although the evidence supporting the early forms of this claim have been questioned on the ground that more that single neurons are involved in such processes, the essentials of the theory has been shown to hold. Naturally, we don't need a scientific proof to intuitively know that our body resonates, so to speak, with other human bodies in action. The process of entrainment is ever present in social groups in which individuals tune their movements to one another, let it be dance, sport, protest march, or warfare. A traditional circus's live performance is a crucible of synergy and empathy. The physical displays of extreme strength and balance are not happening on the separate, parallel space of a stage or a screen but in the very midst of the enveloping audience that vibrates in synchrony with transformative power. It creates a wave that surges and reaches a climax before crashing in tumultuous applause.

In contemporary cultures, though, several social and technological changes are undermining the experiential and ritualistic quality of the traditional circus's acrobatic performances. At least three factors are responsible for this transformation. The first is the democratization of acrobatics through the teaching of circus schools. The second is the rise of information technology and the spread of virtual reality as a common mode of perceptual experience. The third, that derives from the latter, is the abundance of readily accessible erotic visual stimulations.

First, the democratization of acrobatics has contributed to trivialize the magic of the circus. When, in the mid-twentieth century, the traditional circus started to lose some of its popular appeal with the competition of powerful mass media, it nevertheless remained attractive as a fantasized mode of life for many youngsters. Under economic pressure, some circus families decided to cash on this fad by creating basic training programs in several acrobatic specialties. This had two advantages: on the one hand, the fees they charged became a needed financial compensation for their declining business income; on the other hand, those of their "students" who had acquired a reasonable level of acrobatic proficiency provided a cheap labor force to beef up their spectacles. They were willing captives of their fascination for the circus. However, the circus owners were making sure that they would not transmit the most coveted training secrets of their trade and thus create true competition through developing more expensive talents. A seasoned acrobat who had been hired by one of these circus families as a "professor" told me that he once was scolded by the head of the company when they discovered that he was taking his task too seriously and was aiming at perfecting the tricks of some gifted students as if they were his own children. He was told: "Don't teach that! Keep it for ourselves!" To understand this reaction, we must remember that, for circus folks, the ancestral knowledge to acquire these body skills is often the only asset that has helped them survive for generations in a hostile world.

This pedagogical dynamic took a more dangerous turn for the traditional circus when state-sponsored circus schools became a part of the educational landscape in many countries. The training became more rational and inclusive, accompanied by medical monitoring, and capped by esthetic norms that eschewed the sensationalist style of traditional circus performances. A few students from these schools achieved high degrees of acrobatic proficiency and succeeded in making decent careers as circus artists. Many decided to create their own "circus" companies providing strictly acrobatic programs that were characterized by a blend of athletic prowess and choreographic perfection, at times with a touch of innocuous comic interludes. Most of these "new circuses" or so-called "contemporary circuses" were categorized as highbrow "cultural activities" and were generally performing on stage. Many started touring the world thanks to state subsidies for the sake of cultural politics as they could not sustain themselves through admission fees alone. They created innovative names to brand their business and they catered mostly to elitist audiences. Their public was overlapping with concert and ballet rather than with the actual circuses with which they aimed to compete by exploiting the symbolic capital of the word "circus". They foregrounded their difference through promotional strategies markedly different from the traditional circus they were claiming to reinvent and replace. They often framed their performances within narratives that were making up for the lack of the traditional dynamics and excitement of the Gypsy circuses and raised their status to quasi-literary levels. They often blended creative music and poetry with acrobatics. The formal perfection of their body technique was foregrounded and secured by safety devices aimed at excluding the possibility of crippling or mortal accidents.

Another staging strategy that is frequently observed in the contemporary acrobatic circus is the duplication or even multiplication of identical acts in the arena. It is based on the mistaken assumption that a breathtaking aerial or juggling act will be doubly more effective if it is performed by two or more individual artists. Sometimes, this move is designed to fill more visual space when a show is presented in a huge arena. This kind of staging undermines the meaning of the acts that lose their uniqueness and, by the same token, their ritualistic significance. If two or more people can do the same thing, whatever the apparent or real difficulty may be, it ensues a commensurate trivialization and devaluation of these achievements in the eyes of the audience.

In the minds of a large segment of the population the meaning of the word "circus" has now become associated with this kind of performance that is considered up to the standards of a civilization that eschews the use of wild animals and the staging of extreme situations in live spectacles. As I raised this issue recently with an archaeologist friend of mine, I received symptomatic comments of the current attitude toward the traditional circus. After questioning the justification of the apparently pessimistic title of my book on the ground that he had recently witnessed in Florida a show that was fun to watch, he added: "The kids were happy with goats, no need for lions. Performances were good, close to ballet and gymnastics, but with a flair for showing off, just a few intense or very beautiful moments rather than whole artistic performances. The artists were also either based on the new fixed tent or having a set schedule, and not traveling around.

No number was overhyped or extreme, but everything worked. If you think of the circus as a set of performances and exhibitions for fun, then the circus is still alive. The taste of people about what is fun has changed, that's all. [...] I am happy to see that the circus not only survives, but thrives without caged animals, because I could not stand that and for many years I simply refused to go and watch any circus performances because of that." (Andrea Vianello, 2020, personal communication).

The traditional circus is confronted by the emergence of a new genre that exploits some of its ancestral resources, appropriates selectively its body techniques, and captures its symbolic capital. For the new generations which never had an opportunity to experience the magic of the traditional circus and was brought up in the belief that the presence of trained animals tainted its cultural legitimacy and human integrity, the semantics of the circus has lost its capacity to generate meaningful emotions and has flattened itself, so to speak, as a form of theater devoid of all sense of heroism and tragic uncertainty as Vianello's comments quoted above vividly suggest.

The second factor that undermined the relevance of the traditional circus acrobatics is the development of technologies that impacted both the style of performances and the visual experience of the spectators. Ground and horseback acrobatics have not been affected but aerial specialties have been staged increasingly, in the new industrial circus, with the help of mechanical and electronic devices aimed at speeding up the development of some acts and at enhancing materially their grand spectacular effects. When artists are swiftly lifted from the ground to their trapeze through a system of cables and pulleys instead of climbing a rope or a rope ladder, a slight sense of artificiality is inserted into the performance itself. Similarly, the trapezes or straps can be lowered to ground level so that acrobats can reach them by stepping forward without the efforts of gaining altitude through the muscular strength and rhythmic pulse of their arms, and the whole apparatus is then made to ascend by people pulling the cables or through an electronic command. In those cases, the needed mechanical tools are hidden backstage or unobtrusively located outside the reach of the spotlights, thus further erasing the human dimension of the event. This provides an illusion of dreamlike unreality and saves both time and effort, but it skips an important stage of the act: the physical conquest of gravity through muscular strength and moral determination.

In modern industrial and state circuses, great use is made of these devices that tend to convey a sense of bodily weightlessness akin to the movements that are visually generated by information technology in video games, animation films, and popular movies. Flying superheroes saturate contemporary visual cultures, including documentaries showing astronauts floating in zero-gravity environments. As a consequence, it is probable that the quasi-constant presence in the media of these virtual human icons that appear to be immune to the danger of falling desensitizes, or at least biases, the visual perception system that interfaces, through the brain's mirror neurons, with the experience of the weighty body in real space. This amplifies, perhaps a step too far, the circus rhetoric that, through words and images, traditionally makes use of aerial metaphors to propel the acrobats in the realm of dream and magic. In the performances themselves, the long background of efforts, anxieties, and failures during the training are as much as possible glossed over thanks to the choreography, the music, and the smiles that signal pleasure and facility.

The familiarity of the audience with virtual reality further contributes to defuse the acrobats' power of wonderment that used to border sheer magic. Contemporary humans live in a hybrid space that blends virtual and real dimensions, in which the apparent lightness or weightlessness of acrobats do not create the same wonderment than it did many generations ago when the suspicion of magical power was haunting popular consciousness. The actual "flying part" of a modern "flying trapeze" act is a triumph of human courage and ingenuity but it lasts a mere fraction of a second. The direct visual experience of bodies literally within the jaws of gravity is breathtaking, even if the presence of a safety net tempers the fear of witnessing a fatal accident. However, it has become frequent that these movements are filmed and played back in slow motion, thus allowing a better appreciation of the skill and esthetic of these feats while further contributing to the virtual mode of apprehension of an action deprived of the primal uncertainty that is inherent in its live, actual time performance. Furthermore, artists are now prone to advertise their acts by posting videos of their best performances in social media, thus conveying the impression of a constant safe outcome. The same is true of high- or low-wire walking acts that consistently trigger anxiety in their audience. When electronic versions of these acts can be contemplated, their existential dimension and ritualistic values vanish. Then, there always can be the suspicion of image manipulation.

In June 2017, as I was preparing a conference paper on the semiotics of hybrid spaces, a neighbor who was running a virtual reality laboratory, invited me to get a direct experience and kindly led me through a recording session in his studio. I was asked to stand within an octagonal tower while dozens of micro cameras were flashing around me. This process eventually produced an avatar of myself to which various algorithms could be applied. One of the end results turned out to be a surprising video of myself performing a flawless somersault. This technology is now commonly used in the making of fantasy films that feature celebrity actors and actresses leaping over abysses and jumping to the top of high-rises. Such stunning, albeit illusory, imagery surreptitiously defines new perceptual standards of human dynamic capability.

Before electric lighting was introduced in the staging of circus performance, nocturnal displays of wire walking could verge on the supernatural. It is probable that early shamans used the same techniques to convincingly persuade their devotees that they were ascending to successive levels of heavenly realms through the mere force of their mystical power. Later nomadic entertainers perpetuated this skill to establish their credentials as magicians. Much later, the audiences in fairgrounds and on village squares would be equally flabbergasted by the apparent unsubstantiality of seductive bodies bouncing and dancing on unobtrusively thin metal wires.

For Your Eyes Only: Eros at the Circus

The circus has been traditionally a powerful erotic magnet even if the ethos of the circus family, congruent with the fundamental conservatism of patriarchal Gypsy culture, tends to implement restraints on actual licentiousness and promiscuity. Erotic teasing is nevertheless one of the visual arguments of its marketing drives with various degrees of explicitness and provocation. The iconography of ancient parades on scaffoldings erected in front of the circuses and menageries includes female dancers and equestrians who are tasked with enticing spectators to purchase admission tickets. A review of advertising banners and posters provides ample evidence that the representation of the artists as sexualized icons is a powerful strategy of the circus trade. In *Circus Bodies*, Peta Tait's (2005) outstanding work dedicated to exploring the history and meaning of aerial performances, the whole array of "body offerings" is reviewed and discussed, from the "graceful manliness" of "erotic gods" to "gender tricksters" and "androgynous charm." In the last chapter of the book, titled "Ecstasy and visceral flesh in motion", Tait suggests that "aerial bodies are received bodily and viscerally" by the spectators.

The arousing attractiveness of revealed bare skin and fleshy curvatures is proportionate to the rarity of its availability. For long, the circus has offered only occasional chances of visual consumption of sexual fantasies in cultures that insisted on wrapping the female body in layers of obstructing fabrics. The testimony of Indian colleagues who once confided to me that, in their student years, they would never miss a show when a circus was in town not really because they were circus fans, as I first interpreted this information, but because that was the only opportunity they had to stare, even ogle at women's bare thighs and legs in a society in which saris or ample trousers were the norms of female attire, whether they were Hindu or Muslim. Most acrobats in traditional Indian circus are indeed girls and young women from lower social status or coming from other Asian countries (Bouissac 2012: 171).

Traditionally in western cultures, the whole array of the performing arts from popular theater and circus to opera and ballet have more or less ostensibly included an erotic, even lewd dimension contained within a socially accepted framework. The technological evolution that now makes available to anybody an abundance of uncensored pornographic images and films on the screen of their computers and cell phones has seriously undermined one of the tacit assets of the traditional circus. This sensual affordance more or less covertly persists in the staging of acrobatic acts in spite of the modern tendency to build a veneer of respectability compatible with the circus's appeal to children who have become one of the main targets of its marketing drive. Historian Brenda Assael (2005) has shown how the nineteenth-century circus has strived to emerge from the disreputable milieu of the fairground and ambiguously construe itself as an educational institution aimed at young spectators. Compared to the highbrow esthetics that prevail in the academic circus that is usually geared to promote political correctness, the traditional circus still features attractive bodies in potentially suggestive postures and movements in a context of relative visual proximity. However, this offering has been mostly pre-empted by the evolution of permissiveness and the mass commodification of sexual imagery, to the extent that the traditional ring of desire has become hardly relevant on a significant demographic scale.

From Ritual to Spectacle

Ritual actions do not produce a practical result on the external world—that is one of the reasons why we call them ritual. But to make this statement is not to say that ritual has no function ... it gives members of the society confidence, it dispels their anxieties, and it disciplines their social organizations.
George C. Homans, ***Anxiety and Ritual***, 1941.

Circus acrobatics of all sorts are designed to entertain people, let it be the few pedestrians who stop to watch a brief street performance that they may reward with some change, or the larger audience that flock to a big top and pay an admission fee for the privilege of attending the show. There is no doubt that these kinds of entertainment broadly speaking belong to the category of spectacle. They capture the attention of their public and gratify their craving for narratives. Circus, though, provides a qualitatively different sort of experience because it involves an immediacy that is absent from other visual dynamic displays such as theater or cinema. In the latter, the game is already over. The story has already been written. The suspense is artificially created by the skill of the authors and directors. At the end, which we can endlessly read again or replay, both heroes and villains die fictitious deaths or meet imaginary destinies. We may be moved but not to the point of fearing an irreparable outcome. Our emotions are real but only to a point. In any case, in our modern mode of passive consumption of entertainments, the spectacles occur in a virtual space parallel to the one we occupy, where we play our part in our real-life environment on a different level.

By contrast, circus by its very nature compels its audience to be complicit in the actions that unfold at a close range or relatively short distance, ensconced in a well-defined place. Should something bad happen, we could be theoretically implicated as witness, even perhaps as guilty of non-assistance to person(s) in danger, if not worse. It is because we have paid a set price, in full knowledge of the risks at stake, that human beings are engaging in actions that threaten their own life. We cannot plead ignorance since the banners, posters, and the programs spell out the possibility of a lethal outcome as a part of their rhetoric to incite us to become spectators. We may believe that this is all bluff and hope that all will be fine at the end, but we can never be absolutely sure. The circus artists themselves may display various attitudes, from self-confidence to anguish and fright, as a part of their performance in order to arouse our emotions, but, ultimately, they have to overcome their own inner anxiety when they step into the ring or climb a rope to meet whatever challenge is their specialty, let it be a group of predators, the crowd that must be made to laugh, or gravity. As a trapeze artist told me once: "When I leave the backstage to enter the ring, it is like marching up to the front line in a war. I am never sure that I will come back". And she added: "But we get use to that feeling."

It is obvious that the circus is more than a mere spectacle. It is akin to a ritual, even to a sacrificial ceremony in which the victims would commit themselves to self-immolation or, at least, to a voluntary ordeal through which they do all that is necessary to survive the challenge in full cognizance of the odds against them. At the end of their successful performance, they bask in the glory of the applause that acknowledges their achievement but also in the gratifying feeling of their own triumph over themselves. However, for this dimension of the circus to be shared by a participating audience, they must be spatially enveloped in a common place.

Proximity is a crucial factor in human communication. Beyond a certain distance we lose contact with the multi-sensorial perception of all the variations of human expressive resources. The cinema makes up for the "coldness" of the purely visual medium by bringing in close-ups at intense nodes in the narratives. The traditional circus, either in the primal form of street entertainment or in the structural apparatus of its traveling and stable venues, ensures an optimal contact between performers and audience. The spectators may be staggered around what could be described as a pit of various amplitude, but the contact with the artists is live and vibrant within a unified social fabric flooded with signs, while maintaining, at the same time, between the artists and the audience, a kind of ontological divide that cannot be casually bridged and might be considered as the hallmark of the sacred.

All those pragmatic features combine to establish the ritualistic nature of the circus experience. There are also numerous formal characteristics that bring the unfolding of circus acts close to the ways rituals are performed (Bell 1997; Bouissac 2012: 23–7). Students of rituals have concurred that the first characteristic of these ubiquitous social behaviors is that they consist of well-defined actions that are not designed to directly produce practical results on the external world (e.g., Homans 1941). It is, however, generally agreed that rituals are socio-psychologically effective in the way they impact their participating audience. At least three adaptive outcomes have been identified: emotion regulation, goal regulation, and social regulation (Hobson et al. 2017). All three can be considered relevant to the case of the traditional circus. First, the empathetic involvement with the ordeal of the artists redirects attention away from one's own emotions; second, the vicarious identification with the successful completion of a structured action sequence channels the goal-oriented motivation of the spectators; third, the collective experience of sympathetically watching challenging performances along a compelling temporal framework creates a psychological fusion that translates at the end into unanimous applause and, often, spontaneous standing ovations. These combined effects produce a deep feeling of gratification through the stimulation of the reward centers of the human brain. It is in this sense that the circus has been at times defined as food for the heart and the mind.

But does this apply to the contemporary forms of delivery of the circus message? Three principal changes with unintended consequences have contributed to interfere with the ritualistic functions of the traditional circus: the expansion of the physical apparatus, the underplaying of risk, and the addition of supplementary narratives. The first change is the drastic increase in the size of the venues in order to accommodate much larger audiences and maximize profit. This transformation of the venues' structure expanded the distance of the public to the performers beyond the critical threshold that allows a measure of human contact. To compensate for this relative information deficit companies such as the earlier American circuses multiplied the number of areas in which acts were performed simultaneously, thus precluding the possibility of focusing one's attention on individual artists. Later, global enterprises like the Cirque du Soleil or the new Russian and Chinese circuses that strive to compete with the former, replaced the traditional ring with elaborate construction, and multiplied the sources of information by adding extra figuration to individual artists so that the spectators' perception would be saturated. Typical examples include the supreme rola bola act of Vladimir Omelchenko who performed in *La Nouba*, a Cirque du Soleil production, surrounded by dancers and assistants, all dressed in attention-getting costumes, or Russian Gia Eradze's staging of an outstanding handstand act on a white grand piano with a dozen or so dancers cavorting around. As a result, the action is distributed across multiple actors and the uniqueness of the acrobatic act is devalued for the benefit of a spectacular distracting display.

The second change was introduced by the flooding of circus shows with acrobats spun out by the countless circus schools. They usually perform with athletic competence but they too often lack showmanship as a deliberate esthetic decision to steer clear of the "vulgar" traditional circus style. They refrain from "selling their act" through producing willfully seductive or dramatic signs while completing their routine, or they are simply unable to do so because their non-circus family upbringing has molded their behavior into a different habitus and ethos. In addition, as a rule, they reduce the risk factor to a minimum in a way that is so obvious that any attempt to claim that their life is in danger would be preposterous. Acrobatics, then, ceases to be a ritual and is degraded to the status of mere spectacle.

The third modification in the delivery of contemporary circus shows is the tendency to introduce an external narrative thread as an overall interpretation of the program. The lack of understanding of the logic of traditional circus acts prompts the creation of story-based performances that distract the audience from focusing on the core narrative that subtends every act: *the confrontation of a vital challenge that is overcome in several steps of increasing difficulty to conclude ultimately with the triumph of a human hero or a heroic team*. These complex actions are achieved with formal perfection by agents who have no other explicit purpose than the completion of the actions themselves. They are their own reward. They meet the criterion of absolute beauty, as it was defined by Immanuel Kant in his *Critique of Judgement* (1914 [1892]), by being paradoxically "purposive without purpose", meaning that they are not motivated by the external practical results that any action usually has although they are performed with utmost attention to their accomplishment. *They are achieved by artists who have first transformed themselves into icons through careful grooming and special costumes like priests being prepared for sacred rituals.* Naturally, these circus acts are embedded within an institution through which artists are working toward securing their own practical means of survival, as priests in any religion do. Circus artists refer to their performances as "work" but they hold the belief that circus is unlike any other kind of work. Audiences refer to their work as "play", thus indicating that they intuitively sense the specificity of the actions they contemplate.

Overarching narratives that are imposed upon traditional circus acts drown, so to speak, their ritualistic quality into a sea of external interests and motivations and transform circus programs into a succession of episodes toward the resolution of the theatrical fiction that is being staged, let it be a travel around the world or the adventure of a child coming of age. Often, the staging requirements force acrobats, trainers, and clowns to don costumes and represent values that conform to the logic of the storytelling but adulterate their artistic persona. The ritual is thus degraded into a spectacle obeying the forces of the contemporary commodification of mass entertainments and has to compete with other spectacles on their own terms.

6

Coda

Sforzando

"*Things fall apart; the centre cannot hold*"
"*Mere anarchy is loosed upon the world*"
  W. B. Yeats, *The Second Coming,* **Michael Robartes and the Dancer,** 1921

"*Travellers' places always make me think we'd do relatively well in the event of the apocalypse or a zombie invasion.*"
  Damian Le Bas, **The Stopping Places**, 2018.

Resistance and Resilience

The four movements that form this book have explored the nature and current evolution of the main components of the traditional circus from their origin in human ingenuity and resilience to the deployment of specialized performing skills that provided their audience, over millennia, with exhilarating and thrilling experience through spectacles akin to rituals. The synergy of animal training, transgressive humor, and acrobatics has produced a constant source of wonderment and merriment for countless generations that have been inspired and aroused by its performances in both small and large formats. However, over the last decades, the circus in its ancestral form has been under relentless attacks to the point that its disappearance has become plausible in view of the political and ideological forces that now target its very existence.

The purpose of this book was first to document this evolution and, second, to raise the issue of its causes, aiming at looking beyond the immediate circumstances that may account for local or temporary factors, to propose more general hypotheses regarding deeper cultural changes with far-reaching consequences. Only by understanding this wider context will we be able to anticipate possible future evolutionary transformations, and contemplate the resurgence of the circus through the combined effects of resistance and resilience. This concluding chapter, under the sign of forceful reaction (*Sforzando* means a "sudden, strong emphasis" in the Italian musical jargon) is indicative of both the seriousness of the situation and the resolve of its confrontation. It will necessarily evoke a long-term, risky, and possibly tragic horizon.

The Downfall of the Traditional Circus

Op-Ed: The forces that shut down Ringling Bros. want to end a lot more than animal abuse.
Charlotte Allen, Los Angeles Times, May 22, 2017.

This book has endeavored to take the long view on the emergence and destiny of the circus, under any other name, in the cultural fabric of the Eurasian continent, and to understand its present predicaments in the context of semiotic evolution, that is, the way in which the processes of meaning-making shift over time as the forces at play in the social and physical environment undergo transformations that impact human life. Nowadays, a recurrent topic in the press and the media is the demise of what has been known for some three centuries as "the circus"—now increasingly referred to as "the classic or traditional circus" by opposition to new emerging forms that have appropriated the name and its symbolic capital as a shell that still serves promotional purposes. Efforts are made to redefine; some will brashly say "reinvent" the circus. In the meantime, country after country, like a domino effect, prohibits, in the name of an ideological or ethical agenda, the use of wild animals, ultimately any animals, as parts of any spectacle, thus undermining both the economics and the significance of the ritualistic performances of the traditional circus. This trend combines with the abasement and censoring of the clowns' transgressive humor, and the democratization and trivialization of acrobatic displays that avoid excessive risks and eschew any form of sacrificial staging.

Occasional popular resistance to this movement is noticeable but remains marginal in spite of the collective efforts of some associations of circus fans and professionals to go against the flow. Temporary successes often depend on the genuine or opportunistic commitment of institutions or individuals who yield some significant economic or sociopolitical influence. But circus is for them a pleasurable entertainment, not their exclusive means of existence, and their commitment remains fragile and vulnerable to circumstances that may weaken their power through electoral upsets or economic crises. Symptomatically, circus themes have mostly disappeared from the promotional campaigns of local, national, and global business companies. Once a symbolic asset, the imagery of the traditional circus has lost its popular appeal to the point of becoming a liability.

Those who attempt to resist the onslaught on the traditional circus tend to belong to an elitist constituency. The crowd that flocks to Monte Carlo every year for the international festival may give the illusion that the circus remains culturally robust and popular, but traveling to this expensive Mediterranean Principality for the duration of its week of performances in the month of January implies a lifestyle based on a sizeable disposable income that excludes the working- and middle-class folks who used to provide huge audiences for the traditional circus in its heyday during the nineteenth and twentieth centuries. Something has obviously happened that goes beyond the mere competition of other means of entertainment. Festivals are some kind of artificial life support, the last colorful effect of the circus's sunset. These festivals can be organized through the passionate commitment of a few individuals who happen to have access to the levers of administrative power and the corresponding budgets in large cities, and can convince other officials that such festivals raise the cultural profile of the region, please their constituents, and attract tourists with their expected economic bonanza. A festival can also be created and supported for the pleasure and glory of a prince, perpetuating the ancient monarchic tradition of welcoming exotic entertainers in their royal court. This obsolete model, though, cannot be a substitute for the sustainable flow of truly popular audiences commensurate with the crowds that nowadays flock to oversized arenas for sport events and rock music concerts.

In fact, for a great many, the circus with its strong component of trained wild animals, as it has prospered on various levels in the previous centuries, is now considered barbaric and irrelevant, and it is commonly, but abusively lumped together with the Spanish corrida and ubiquitous cock fights. The rhetoric of its detractors often targets the Gypsies who have fostered the circus arts for immemorial times and remain widely stigmatized in Europe. The mainstream population is prone to conflate their ideological reprobation of the circus with their racist prejudices. However, such a radical shift in the popular attitude toward an ancestral tradition deeply rooted in the transnational culture of the West cannot be explained away by a simple change of taste with underlying xenophobic overtones. Circus fans cannot take solace from the sporadic existence of successful traditional circuses that prosper thanks to the protection of authoritarian regimes or temporary legal victories. These are fragile oases in a sea of advancing dunes. In the near future, the fate of the traditional circus is written on the wall. Something more is bound to be at stake in this semiotic landslide. Let us try to tentatively identify some of the factors that may account for such a cultural evolution if not revolution.

The Anthropocene Delusion

> *"Humans are now living in a new geological epoch of our own making: the Anthropocene. Or so we're told.*
>
> Peter Brannen. **The Anthropocene is a Joke.** theatlantic.com

As we have seen in the previous parts of this book, the circus flourished at times when humans were challenged by pervasive uncertainties. In such a context, rituals that affirmed and proved by proxy the possibility of overcoming endemic physical and social threats provided precious symbolic and emotional resources, a kind of existential entrainment. Whether these spectacular triumphs against all apparent odds were genuine or skillfully produced as credible illusions is irrelevant. Literate humans equally get life-transforming inspirations from reading pure fiction or listening to fancy tales. Circus rituals may have had such a profound function in times when their audiences were mostly illiterate. It appears that, with the advent of modernity, the sense of uncertainty has been considerably, albeit not totally reduced.

The industrial revolution of the last few centuries has brought to a climax the relentless efforts of humans to transform their natural environment in order to adapt it to their perceived needs. Most organisms, from social insects like the bees and the termites to industrious mammals like the beavers, for example, tend to modify their surroundings to lesser or greater extents by reshaping the space within which they are embedded in a way that is adaptive to their immediate survival. Humans are no exception but, during the twentieth century, geologists have taken notice that the impact of industry and technology on the environment has reached such a magnitude that earth has entered a novel epoch they dubbed the "Anthropocene", a word they coined on the model of the previous "Pleistocene" and "Holocene" epochs, using the Ancient Greek word *Anthropos* that means "man" in the sense of "human" rather than "male". The Canadian documentary film, *Anthropocene: The Human Epoch* vividly illustrates the gigantic excavations, re-directions or damming of rivers, deforestations, and drastic reshaping of landscapes that have transformed the planet during the last 100 years (Burtynsky et al. 2018).

These impressive albeit worrisome transformations, although they cannot compare with the geological events that have raised the Alps, the Andes, and the Himalayas for instance, have a definite impact on human minds: the delusion of absolute control, actual or potential, upon challenges to our well-being or even to our very existence. The world had been made to suit us and whatever is still beyond our control takes the form of an engineering challenge that generates projects. It is symptomatic that when the Covid-19 pandemic flared up in early 2020, the immediate reaction was that it was only a matter of time until a vaccine able to eradicate that danger would be created. For contemporary mentalities, the emergence of uncontrollable, irreversible devastations is reserved to the domain of science fiction. Uncertainty is conceived as being a mere stage in the heuristic process that leads to efficient adaptations. Predictability, or at least relative predictability, is assumed and directs the planning of our individual and social lives. Unpredictable, incontrollable absolute novelty is not on the cards. This applies not only to our cosmology but also to our social lives.

The civilizing process, so aptly described and documented by Norbert Elias (1939), and amplified in the twenty-first century by the ethos of tolerance and inclusiveness has reduced the level of uncertainty with which contemporary humans have to cope during their lives. At least, international legislation and in many cases national laws have established legal standards that offer a virtual protection against exclusion and discrimination. The relative homogeneity of interactional manners ruled by conventions, the actual or virtual contractual relations between individuals and states, and the technological exploitation and control of the environment have led to a fairly new secure sense of predictability. The anthropological notion of culture can be minimally characterized as the nurturing in society of a feeling of a rather comfortable certainty that makes possible both short- and long-term planning along agreed-upon rational, or at least commonsensical constraints. Socialized humans make basic common assumptions about themselves and the world. The artificial semiotic sphere they have spontaneously constructed over the last few centuries allows for an apparently reliable universal database of translatable meanings. There are, of course, tensions, crises, and conflicts which are mostly managed by negotiations and transactions aimed at recovering some degree of stability. Even when extreme, lengthy violence has erupted in the process, scripts for how to terminate a war are available in the collective memory and in the playbook of nations.

The globalization of trade and communication has greatly expanded in the world's populations the representation of potentialities and possibilities that circumscribe the range of expectable future events and their consequences. This attitude is implied in the commonsense knowledge that motivates decisions and planning from individual to international levels. Correspondingly, general policies are driven by powerful statistical models allowing for the projection of forthcoming states of the world that may quantify some degree of uncertainty but generally exclude, with some exception, the total collapse of civilization. The tacit assumption that sustains the belief of ever-expanding predictability is that humans have succeeded in asserting an absolute control of the forces and resources of the planet earth.

Humans have come to broadly consider that they own the earth and the various forms of life that have evolved on it. At least, this is implied by their behavior. This delusionary feeling may be colored by diverse metaphors such as the "conquest of frontiers" or, in other words, the grabbing of space to be explored and exploited; the "eradication of pest and predators", a kind of sanitation or house cleaning; the "management of the environment", somewhat like the rational cultivation of one's garden for optimal pleasure and utility; "the protection of species" threatened by extinction, being understood that this investment is selectively reserved to some organisms at the exclusion of others; the conceptual and emotional construal of the earth as "mother nature", that implies the fantasy of the fundamental benevolence of a forgiving provider, notwithstanding occasional rough treatment in the form of storms or droughts that are interpreted as mere angry tantrum but excluding in principle the blind, haphazard destruction of the human species. This list could be expanded to include the beliefs that the earth was given to humans, for their exclusive use, by some divine power, or that they have been entrusted with the task of taming its forces and protecting its animals.

Another pervasive tacit metaphor is "nature as spectacle". This mental attitude has generated the rich literary tradition of travelers' accounts of their peregrinations in exotic countries, or even what they witnessed in their own backyards. Global tourism in recent centuries has fed the delusion that nature, including predators and their prey, is something to be seen, painted, or photographed. Nowadays, films and documentaries provide a constant flow of images representing esthetically or dramatically pleasing scenes and actions. Self-representations in a natural environment implicitly assert our safe control of the natural world. This presupposes that humans see themselves as virtually located outside the reach of natural predators among other menaces that for eons took a lethal toll on humans. As we recalled earlier in this volume, a mere few centuries ago, European populations that were then mostly rural lived in the constant fear of wolves which were roaming the forests and the countryside, and were prone to catch toddlers who would wander out of the watch of their caretakers; sheep, of course, were relatively easier prey in spite of the shepherds and their dogs. In today's India and Sumatra, for instance, death by tiger attack is an almost daily occurrence that does not always make the news. However, such killings are considered to be anecdotal and, as we saw in the second part of this book, generally blamed on the people who encroached on the predators' territories, thus casting "nature" as a kind of zoological display with safe compartmentalization. Those who visit African safaris from the assumed safety of Land Rovers or tourist busses are driven on virtual parallels to the contained wildness of nature, feeling immune to the brute forces that lurk beyond the glass of their cars and the illusion afforded by the fragile metaphors they live by.

Such metaphors, though, are sustainable only as long as human societies and their cultures remain relatively stable, both technologically and semiotically. People, then, feel confident that they can account for disruptions in the environment through meaning-making narratives of a mythical or scientific nature.

Naturally, as we repeatedly pointed out in earlier chapters of this book, what anthropologists call a culture is not a totally consistent whole that determines the understanding and behavior of every single member of a society. Its systematicity is variegated and flexible due to the fact that it is in constant flux within some constraints from heterogeneous origins. The degree of knowledge and the set of beliefs held by individuals or groups depend on their position with respect to the core register of the mainstream population. There is nevertheless, in the current global culture, a dominant key: the sense that humans have achieved actual, or at least potential, control over the complex ecosystem in which we live, either directly or by proxy. Humans keep wildness in check and manage the profitable husbandry of the cattle they own and the socializing of the pets they love. Some people are keen on posting on the social media videos of men and women, even children interacting peacefully and playfully with cubs and sub-adults of predators which they have raised as pets, thus hinting at a new cross-species complicity that is the sign of the new age. The scenes always suggest that humans are in control but also imply that the beasts are willing benevolent partners in those games. As we saw in the part of this book devoted to animals, the fountain heads of contemporary anthropomorphism, such as primatologists Jane Goodall and Frans de Waal, have inspired a broader than intended shift of attitude toward wild species in a vast human population that has no direct experience of predators.

The hypothesis that this book has developed contends that the demise of the traditional circus can be in part accounted for by more general factors than the hostility of "animal rights" and "animal liberation" movements or local economic circumstances. In the context of the Anthropocene, the whole semiotic scaffolding that had sustained the ritualistic power of the circus for millennia has progressively collapsed. The immemorial emergence of the circus, under any other name, rested upon the experience of the world as a constant confrontation with uncertainty and life-threatening challenges. The traditional circus skills such as the mastery of predators and the triumph over gravity embodied the heroic or magic reduction of the uncertain outcomes that were ever lurking at every turn in human lives. Supernatural powers rather than technology were the mantra of the time.

The Reign of Anthropomorphism

Few Americans fear predators simply because most of us no longer live in areas where we can be part of the food pyramid. [...] In parts of southern Tanzania, a legacy of fear continues. Between 1932 and 1947, a total of 1,500 villagers were reportedly killed by lions. [...] During 2001 and 2002, there were 22 attacks that resulted in 14 human fatalities.

Joel Berger, **The Better to Eat You With: Fear in the Animal World**, 2008: 105–6.

The industrial revolution and the consequential rise of urbanization have ushered in a fallacious sense of control and predictability. Around the same time, Romanticism raised a counter-reaction, idealizing "nature" and promoting the genuine goodness of the "noble savage", a phrase coined by British poet John Dryden in the seventeenth century but later associated with French philosopher Jean-Jacques Rousseau, who promoted the idea of the natural goodness of humans before civilization corrupted them. This notion has now been expanded to include "the noble animal" and, implicitly, the "good predator" that is actually only good at killing anything that moves and is palatable.

As the fear of the local European fauna, principally the wolves, faded away, tales from the colonial conquest brought to the forefront of popular imagination icons of terror such as man-eating tigers and lions. The wild-animal trainers of the traveling menageries and the circuses provided heroic and romantic postures that fed, for close to two centuries, a visual and literary esthetic of the sublime until the haunting fear of these exotic predators succumbed to the reverse anxiety of species extinction. Today, in Europe, the wolf and the bear have become, for city dwellers, kinds of romantic heroes whose return in our midst is welcomed by the ecological cohorts at the dismay of sheep breeders. Similarly, the protection of threatened lions, tigers, and other predators commands vast conservation budgets, irrespective of the death and devastation they still cause in their native areas. The victims are the collateral damage of virtuous policies.

The traditional symbolism of the circus arts, at least from the Greek and Roman Empires to the end of the European colonial era, was consistent with the grand narrative that supported the Western cultural expansion under its many forms. Hyperbolic expressions such as "tigers recently captured in India" or "jungle-bred lions" now would trigger alarm rather than awe, and even call for legal prosecutions, as do discriminatory characterizations of other humans as savage or uncivilized, a patent violation of universal human rights.

The demise of the traditional circus may be sporadically resisted by those who still make a living from this trade along the lines of an economy of subsistence, and by a minority of the population in which the nostalgic memory of their childhood wonderments survives. This constituency keeps providing a sufficient income for most family circuses to survive thanks to a combination of resilience and compromise. However, many had to discontinue the keeping of wild animals. There are, though, a few exceptions in countries in which the political power of conservative parties opposes the ecologist zeitgeist, but these are zones of resistance at the mercy of an electoral change. It is symptomatic that the current leaders of some of the most prestigious, multi-generational circus lineages have already yielded to the pressure of activists. The presentation of predators, as well as elephants, has disappeared from their programs. Typically, the French magazine *Bretagne Circus* that appeared in March 2020 reports that there were only a very few trained animals, mostly dogs, cats, birds, and some horses in the latest Christmas circus festivals that have become the main performing events in many French cities during the end-of-year holidays. Another symptom is obvious if we consider the programs of the Monte Carlo International Circus festivals: in its early years, over four decades ago, up to four or five wild animal acts were featured in the competition but only one such act has been scheduled each year during the last ten years. As a symbolic token of support for the tradition, this single act has always received one of the most prestigious prizes. In years to come, though, this kind of act will likely disappear from the programs. There is also a dearth of robust clowning in the trade and the fear to offend flattens the permissible humor. Progressively, the grand staging of acrobatics offsets the ritualistic value of daring individual acts in favor of spectacular collective displays.

The Romantic perception of the circus lingers in contemporary popular cultures but the powerful historical and symbolic scaffolding that sustained its deeply human relevance has mostly collapsed. In twenty-first-century Europe and America, the traditional circus has been eradicated, or adulterated under a variety of ideologies that led a cultural war against its ritualistic celebrations of the conquest of the wild; the sublime strength, beauty, and vulnerability of the human body; and the capacity to confront the fragility of arbitrary norms.

"The Return of the Hyenas"

Even if history does not truly repeat itself, life on earth is subject to recurring unexpected catastrophic events as geology and paleontology amply demonstrate. twenty-first-century humans, in spite of some dissonant voices, have come to assume the stability of their cosmological niche, looking at climate and tectonic upsets as things from a bygone past. The Covid-19 crisis, still in progress as these lines are written, tragically revealed the vulnerability of the global society that has engineered over the millennia an apparently predictable and controllable environment. A pandemic, though, is only one of innumerable surprises that nature or fate may keep in store. The evolution of life on earth breeds uncertainty and the underlying physical forces at work inside and above the planet never rest. In addition, humans have built risky tools of commodity and domination such as nuclear facilities and weaponry, deep earth drilling and exploitation, and ever-advancing artificial intelligence. The sheer complexity of the numerous interconnections that sustain our livelihood and the sense of security and predictability that allows us to make plans and anticipate future states of the world is what renders this meaningful stability fragile and vulnerable. Some linkages in the networks might be more resilient than others but do not guarantee absolute resistance in front of an eventual convergence of multiple failures. In many countries, the 2020 pandemic brought health care institutions to the brink of collapse but there is no necessity, not even likelihood that pandemics always come one at a time. Infinite swarms of viruses have a dynamic of their own and freely mutate under the wind of chance. Beyond a certain threshold, these are non-negotiable forces.

These considerations have prompted some scientists and philosophers to reflect upon the eventuality of the total collapse of civilization under its many forms as we have known it as far as we can remember. Their diverse research and calculations have converged and have been encapsulated in the term "collapsology", that is, the science of collapsing (e.g., Tainter 1988; Servigne and Stevens 2020). Apocalyptic narratives have long haunted the religious and literary imagination of humans, but the examination of actual trends and transformations that are observable and quantifiable in the dynamics of the planet have given substance to this ancestral fear (e.g., Clark 2018).

Relentless human industry has modified our environment so drastically that we have entered a new bio-geological era, a period dominated by the irreversible impact of humans on the earth. The correlate of this state of affairs is that, as it was pointed out above, humans have nurtured a sense of predictability and infinite progress toward the absolute control of all the antagonistic forces that challenge their physical, biological, and cultural stability.

The hypothesis that I have attempted to develop in this volume—or let us say rather the tentative theory, since a hypothesis that is not falsifiable is merely a view of the mind—considers the traditional circus as a ritual that produces meaning in a context of uncertainty. The heroic control of predators, gravity, or social chaos for instance, presupposes that these challenges to human life are a potentially lethal presence in the immediate environment. If a feeling of security and predictability dominates the experience of life, the uncanny skills of circus folks lose their informative and practical values and become redundant. It is in this sense that we can understand the "end" of the circus, not as a sudden death but a slow march toward obsolescence due to a progressive lack of relevance.

However, as the collapsologists contend, the stability of the earth systems and the cultural bedrocks of civilization provide humans with a delusional sense of certainty that can be shattered any time. The Covid-19 pandemic has caused as much mental distress as physical illness and death. It overwhelms our capacity to make sense as much as it challenges the health institution facilities. It adumbrates the possibility of the radical return of uncertainty, the dreaded "free energy" or "unbounded information" that threatens meaning itself.

The traveling entertainers, circus and fairground folks, Gypsies and others whose life depends on the capacity of attracting crowds to their temporary performing space, felt the pandemic as an existential tragedy. My Facebook friend, Robert Gasser, one of the scions of a German Swiss lineage that goes back countless generations, expressed his sorrow by broadcasting a poignant poem in his native language and several automatically translated versions:

This misfortune came very quickly and quietly to us, on the journey.
For the moment everything stands still, everything nobody wants.
An invisible enemy is bringing us to our knees right now.
We never believed in anything like that.
We want to bring joy to everyone's life, that is our aspiration.
Never will we give up.
We are born for the journey. Our lives are way too quiet now.
She will come back again, our golden hour. We will be on everyone's lips.
We will rise from the ashes and soon will see bright children's eyes again.
Also, the carousels, they will turn again.
Everything will be bright when we all meet again.
There will be hugs and countless friends' tears because we love life.
Joy and sorrow is the way of the world, even if we don't like it.
Every enemy is to be defeated.
Don't let us down, come back, and there will be peace again.

In the first draft of this conclusion, that I sketched about a year before Covid-19 struck the planet, I tried my hands at the fictitious depiction of a forthcoming, perhaps unstoppable dystopia. The idea was to ask, in the form of a thought or emotion experiment: what if civilization actually collapsed? I titled this concluding part "The return of the hyenas", as a radical metaphor of the uncontrollable resurgence of the wild in the ruin of our lost life world. I described this moment in anticipated human trajectory from the local point of view of my own neighborhood in the city where I live because, at the time of such collapse, all global communication systems would have faltered and nobody could have knowledge of what was happening beyond their immediate experience of survival and desperation. I mentioned, in slow motion because things would have occurred irrevocably at their own pace, the progressive night caused by more or less simultaneous gigantic volcanic eruptions; forest and taiga fires; explosions of nuclear facilities and stocks of decaying military bombs and rockets; cumulative chemical densification of the atmosphere produced, among other causes, by the raging industries that tried to create profitable solutions to the creeping night that was enveloping the planet such as building artificial suns or moons. Like the efforts of a mammoth trapped in a mud swamp, every move had started to make things worse. The social order had been the first victim of this process of deterioration that had led to the inability to make sense of anything beyond finding something to eat and avoiding to be eaten. It was the way things can be expected to go with the flow when free energy escape control and run the world. The city zoo had been deserted in panic after the nearby nuclear power plant had collapsed, and some of the animals had survived and escaped.

The hyenas had proliferated and troupes of them were roaming the ruined city, feeding on the corpses that were left out since burials, let alone burial rituals were out of the question. Those humans who had decided to survive lived in fear of these hyenas that, fortunately, could not be everywhere at the same time. The monitoring of their movements was the most pressing duty of whatever was left of resilient civility confronted to the specter of maximal uncertainty.

Some humans, though, because of their ancestral culture that was rooted in the depth of time, had better chance of survival. My fable was ending with a faint hope of human—and perhaps circus—resurgence, as pages of a diary from a time when we had lost the sense of a future:

2035: Ragnarok in Slow Motion

The age of fear has come upon us. It started long ago, perhaps a century, perhaps more. At first, it was a vague menace that haunted some artists' imagination. There were novels and movies in which characters wandered through a wasted land but we knew that the actors and the writers actually were living in luxurious mansions near the sea in balmy climates. Then, the experts fed us with statistics and curves that were leading straight up to the top right corner of the page or the screen, the point beyond which all hope would disappear. This seemed too abstract, though, or too dramatic for being a matter of real concern. We thought that, anyway, we would be dead before the line would reach that final zone. However, for the sake of future generations, we started recycling plastic bottles and batteries with a sense of self-righteousness. In the meantime, the summers became too hot, the winters too stormy, but had not nature always been whimsical? At times, we were anxious and stored more food and water than we needed in our pantries and freezers, just in case. We could not ignore those who were claiming in the media that with a few more degrees Celsius civilization would collapse and the earth would become inhabitable but we dismissed the credibility of these prophets of doom: we had heard that before. Now, only the oldest survivors can remember those days. Some call this a creeping Apocalypse, others, in the North, a rotten Ragnarok.

2039: The Return of the Hyenas

Some years ago, when the darkness of the day had settled on the region, we heard that the hyenas of the zoo had escaped by digging a tunnel under their enclosure.

Driven by hunger after their keepers failed to show up for work, They had killed and eaten some horses and zebras. At the time, there were still a couple of local tabloids. The hyenas did not make the front page. We were more concerned, then, about the leaks that had been discovered in the Pickering nuclear facility. Our electricity was rationed and erratic. Anyway, these animals could be easily shot or captured. We soon forgot about them. As darkness thickened, other priorities piled up. In the meantime the hyenas had colonized the Don Valley, fed on wildlife and prospered on scavenging our garbage which was, then, picked up only once a week. This was the year before the total collapse of municipal services. First at night, but soon under the faint light of the day, the hyenas started roaming freely in the city in search of food.

2045: A Last Dream as Night Falls

Maybe, far away down South, a pregnant mare is pulling an old van, helped by two rough looking men along a deserted road. Perhaps, a woman and two young children look through the dusty windows of the van that has lost its tires. The wheels have been wrapped with rags. They have been struck on their journey, quickly and quietly, but they had inherited the will and the skill to survive misfortunes. Soon, perhaps, they will stop close to a stream of clear water. While the mare grazes, the woman will make a fire under the somber sky and will brew some dry leaves. The men will come back with some meaty animals they have caught along the overgrown edge of the path. Perhaps they will sit down in peace and eat, and drink, telling stories to the children, remembering circus days. Perhaps, faintly, in the distance, I can hear them speak a Romany dialect.

Bibliography

Adorno, Theodor. 1996. Chaplin Times Two. *Yale Journal of Criticism* 9(1): 57–61.

Armandi, Pierre. 1843. *Histoire militaire des éléphants depuis les temps les plus reculés jusqu'à l'introduction des armes à feu.* Paris: D'Amyot

Assael, Brenda. 2005. *The Circus and Victorian Society.* Charlottesville: University of Virginia Press.

Basalla, George. 1988. *The Evolution of Technology.* Cambridge: Cambridge University Press.

Beadle, Ron. 2019. "Response to Consultation on Wild Animals in Circus (Wales) Bill WA 10", National Assembly for Wales Climate Change, Environmental and Rural Affairs Committee. https://business.senedd.wales/documents/s93141/WA%2010%20 Professor%Ron%Beadle.pdf

Beffa, Marie-Lise and Marie-Dominique Even (eds.). 1995. Variations chamaniques 2. *Etudes mongoles et sibériennes* 26.

Bell, Catherine. 1997. *Ritual: Perspectives and Dimensions.* New York: Oxford University Press.

Bensimon, Agnès. 2005. Les Pauwels. Histoire d'une famille juive du cirque. *Les Cahiers de la mémoire contemporaine* 6: 239–47. https://doi.org/10.4000/cmc.987

Berger, Joel. 2008. *The Better to Eat You With: Fear in the Animal World.* Chicago: University of Chicago Press.

Berger, Joel. 2018. *Extreme Conservation: Life at the Edges of the World.* Chicago: University of Chicago Press.

Bergson, Henri. 1911 [1901]. *Laughter.* London: Macmillan.

Berland, Joseph. 1982. *No Five Fingers Are Alike: Cognitive Amplifiers in Social Context.* Cambridge, MA: Harvard University Press.

Berson, Josh. 2019. *The Meat Question: Animals, Humans, and the Deep History of Food.* Cambridge MA: MIT Press.

Bhat, G. K. 1959. *The Vidûshaka.* Ahmedabad: The New Order Book Co.

Borrow, George. 1991 [1851]. *Lavengro: The Scholar, the Gypsy, the Priest.* Mineola NY: Dover.

Bouglione, Firmin. 1962. *Le Cirque est mon royaume.* Paris: Presses de la cité.

Bouissac, Paul. 1958. *Animaux de parade et animaux dressés dans les jeux de l'amphithéâtre.* Thèse pour le diplôme d'études supérieures. Université de Paris-Sorbonne.

Bouissac, Paul. 1973. *La mesure des gestes: prolégomènes à la sémiotique gestuelle.* The Hague: Mouton.

Bouissac, Paul. 1992. Technological Innovations and Cultural Semiosis: The Ritualistic Appropriation of the Bicycle by the Circus. In Marlene Landsch, Heiko Karnowski, and Ivan Bystrina (eds.) *Kultur Evolution: Fallstudien und Synthese*. Frankfurt: Peter Lang.

Bouissac, Paul. 2010. *Semiotics at the Circus*. Berlin: De Gruyter.

Bouissac, Paul. 2012. *Circus as Multimodal Discourse: Performance, Meaning, and Ritual*. London: Bloomsbury.

Bouissac, Paul. 2013. The Legal Status of Animals: From Perpetrators of Wrongs to Victims of Abuses. In B. Wojciechowski, P. Juchacz, and K. Cern (eds.) *Legal Rules, Moral Norms, and Democratic Principles*. Frankfurt am Main: Peter Lang.

Bouissac, Paul. 2015. *The Semiotics of Clowns and Clowning: Rituals of Transgression and the Theory of Laughter*. London: Bloomsbury.

Bouissac, Paul. 2018. *The Meaning of the Circus: The Communicative Experience of Cult, Art, and Awe*. London: Bloomsbury.

Bourdieu, Pierre. 2013 [1977]. *Outline of a Theory of Practice*. Translated by Richard Nice. Cambridge: Cambridge University Press.

Burtynsky, Edward, Jennifer Baichwal, and Nick De Pencier. 2018. Anthropocene: The Human Epoch. Documentary. Mercury Films. Theanthropocene.org/film.

Canestrelli, Ottavio. 2016. *The Grand Gypsy: A Memoir by Ottavio Canestrelli with Ottavio Gesmundo*. Milton Keynes: Lulu Publishing Services.

Carmeli, Yoram. 1989. Wee Pea: The Total Play of the Dwarf in the Circus. *The Drama Review* TDR 33 (4): 128–45.

Carmeli, Yoram. 1991. Performance and Family in the World of British Circus. *Semiotica* 85 (3/4): 257–90.

Carmeli, Yoram. 2003. Lion on display: culture, nature, and totality in a circus performance. *Poetics Today* 24 (1): 65–90.

Chalier-Visuvalingam, Elizabeth. 2003. *Bhairava: Terreur et Protection: Mythes, Rites et Fêtes a Benares et Katmandou*. Bern: Peter Lang.

Chambers, Edmund Kerchever. 1903. *The Mediaeval Stage*. Oxford: Clarendon Press.

Chipperfield, Thomas. 2015. Why Lions Attack Their Trainers. *The Telegraph*. February 10. https://www.telegraph.co.uk/news/earth/wildlife/11402840/Why-lions-attack-their-trainers.html

Christinger, Raymond and Willy Borgeaud. 1963. *Mythologie de la Suisse ancienne*. Genève: Musée et Institut d'Ethnographie de Genève, Georg et Cie.

Clark, William C. (ed.). 2018. *Trajectories of the Earth System in the Anthropocene*. Cambridge, MA: Harvard University Press.

Conway, David. 2020. *Magic: A Life in More Worlds than One*. London: Rose Ankh.

Cooke, Steven J. 2017. What is Innate Releasing Mechanism (IRM) Regarding Animal Behavior? *Socratic.org*. https://link.springer.com/referenceworkentry/10.1007%2F978-1-4020-8265-8_200148

Course, Magnus. 2013. The Clown Within: Becoming White and Mapuche Ritual Clowns. *Comparative Studies in Society and History* 55 (4): 771–99.

Cuisenier, Jean. 1985. Sur un conte, du mythe et un rituel: les ursitoare de Roumanie. In Herman Parret and Hans-George Ruprecht (eds.) *Exigences et perspectives de la sémiotique: Recueil d'hommages pour A.J. Greimas/Aims and Prospect of Semiotics: Essays in honor of A.J. Greimas.* Amsterdam: John Benjamins, 905–26.

Deleuze, Gilles. 1971. *Masochism: An Interpretation of Coldness and Cruelty.* Jean McNeil, translator. New York: George Braziller.

De Waal, Frans. 1982. *Chimpanzee Politics.* London: Jonathan Cape.

De Waal, Frans. 1989. *Peacemaking among Primates.* Cambridge MA: Harvard University Press.

Disher, Maurice Willson. 1968 [1925]. *Clowns and Pantomimes.* New York: Benjamin Blom.

Dolensek, Nejc, Daniel A. Gehrlach, Alexandra S. Klein, and Nadine Gogolla. 2020. Facial expressions of emotion states and their neuronal correlates in mice. *Science* 368 (6486) (3 Avril): 89–94.

Douglas, Mary and Aaron Wildavsky. 1982. *Risk and Culture.* Berkeley: University of California Press.

Dwyer, Colin. 2019. "McJesus" Sculpture to Be Pulled from Israeli Museum after Violent Protests. *NPR Daily* Newsletter. January 17. https://www.npr.org/2019/01/17/686199231/mcjesus-sculpture-to-be-pulled-from-israeli-museum-after-violent-protests

Ekman, Paul. 1979. *Darwin and Facial Expression: A Century of Research in Review.* New York: Academic Press.

Ekman, Paul, P. W. Friesen and P. Ellesworth. 1972. *Emotion in the Human Face.* New York: Pergamon Press.

Elias, Norbert. 1997 [1939]. *The Civilizing Process.* London: Blackwell.

Emerson, Ralph Waldo. 1838. *Nature.* Boston: James Munroe

Ernout, Alfred and Antoine Meillet. 1967. *Dictionnaire étymologique de la langue latine.* Paris: Klincksieck.

Frank, Roslyn. 2008. Recovering European Ritual Bear Hunts: A Comparative Study of Basque and Sardinian Ursine Carnival Performances. *Insula-3: Quaderni di Cultura Sarda* (June): 41–97.

Frank, Roslyn. 2015. Bear Ceremonialism in Relation to Three Ritual Healers: the Basque *salutariyua*, the French *marcou* and the Italian *maramao*. In Enrico Comba and Daniele Ormezzano (eds.) *Uomini e Orsi: Morfologia del Selvaggio.* Torino: Accademia University Press, 495–512.

Fraser, Angus. 1992. *The Gypsies.* Oxford: Blackwell.

Fridlund, A. 1994. *Human Facial Expression: An Evolutionary View.* San Diego: Academic Press.

Friston, Karl. 2010. The Free Energy Principle: A Unified Brain Theory. *Nature Review. Neuroscience* 11 (2): 127–38.

Friston, Karl. 2013. Life as We Know It. *Journal of the Royal Society. Interface/The Royal Society* 10 (86).

Fuchs, Christian. 2016. *Critical Theory of Communication: New Readings of Lukacs, Adorno, Marcuse, Honneth, and Habermas*. London: University of Westminster Press.

Gmelch, Sharon Bohn and George Gmelch. 2014. *Irish Travellers: The Unsettled Life*. Bloomington IN: Indiana University Press.

Golden, Leon. 1984. Aristotle on Comedy. *Journal of Aesthetics and Art Criticism* 42 (3): 283–90.

Goodall, Jane. 2000. *Through a Window: My Thirty Years with the Chimpanzees of Gombe*. New York: Houghton Mifflin.

Gorman, James. 2013. Rights Group Sues to Have Chimp Recognized as Legal Person. *The New York Times*. December 2. http://www.nytimes.com/2013/12/03/science/rights-group-sues-to-have-chimp-recognized-as-lrgal-person.html

Grellmann, H. M. G. 1810. *Histoire des Bohemiens ou tableau des moeurs, usages et coutumes de ce peuple nomade*. Paris: Joseph Chaumerot Libraire

Hachet-Souplet, Pierre. 1895. *Le dressage des animaux*. Paris: Firmin-Didot.

Hall, Edith. 2018. Hephaestus the Hobbling Humorist: The Club-Footed God in the History of Early Greek Comedy. *Illinois Classical Studies* 43 (2): 366–87.

Hancock, Ian. 2002. *We Are the Romani People: Ame Sam e Rromane Dzene*. Hatfield: University of Hertfordshire Press.

Hancock, Ian, Siobhan Dowd, and Rajko Djuric. 2013 [1998]. *The Road of the Roma: A Pen Anthology of Gypsy Writers*. Hatfield: University of Hertfordshire Press.

Hatab, Lawrence J. 1988. Laughter in Nietzsche's Thought: A Philosophical Tragicomedy. *International Studies in Philosophy* 20 (2): 67–79.

Hediger, Heini. 1961. *Beobachtungen zurTierpsychologie im Zoo und im Zirkus*. Basel: Fredrick Rienhardt

Hediger, Heini. 1962. Clefs et secrets des dompteurs. *Science et Vie* 356 (Mai 1962): 53–64 and 151.

Hediger, Heini. 1964. Man as a Social Partner of Animals and Vice-Versa. *Animal Behaviour* 12 (3–4): 291–300.

Heinrich, Bernd. 1999. *The Mind of the Raven*. New York: Harper Collins.

Hermann, Arnold. 1983. *Fahrendes Volk: Randgruppen des Zigeunervolkes*. Luwigschafen: Pfalzische verlagsanstalt.

Hiltebeitel, Alf. 1989. *Criminal Gods and Demon Devotees: Essays on the Guardians of Popular Hinduism*. Albany NY: State University of New York Press.

Hobson, Nicholas M., Juliana Schroeder, Jane L. Risen, Dimitris Xygalatas, and Michael Inzlicht. 2017. The Psychology of Rituals: An Integrative Review and Process-Based Framework. *Personality and Social Psychology Review* 22 (3): 260–284.

Homans, George C. 1941. Anxiety and Ritual: The Theories of Malinowski and Radcliffe-Brown. *American Anthropologist* 43: 164–72.

Horkheimer, Max and Adorno, Theodor. 2002 [1947]. *Dialectic of the Enlightenment*. Redwood City, CA: Stanford University Press.

Isocrates. 1980. Isocrates with an English Translation in three volumes, by George Norlin, Ph.D., LL.D. Cambridge, MA, Harvard University Press; London, William Heinemann Ltd.

Jando, Dominique. 2018. *Philip Astley: The Horseman Who Invented the Circus*. San Francisco, CA: Circopedia Book.

Julliard, François and Christophe Nobili. 2015. La foundation d'aide aux animaux qui se soigne sur la bête. *Le Canard enchaîné*. February 11 (reprinted in lejpa.com).

Kant, Immanuel. 1914 [1892]. *Kant's Critique of Judgement*. Translated by J. H. Bernard. London: Macmillan.

Karanth, Dileep (ed.). 2010. *Ian Hancock. Danger! Educated Gypsy. Selected Essays*. Hatfield: University of Hertfordshire Press.

Katz, Jon. 2017. The Death of the Circus: An American Tragedy: "Losing Our Jobs, Our Homes, Our lives." *Bedlam Farm Journal*. January 16. https://www.bedlamfarm.com/2017/01/16/the-death-of-the-circus-an-american-tragedy-losing-our-jobs-our-homes-our-lives/

Kiley-Worthington, Marthe. 1990. *Animals in Circuses and Zoos: Chiron's World. Independent Scientific Report*. Harlow: Little Eco-Farms Publishing.

Kirby, E. T. 1974. The Shamanistic Origins of Popular Entertainment. *The Drama Review* 18 (1): 5–15.

Krasskova, Galina. 2010. http://www.patheos.com/blogs/pantheon/2010/05/demonization-of-loki-part-1

Kruuk, Hans. 2002. *Hunter and Hunted: Relationship between Carnivores and People*. Cambridge: Cambridge University Press.

Kuiper, F. B. J. 1979. *Varuna and Vidushaka: On the Origin of the Sanskrit Drama*. Amsterdam: North Holland Publisher.

Laude, Patrick. 2005. *Divine Play, Sacred Laughter, and Spiritual Understanding*. New York: Palgrave Macmillan.

Leathers, Victor. 1959. *British Entertainers in France*. Toronto: University of Toronto Press.

Le Bas, Damian. 2018. *The Stopping Places: A Journey through Gypsy Britain*. London: Chatto & Windus.

Lee, Jonathan. 2019a. How the Nazis Wiped Out the Romani Middle Class. *The Norwich Radical*. January 25. https://thenorwichradical.com/2019/01/25/how-the-nazis-wiped-ot-the-romani-middle-class/

Lee, Jonathan. 2019b. Antigypsyism Will Not Be Cured by Neoliberal Wishful Thinking. *The Norwich Radical*. October 11. https://thenorwichradical.com/2019/10/11/antigypsyism-will-not-be-cured-by-neoliberal-wishful-thinking/

Lee, Patrick Jasper. 2015 [2000]. *We Borrow the Earth: An Intimate Portrait of the Gypsy Folk, Tradition, and Culture*. Pembrokeshire, Wales: Ravine Press.

Lestel, Dominique. 2016. *Eat This Book: A Carnivore's Manifesto*. Translated by Gary Steiner. New York: Columbia University Press.

Lévi-Strauss, Claude. 1971. Race et Culture. *International Social Science Journal* 23: 608–25.

Levi-Strauss, Claude. 1988 [1975]. *The Way of the Masks*. Sylvia Modelski, translator. Seattle: University of Washington Press.

Lieberman, Daniel. 2013. *The Story of the Human Body*. New York: Pantheon Books.
Liégeois, Jean-Pierre. 1983. *Tsiganes*. Paris: Maspero
Liégeois, Jean-Pierre. 2005. *Gypsies: An Illustrated History*. London: Saqi Books.
Lippitt, John. 1992. Nietzsche, Zarathustra and the Status of Laughter. *British Journal of Aesthetics* 32 (1): 39–49.
Little, Kenneth. 1991. The Rhetoric of Romance and the Simulation of Tradition in Circus Clown Performance. *Semiotica* 85 (3/4): 227–55.
Little, Kenneth. 1993. Masochism, Spectacle, and the "Broken Mirror" Clown entrée: A Note on the Anthropology of Performance in Postmodern Culture. *Cultural Anthropology* 8 (1): 117–29.
Lorenz, Konrad. 1966 [1963]. *On Aggression*. London: Methuen.
Loucas, Ioannis. 1989. Ritual Surprise and Terror in Ancient Greek Possession-Dromena. *Kernos* 2 (8): 97–104.
Lucardie, Paul. 2020. Animalism: A Nascent Ideology? Exploring the Ideas of Animal Advocacy Parties. *Journal of Political Ideologies* 25 (2): 212–27.
Makarius, Laura. 1974. *Le sacré et la violation des interdits*. Paris: Payot.
Marsh, Jason. 2012. Do Mirror Neurons give us Empathy? *Greater Good Magazine*. March 29. greatergood.berkeley.edu
Martinez-Cruz, Begoña, Isabel Mendizabal, Christine Harmant, Rosario de Pablo, Mihai G. Netea, Horolma Pamjav, Andrea Zalán, Ivailo Tournev, Elena Marushiakova, Vesselin Popov, Jaume Bertanpetit, Luba Kalaydjeva, Lluis Quintana-Murci & David Comas, and the Genographic Consortium. 2016. Origins, Admixture and Founder Lineages in European Roma. *European Journal of Human Genetics* 24: 937–43.
Matras, Yaron. 2015. *The Romani Gypsies*. Cambridge, MA: Harvard University Press.
Maximoff. Mateo. 1949. *The Ursitory*. London: Chapman & Hall.
McConnell-Stott, Andrew. 2009. *The Pantomime Life of Joseph Grimaldi*. London: Canongate.
McGarry, Aidan. 2017. *Romaphobia: The Last Acceptable Form of Racism*. London: Zed Books.
McPherson, Douglas. 2014. Thomas Chipperfield: Britain's Last Lion Trainer. *The Telegraph*. May 29. https://www.telegraph.co.uk/culture/theatre/10862398/Thomas-Chipperfield-Britains-last-lion-tamer.html
Meishar, Stav. forthcoming. *The Lorchs: The Rise and Fall of a Jewish Circus Dynasty*. https://www.kickstarter.com/projects/stavmeishar/the-lorchs-the-rise-and-fall-of-a-jewish circus-dynasty/posts/3134151/.
Müller-Wille, Staffan. 2010. Claude Lévi-Strauss on Race, History, and Genetics. *Biosocieties* 1: 5 (3): 330–47.
Narayan, R. K. 1983. *A Tiger for Malgudi*. New York: Viking Press.
National Animal Interest Alliance (NAIA). 2000. Deception in the Name of Animal Rights. http://www.naiaonline.org/article/deeption-in-the-name-of-animal-rights#sthash.BCiEdyBR.dpbs
Nguimfack-Perault. 2015. *Le costume de clown blanc: Gérard Vicaire, la passion pour un seul habit*. Bruxelles: Chapitre Douze

Nietzsche, Friedrich. 1995 [1885]. *Thus Spoke Zarathustra: A Book for All and None.* Translated by Walter Kaufmann. New York: Penguin Random House.

Ohlheiser, Abby. 2017. PETA Wanted a Fake Cat Video to Go Viral. It Didn't Exactly Turn Out as Planned. *The Washington Post.* June 7. https://www.washingtonpost.com/news/the-intersect/wp/2017/06/07/peta-wanted-a-fake-cat-video-to-go-viral-it-didnt-exactly-turn-out-as-planned/

Okely, Judith. 1983. *The Traveller-Gypsies.* Cambridge: Cambridge University Press.

Oltermann, Philip. 2019. Austria Struggles with Marauding Krampus Demons Gone Rogue. *The Guardian.* December 8. https://www.theguardian.com/world/2019/dec/08/austria-struggles-with-marauding-krampus-day-demons-gone-rogue

O'Neill, Grace Claire. 2020. I'm a Romany Gypsy – Why Is Racism against Us Still Acceptable? *The Guardian.* June 15. https://www.theguardian.com/commentisfree/2020/jun/15/romany-gypsy-racism-britain-prejudice-roma-travellers

Otte, Marline. 2006. *Jewish Identities in German Popular Entertainment 1890-1933.* New York: Cambridge University Press.

Parikh, J. T. 1953. *The Vidûshaka Theory and Practice.* Shri Chunijal Gandhi Vidya Bhavan Studies 2, Surat.

Pechon, de Ruby. 2019 [1596]. *La vie généreuse des mercelots, gueux & bohémiens.* Paris: Allia.

Peterson, Jordan. 1999. *The Pragmatics of Meaning.* https://semioticon.com/frontline/jordan_b.htm

Porcher, Jocelyn. 2017. *The Ethics of Animal Labor: A Collaborative Utopia.* London: Palgrave Macmillan.

Reeve, Dominic. 2003. *Smoke in the Lanes.* Hatfield: University of Hertfordshire Press.

Rémy, Tristan. 1986. *La vie malheureuse de Rhum, clown inspiré.* Paris: Le Flexatone.

Rémy, Tristan. 2002 [1945]. *Les Clowns.* Paris: Grasset.

Roth, Wolfgang. 2021. Circus Lorch Eschollbruken 1876–1905. Plungstadt: Selbstverlag.

Roth, Wolfgang. 1996. Juden in Eschollbrucken. Pfungstadt: Selbstverlag.

Rousseau, Jean-Jacques. 2008 [1755]. *Discours sur l'origine et les fondements de l' inégalité parmi les hommes.* Paris: Flammarion.

Serboianu, C. J. Popp. 1930. *Les Tsiganes.* Paris: Payot.

Servigne, Pablo and Raphael Stevens. 2020. *How Everything Can Collapse: A Manual for Our Times.* Cambridge: Polity.

Siegel, Lee. 1991. *Net of Magic: Wonders and Deception in India.* Chicago: Chicago University Press.

Simonet, Alain. 2009. Le Cirque Bureau: Direction Jules Glassner. *Dossiers de l'histoire du cirque*, 9. Paris: Arts des Mondes.

Singh, Manvir. 2018. The Cultural Evolution of Shamanism. *Behavioral and Brain Sciences* 41: 1–62.

Snyder, Gary. 1990. *The Practice of the Wild.* Berkeley: Counter Point.

Steffen, Will, Jacques Grinevald, Paul Crutzen, and John McNeill. 2011. The Anthropocene: Conceptual and Historical Perspectives. *Philosophical Transactions of the Royal Society A* 369 (1938). https://royalsocietypublishing.org/doi/full/10.1098/rsta.2010.0327

Stewart, Michael. 1997. *The Time of the Gypsies*. Boulder, CO: Westview Press.

Stoddart, Helen. 2000. *Rings of Desire: Circus History and Representation*. Manchester: Manchester University Press.

Tainter, Joseph. 1988. *The Collapse of Complex Societies*. Cambridge: Cambridge University Press.

Tait, Peta. 2005. *Circus Bodies: Cultural Identity in Aerial Performance*. London: Routledge.

Tait, Peta. 2012. *Wild and Dangerous Performances: Animals, Emotions, Circus*. New York: Palgrave.

Tait, Peta. 2016. *Fighting Nature: Travelling Menageries, Animal Acts, and War Shows*. Sydney: Sydney University Press.

Tebbutt, Susan (ed.). 1998. *Sinti and Roma: Gypsies in German-speaking Society and Literature*. New York: Berghahn.

Thoreau, Henry David. 1994 [1863]. *Walking: All Good Things Are Wild and Free*. New York: HarperCollins.

Thoreau, Henry David. 2016 [1854]. *Walden*. Penguin Classics.

Tinbergen, Nicolaas. 1953. *The Study of Instinct*. Oxford: Oxford University Press.

Toffin, Gerard. 2018. Bouffons et clowns sacrés de l'Himālaya. *Revue de l'histoire des religions* 1: 97–131.

Tonnessen, Morten, Kristin Armstrong Oma, and Silver Rattasepp (eds.). 2016. *Thinking About Animals in the Age of the Anthropocene*. Lanham: Lexington Books.

Towsen, John. 1976. *Clowns*. New York: Hawthorn.

Vidyasagar, Aparna. 2018. *What Is CRISPR?* April 21. Livescience.com

Visuvalingam, Sunthar. 1989. The Transgressive Sacrality of the Dîksita: Sacrifice, Criminality, and Bhakti in the Hindu Tradition. In Alf Hiltebeitel (ed.) *Criminal Gods and Demons Devotees*. Albany: State of New York University Press (427–62).

Walker, Shaun. 2020. Europe's Marginalized Roma People Hit Hard by Coronavirus: Pandemic Has Increased Deprivation and Stigmatization of Continent's Largest Minority. https://www.theguardian.com/world/2020/may/11/

Wallace-Wells, David. 2019. *The Uninhabitable Earth: Life after Warming*. New York: Crown Publishing Group.

Ward, Steve. 2014. *Beneath the Big Top: A Social History of the Circus in Britain*. Barnsley: Pen & Sword History.

Ward, Steve. 2018. *Father of the Modern Circus "Billy Buttons": The Life and Times of Philip Astley*. Barnley: Pen and Sword Books.

Wilding, Mark. 2019. Having a Laugh: Is This the End for Clowning. *The Guardian*. December 29. https://www.theguardian.com/global/2019/dec/29/horror-films-and-how-the-clowns-are-fighting-back?CMP=share_btn_link

Williams, Patrick. 2013 [1993]. *Gypsy World: The Silence of the Living and the Voices of the Dead*. Translated by Catherine Tihanyi. Chicago: Chicago University Press.

Wilson, David A. H. 2015. *The Welfare of Performing Animals: A Historical Perspective*. Berlin: Springer.
Yeats, William B. 1921. *Michael Robartes and the Dancer*. Dublin: Cuala Press.
Yoors, Jan. 1987 [1967]. *The Gypsies*. Long Grove: Waveland Press.
Zeller, Anne. 1981. Primate Facial Gestures: A Study of Communication. *International Journal of Human Communication* 13: 505–606.

Index

Acharia, Mahuya 76
Adorno, Theodor 146
Aelian (Claudius Aelianus) 105–7, 109
agriculture 47
amphitheater 104
Androclus, Androcles 110
Animal complicity 119
animalists 100–3, 128
animals 36, 53–129
Ansdell, Richard 70
Antarès 182
Anthropocene 218
Anthropomorphism 222
Apollo circus 78
Aristotle 140
Armenian Circus 111
Arnaud, Yann 187
Astley, Philip 7, 27–34
Atkinson, Rowan (Mr. Bean) 149
Aulu-Gelle (Aulus-Gellius) 110
Axt, Elizabeth 173

Bhairava 140
Basque 64
Beadle, Ron 116
bear 63–5, 91
Berger, Joel 59, 61–2, 222
Bergman, Ingmar 2
Bergson, Henri 148
Berland, Joseph 15
Black face 159
Blake, William 3, 74
Blankard, Catherine 201
body 6, 172–213
Bombled, Charles 69–71
Borrow, George 19, 41
Bouglione, Firmin xvii, 37, 46, 57, 88
Bouillon, Patricia 37
Bretagne Circus 223
Bureau, cirque 53

Cairoli, Charlie 156
Canestrini, Duccio 45

Carl, George 163
carnivores 59
Chaplin, Charlie 143–7
Chickys (the) 138
chimpanzees 117
Chipperfield, Thomas 86–7, 114
Chocolat 160
Circopedia 88
Cirque du Soleil 33
Clown theory 151
clowns 5–6, 132–69
collapsology 225
colonial discourse 113, 161
concentration camps 17–19
contemporary circus 205
contortionist 172
Conway, David 202
costume (white face clown) 154–9
coulrophobia 140
crocodiles 93
Crucifixion 161–4
Cultural entropy 125
cultural evolution 122, 124, 139, 141
culture 49–51, 61–3, 125, 204, 219–21
Culture wars 129

Dantès, Henri 87–9, 201
Davison, Jon 159
De Waal, Frans 83–4
Deleuze, Gilles 141
democratization of circus 204
Descartes, René 83
Dionysos 140
discrimination 20
domestication 47
Douglas, Mary 191
dualism (Cartesian) 127
dynamic systems 126

Edon, Gérard 178–81
Ekman, Paul 132
elephants 103–8
Elias, Norbert 219

Emerson, Ralph Waldo 85
entropy 50, 126
Eötvös-Dobritch, Christopher 172–5
Epiphanies 183
Eros 208
ethics 114
ethos 48, 114
evolution 203

face 132–4
fear 59–61
Fellini, Federico 2
Ferreri, Miguel 195
festivals (circus) 217, 223
fitness 35
Flanagan, Gerry 151
Folies Bergère 72
Footit 160
Frankfurt School 146
free energy 49, 127
Frène, Théophile 54–5
Fridlund, Alan 132
Friston, Karl 49, 125, 127, 142

Gadje 19
Gardin, Arthur 145
Gasser, Robert 225
Gemini Circus 79
Geraldos, the 184–90
Glassner, Jules 53
globalization 220
Goodall, Jane 83–4
Gorgios 19
Grimaldi, Joseph 131, 136–7, 139
Gypsies 1–3, 12–19

Hachet-Souplet, Pierre 119, 120
Hediger, Heini 119, 120
Heinrich, Bernd 61
Hephaistos 140
Hippisley-Coxe, Antony 184
Holi 142
Homans, George 209
hominins 59
horsemanship 28, 32
Hoskins, Bob 46
Houcke, Gilbert 95
Hugo, Pieter 66
Humberto Circus 191
humor 149

hunger 57–63, 77
hunter-gatherers 24, 47
hyenas 65–7, 224

Ichikawa Ebizo 194
identity 133
ideology 73, 85
India 26
information 49–50
Isocrates 109

Jando, Dominique 27, 29
Jenu Koruba 176–7

Kabuki 194
Kahn, Gustave 33
Kant, Immanuel 213
Kobukada, Arashi 194
Konyot, David 165–9
Krampus 135
Kremo, Bela 195
Kruuk, Hans 60, 77

laughter 147–9
Le Bas, Damian 20, 43, 216
Lee, Patrick Jasper 23
Leinonen, Jani 163
Lesiak, Christine 159
Lichner, Alexander 193, 196–200
Lichner, Denise 200
Lieberman, David 46
Liégeois, Jean-Pierre 21
Lion King 82
lions 63, 92
Little, Kenneth 153
Loki 142

magic 172–5
Makarius, Laura 141
Mallarmé, Stéphane 110
man-eater 96, 124
Martha-la-corce (Corsican) 123
Martial (Marcus Martialis) 110
Martinez Brothers 194–5
mask 132–5, 137
McDonald, Ronald 163–4
metaphor 220
Micheletty, Romina 172
migration 17, 25
Mohammad Abdullahi 67

Nagarahole National Park 177
Narayan, Kikkeri 176
Narayan, R.K. 81–3
National Animal Interest 118
Navratil, Hynek 191
Neolithic 40, 64
Nguimfack-Perault, Sylvie 154–5
Nicephorus Gregoras 15
Nietzsche, Friedrich 140
nomads 2, 23, 35, 48

Odin 142
Omelchenko, Vladimir 212
O'Neill, Claire 21–2
Orpheus 110

Paleolithic 63–4
pandemic 225
Pechon de Ruby 19, 40
persecution 8, 17–19
Peterson, Jordan 114–15, 122, 165–6
pilgrims 16
Pinita Del Oro 177
Pipo 195
Plutarch 105
predators 58–9, 109–11, 118
prohibition 117
Punakawans 143

racism 7
Raggedy Rawney 44
Ragnarok 227
Ramuz, Charles-Ferdinand 183
Ranthambore National Park 74
religion 37–9
Remy, Tristan 156
resilience 216
revolution (industrial) 218
Rhum 156
risk 203
ritual 6, 209, 211–12, 218, 225
Rivel, Charlie 145
Roche, Rudesindo 71–2
Rome 104
Roncalli Circus 150
Rossi, Yann 157
Rousseau, Jean-Jacques 85

sacred clowns 134
Saint Sarah 39
Sanskrit drama 140
Santus, Sascha 149
Sasunti Davit 111
Serboianu, C.J. 47
shaman 134
Shub Peter 150, 162
snakes 96
space 46
Stewart, Michael 40
Strehly, Georges 34

Tait, Peta 87
Taras Bulba 94
Thoreau, David 85
tigers 74–83, 92
Toni Alexis Trio 157
Torralvo-Quiros, Nuria 197
Towsen, John 159
trickster 149, 165
Turkey 25

uncertainty 225
Ursitoare 39
Utopia 112

vagrancy 23
Van Been, Joseph 90
Venus Circus 79
Vianello, Andrea 206
Vicaire, Charles 155
Vicaire, Gerard 155
Vidûshaka 139–43
virtual reality 207
Visuvalingam, Sunthar 142

Wallenda, Karl 184
Ward, Steve 27, 29
Washington trapeze 178–81
Wayang 143
white-face clown 153–8
wilderness 112, 123
Wilding, Mark 162
wolves 68–74

Yeats, William B. 216
Yoors, Jan 19, 34, 40–1

www.ingramcontent.com/pod-product-compliance
Lightning Source LLC
Chambersburg PA
CBHW062132300426
44115CB00012BA/1894